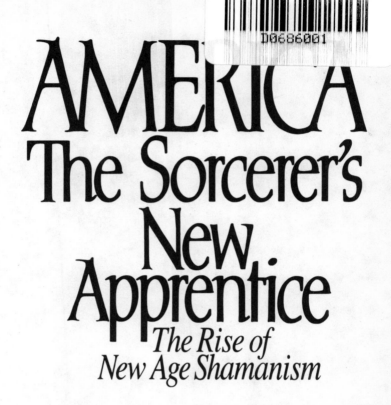

AMERICA
The Sorcerer's New Apprentice
The Rise of New Age Shamanism

DAVE HUNT
T.A. McMAHON

HARVEST HOUSE PUBLISHERS
Eugene, Oregon 97402

AMERICA: THE SORCERER'S NEW APPRENTICE

Copyright © 1988 by Harvest House Publishers
Eugene, Oregon 97402

Library of Congress Catalog Card Number 87-082791
ISBN 0-89081-673-5 (Cloth edition)
ISBN 0-89081-651-4 (Trade paper edition)

Printed in the United States of America.

Contents

AMERICA
The Sorcerer's New Apprentice

The Rise of
New Age Shamanism

1

A Turning Point?

Today's world confronts a strange and growing paradox that could very well mark a pivotal point in human history. Even as the scientific and technological advancement which ushered in the space age is accelerating at an exponential rate, we are witnessing far and away the greatest occult explosion of all time. The evidence seems to indicate that something of unusual historic significance is in process. Primitive pagan religious practices that were generally confined to undeveloped Third World countries (and were regarded in the West with suspicion and ridicule only a few years ago) are now being embraced by increasing millions of enthusiasts worldwide. By some peculiar metamorphosis occultism has become scientific.

The word "occult" (or "hidden") has traditionally referred to an ancient perennial wisdom involving mysterious powers pursued and practiced in secret. Reflecting a recent change in attitude, however, the 1980's brand of occultism is out in the open, having gained wide acceptance and respectability in mainstream America. Commenting upon the pervasive effects of what is clearly a significant change in the belief system of scores of millions of Americans, Robert Lindsey wrote in the *New York Times*:

> Representatives of some of the nation's largest corporations, including IBM, AT&T and General Motors, met in New Mexico this summer [1986] to discuss how metaphysics, the occult and Hindu mysticism might help executives compete in the world marketplace.

9

> . . . a thread of alternative thought . . . scholars say
> is working its way increasingly into the nation's cultural,
> religious, social, economic and political life. On one
> level, they say, it is evidenced by a surge of interest in new
> metaphysical religions, mediums, the occult, reincarna-
> tion, psychic healing, Satanism, "spirit guides," and
> other aspects of supernatural belief. . . .
>
> Leaders [in the movement] contend they are ushering
> in what they call a New Age of understanding and intel-
> lectual ferment as significant as the Renaissance.[1]

The last time anything approaching this mass flight from reason
to mysticism occurred was in the 1920's and 30's. It was very likely
this great occult resurgence in Western Europe, and particularly in
Austria and Germany, which helped to set the stage for Germany's
acceptance of Nazism. Some historians, in fact, have referred to
Hitler as the "Occult Messiah." What anti-Nazi Max Planck (German physicist and Nobel prizewinner) had to say in 1932 would
seem to be remarkably relevant to current developments. Referring
to the peculiar and growing "popularity of occultism and spiritualism and their innumerable variants" in his day, Planck wrote:

> We might naturally assume that one of the achieve-
> ments of science would have been to restrict belief in
> miracle. But it does not seem to be so. . . .
>
> Though the extraordinary results of science are so
> obvious . . . [yet] the tendency to believe in the power of
> mysterious agencies is an outstanding characteristic of
> our own day.[2]

Today's disillusionment with science is apparently even more
widespread than in Planck's time. The present revival of sorcery is
evident in modern trends in art, psychology, medicine, education,
the military, business, music, and especially in the media, from
children's television cartoons to major feature films. The once
seemingly-reasonable hope that the solutions to mankind's problems would all be provided by science has proven false and has been
abandoned by all but a handful of hard-core materialists. Stanford

University professor Willis Harman points out that "the growing interest in such areas as Eastern religious philosophies, yoga and meditation, channeling . . . etc. has made clear the public's dissatisfaction with the scientists' exclusive claim to valid truth-seeking."[3] The United States leads the way in the resultant world-wide occult renaissance (which is also being embraced even in those bastions of scientific materialism, China and the Soviet Union).

Taking "Spiritual" Experiences Seriously

It is especially significant that today's sorcery is no longer generally associated with evil forces or despised as "unscientific." While a few outspoken skeptics stubbornly continue to label psychic phenomena as either hoax or delusion, many competent investigators who were once doubters are reluctantly becoming convinced that the evidence in a significant number of cases is extremely persuasive. A 1983 study by the Library of Congress, for example, concluded: "A number of recent [psychic] experiments have yielded more or less consistent positive results under rigorous conditions of investigation." Both the Soviet and American military establishments are taking paranormal powers seriously enough to invest heavily in psychic research. Philosophy-of-science professor John Gliedman has called attention to the fact that the research of certain leading scientists strongly suggests the existence of "a hidden *spiritual* world." After extensive interviews in Europe and America, Gliedman wrote in *Science Digest*:

> From Berkeley to Paris and from London to Princeton, prominent scientists from fields as diverse as neurophysiology and quantum physics are coming out of the closet and admitting they believe in the possibility, at least, of such unscientific entities as the immortal human spirit and divine creation.[4]

Millions of people who formerly had no interest whatever in psychic phenomena are being caught up in a "new consciousness" that is totally changing their lives. A millionaire sells his five Burger King restaurants and moves to a rural area in Northern California, where he builds a pyramid-shaped house to tap into the energy of the universe. He has changed his lifestyle completely because of the teachings of an alleged 35,000-year-old entity that speaks through a former housewife. "You won't find heart surgeon Ken Eyer at Providence Hospital anymore," begins another newspaper's report on the hard-to-explain transformation which this powerful movement is effecting around the world. The article goes on to relate that Dr. Eyer, in what is becoming an increasingly common story, is now "dedicating his life to a religious philosophy loosely dubbed 'New Age.' " The former successful physician is quoted as saying:

> I made a life decision to take a stand, even though that meant walking away from my medical practice at the peak of my popularity. I knew there was more to the physical universe than my five senses were telling me.[5]

Even psychologists and psychiatrists, whose profession has traditionally ranked among the most skeptical, are now taking "spiritual" experiences seriously. Featured speakers and workshop leaders at recent annual conventions of the Association for Humanistic Psychology have included practicing witch doctors, trance mediums, a Taoist master of Zen and T'ai Chi, and channelers of "spirit entities" (such as Kevin Ryerson, who has "channeled" for Shirley MacLaine and was featured in her TV miniseries in January 1987). This phenomenon, however, has been given a new psychological interpretation. Reflecting this trend, *American Health* magazine reported: "There's a new breed of shrinks in the land. But instead of couches and Rorschach tests, their accoutrements are tarot cards and astrology charts . . . [these are] the shrinks of the yuppie generation . . . belief in the occult is stronger than ever."[6] The *San Jose Mercury News* recently reported:

> Seeing visions. Speaking in tongues. Walking and talking with Jesus. Blissed out on Buddha. Wrestling with Satan. Sighting UFOs.
> It reads like a litany of psychological afflictions— profiles of people who have let their membership in the

sane world lapse and have instead become card-carrying crazies.

Or have they?

At the Institute for Transpersonal Psychology in Menlo Park [California] . . . when their clients discuss mystical experiences, the psychiatrists, psychologists and counselors at the institute do not blink. They are dedicated to recognizing spirituality—even in its most bizarre manifestations—as an important element of the human condition.[7]

What Is Going On?

Within the past two decades there has been an increasing incidence of mystical experiences and psychic phenomena among the general populace that seems to be reaching unprecedented proportions. A recent nationwide poll sponsored by the University of Chicago showed 67 percent of the public claiming psychic experiences.[8] This is up from 58 percent in a similar survey taken in 1973.[9] Confounding skeptics and critics alike, the poll revealed that those having mystical and occult experiences "are anything but religious nuts or psychiatric cases." In a psychological well-being test "the mystics scored at the top." Ironically, "spiritual" experiences that were once considered by psychologists to be a sign of mental illness are now being reported even by "elite scientists and physicians who [still] insist that such things cannot possibly" occur.[10]

Considering the often-bizarre nature of psychic phenomena, it is understandable that many of those who have had such experiences remain skeptical. What has apparently happened to them simply defies rational explanation. At the same time, however, there appears to be no shortage of those who readily believe that the unbelievable has happened to other people. Almost anyone who claims "revelations" from supernatural sources (seemingly the more incredible the experiences, the better) quickly gathers a large and enthusiastic following. "Channeler" J. Z. Knight, who catapulted from obscurity to international prominence almost overnight, is one example among hundreds of persons seriously claiming contact with a variety of "spirit entities."

Knight tells us that she was unprepared by her traditional Christian upbringing for the huge "being of light" that suddenly stood before her in her kitchen and promised to use her as a channel of blessing to the world. This incredible entity allegedly spent a year preparing Knight for her mission and performing miracles to prove its powers. Since then "Ramtha," who claims to be a 35,000-year-old warrior from Atlantis who has become a god, has been "channeling" his ancient wisdom through Knight in seminars and on national television. This public display is a recent development in an ancient phenomenon which has traditionally been presented privately through trance mediums in spirit seances.

Skeptics suggest that Knight and other "channelers" are, through skillful acting, deliberately deceiving millions with a moneymaking scam. It is true that some channelers have become extremely wealthy; and most mediums have at times been caught in fraud. It would be a mistake, however, to assume that the entire phenomenon of channeling can be explained away as a giant hoax. Independently of one another, millions of people widely scattered around the world have had similar experiences. This fact together with the striking consistency in the message eliminates hallucination or coincidence as possible explanations. As two editors familiar with this subject insightfully point out:

> Whatever the method of channeling, it is the content that is most important, and here there is remarkable agreement, even unanimity, among the various channeled entities.[11]

Thousands of people have been convinced by Jach Pursel's channeling of "Lazaris," a disembodied intelligence with no previous incarnations, who claims to be the "consummate friend" of mankind. Then there is "Mafu," a " 'highly evolved' entity from the seventh dimension," that also preaches the same message which Aldous Huxley called *The Perennial Philosophy*.[12] After he (or it) suddenly began "channeling" through Los Angeles housewife Penny Torres, Mafu quickly gained a following among Hollywood's elite.[13] According to Margo Chandley, who studied 50 "channels" in the process of writing her Ph.D. thesis in transformational psychology, there are an estimated 1000 "channels" practicing in the Los Angeles area alone, compared with only two a decade ago.[14] What in the world is going on?

Contact with Spirit Entities?

Like mediumship down through history, today's "channeling" strains common sense. Nevertheless, it has neither been explained satisfactorily nor explained away by science. Freud and Jung both grudgingly admitted its validity and mystery, as did William James. Dismissing it all as hoax or hallucination is too simplistic in view of the competency and reputations of those who have experienced it. Take, for example, Ruth Montgomery. At the height of an illustrious career as one of the most highly honored women journalists of her day, Montgomery was assigned by an editor to investigate the strange phenomenon of communication with alleged spirits of the dead. Surprisingly, she found herself confronted with more than enough evidence to eventually overcome her seasoned journalistic skepticism. As a result, an unexpected transformation occurred: "Spirit entities" began writing books through Montgomery, and she became known as "the Herald of the New Age."[15]

Helen Shucman is another interesting case in point. An atheist psychologist at Columbia University, Shucman was hardly a likely candidate to receive "revelations" from the spirit world. Yet the voice she began hearing (which claimed to be Jesus) persisted in its repeated demand: "This is a course in miracles; take it down!" It was futile to resist. After consulting with some of her colleagues at Columbia, Shucman reluctantly obeyed. When the dictation had finally ended, the "Course" encompassed an astonishing 1100 pages that many psychologists and theologians alike acclaim for its brilliant insights. That seems to be an unreasonably lengthy and lucid "hallucination."

Strangely enough, even though the voice had claimed to be Jesus, it contradicted nearly everything the Bible says about him, according to Kenneth Wapnick, head of the foundation that publishes the "Course."[16] In fact the message which Shucman received was consistent with that being communicated by a wide variety of entities through thousands of "channels" around the world, channels whom Shucman had never even heard of and whose tall tales she would not have believed until she had experienced a similar visitation.

What is the source of these apparent intrusions from some mysterious spiritual dimension? Why is there an explosion of such experiences at this time? And why, in spite of the rich variety in the entities and manner of communication, is there such consistency in the message they bring? We will be examining that message in our attempt to identify its source.

Some Disturbing Possibilities

It took Whitley Strieber years even to admit that his own bizarre experiences had occurred—experiences which he is now convinced are real, yet beyond comprehension. Highly intelligent, well-educated, and already a best-selling author with a reputation to maintain, Strieber is not the kind of person one would suspect of repeated hallucinations, much less deliberate deceit to sell another book. In *Communion*, he meticulously lays out the facts as well as he can piece them together, comprising what he calls "a shattering assault from the unknown . . . an elaborate personal encounter with intelligent nonhuman beings."[17] Do they come to earth from other planets or from another dimension? From his own mind, or from UFO's—from inner or outer space? Strieber still doesn't know, yet the impact upon his life and upon the lives of a growing number of other people with similar experiences has been devastating.[18]

Strieber is angry and still confused. He feels violated. "The visitors," he tells us, "marched right into the middle of the life of an indifferent skeptic without a moment's hesitation." At first he thought he was going crazy. Eventually he came to the point where being diagnosed as insane would have been preferable to believing that what he was experiencing was *real*. But the "three psychologists and three psychiatrists" who gave him "a battery of psychological tests and a neurological examination" declared him to be "normal" in every respect. He also passed with flying colors a lie detector test administered "by an operator with thirty years' experience." Again, neither hallucination nor hoax seems to fit. In his search for truth, Strieber also consulted space scientists, physicists, and an astronaut, only to learn: "To the scientific community, the nature of this phenomenon remains an unresolved question."

Interestingly enough, such an authority as astronomer Robert Jastrow holds (along with a number of other leading scientists) a theory which could explain at least some of the contacts with nonphysical entities. Jastrow, who set up and directed the Goddard Institute for Space Studies (which played a key role in the Pioneer, Voyager, and forthcoming Galileo space probes), makes this fascinating suggestion: ". . . life that is a billion years beyond us may be far beyond the flesh-and-blood form that we would recognize. It may be . . . disembodied and has escaped its mortal flesh to become something that old-fashioned people would call spirits. And so how do we know it's there? Maybe it can materialize and then dematerialize. I'm sure it has magical powers by our standards. . . ."[19]

When coupled with telepathy and other psychic powers, Jastrow's theory opens up the frightening possibility that human minds could be invaded or at least influenced and deceived by nonphysical intelligences from out there somewhere. This in turn raises a number of other questions. Who are they, and what could be their motive? If Jastrow's suggestion is correct, would we not have a difficult time even knowing that our minds were being influenced? This seems to agree with the confusion that Strieber and so many others have experienced. And could not this explanation provide at least one viable explanation for "channeling" and other visitations and communications from the apparent "spirit" entities who appear in such a variety of forms, from "ascended masters" to spirits of the dead? The world's major governments and leading scientists take the search for extraterrestrial intelligence (SETI) seriously enough to launch space probes and search programs in an attempt to establish radio communication with intelligent life beyond our solar system. It would seem just as reasonable to take seriously the possibility of psychic contact with nonphysical ETI's.

Ushering in the "New Age"

The sudden and inexplicable explosion of apparent contact with entities from a nonphysical dimension, while only one facet of the current occult revival, seems to represent the major avenue for bringing a transformational message to mankind. This gives peculiar significance to the fact that millions of people are now being trained to contact "spirit (or inner) guides" through such proliferating Eastern meditation techniques as transcendental meditation, and mind dynamics courses such as Silva Mind Control. Many supposedly modern methods for self-improvement now being offered in thousands of courses worldwide are in fact a revival of ancient sorcery under new labels. The generic term for all of these is "New Age."

At the heart of sorcery have always been secret techniques for allegedly contacting spirit entities in order to gain supernatural knowledge and power. These ancient occult methodologies are presently being revived, resulting in renewed contact with the same "helpful spirits" known to occultists for thousands of years. Only now the process is dressed in modern psychological or self-improvement terminology, and the purpose is explained as tapping into an infinite "inner potential." As a result, the exploration of "inner space" in search of mystical powers has become a growing and trendy obsession in the West.

While skeptical observers over the past 20 years have persisted in labeling it a "fad" and predicting its imminent passing, the New Age movement has quietly but relentlessly gathered momentum. Viewing this unprecedented phenomenon with considerable hope, some researchers have called it the most powerful force for positive change in human history. Still others, however, have warned that Eastern mysticism, which is the heart of the "new consciousness," is a Trojan horse that will eventually bring down Western civilization. These critics see in the New Age mentality now sweeping the West the same penchant for a "magical formula" that the popular Indian poet Rabindranath Tagore ascribed to Mahatma Gandhi. That mentality Tagore labeled "the original sin from which all our [India's] ills are flowing."[20]

The idea that magical formulas, not for quick-fix political solutions (as with Ghandi) but for harnessing occult powers and contacting the spirit world, could actually be growing in appeal to millions of well-educated persons in the space age may at first seem unbelievable. We cannot escape the shattering implications, however, by burying our heads in the sand of materialistic dogmatism that demands a *physical* explanation for all phenomena. After all, what is the physical basis for *ethics*? It is astonishing that the mechanistic belief that all human behavior and values can ultimately be explained in physical terms has hung on for so long. As Nobel prizewinning neurophysiologist Sir John Eccles has pointed out:

> But if there are bona fide mental events—events that are not themselves physical or material—then the whole program of philosophical materialism collapses.
>
> The universe is no longer composed of "matter and a void" but now must make (spaceless) room for (massless) entities [i.e. *minds*].[21]

A Ghost in the Machine?

In a clear break with materialism, Eccles has described the human brain as "a machine that a *ghost* can operate." As a result of his research, Eccles is convinced that there is compelling evidence to support the traditional religious belief in the existence of a nonphysical soul and/or spirit—and that this is the "ghost" which actually operates the human brain and through it the body. This would in turn seem to support belief in life after death. It is certainly reasonable to assume that the "operator" could very well survive the death of the "vehicle" it was operating, particularly in view of Jastrow's interesting speculation concerning pure intelligences without physical bodies. Among those joining Eccles in his important conviction are such eminent scientists as Nobel Laureate Eugene Wigner, known as "one of the greatest physicists of the century"; Sir Karl Popper, who has been called "the most famous philosopher of science of our age"; and the late mathematician and quantum mechanics theorist John von Neumann, who has been described as perhaps "the smartest man who ever lived."

There is no escaping the sweeping changes that must be made in scientific theory and practice once the existence of Eccles's "ghost" in the machine is admitted. If the *physical* brain is run by a *spiritual* entity, this would mean that psychokinesis (mind over matter) is not only possible but essential for bodily human existence. This remarkable fact would open the door to the possibility of ESP and other psychic powers, which could then logically operate outside the limitations of the physical laws of the space-time-matter universe.

In fact, psychic phenomena of all kinds might even result from contact with Jastrow's nonphysical entities. This likelihood becomes even more reasonable as a result of Eccles's fascinating experiments, to which we will refer later. In *Beyond the Brain*, clinical psychiatrist Stanislav Grof predicts:

> Western science is approaching a paradigm shift of unprecedented proportions, one that will change our concepts of reality and human nature, bridge the gap between ancient wisdom and modern science, and reconcile the difference between Eastern spirituality and Western pragmatism.

Though many questions still remain, Eccles's "ghost in the machine" would seem to challenge the skeptics with a logical rationale not only for paranormal powers but also for mystical experiences. The possible implications are staggering. Recognizing this fact, psychologist Carl Rogers accepted the reality and predicted the imminent practical application of "such paranormal phenomena as telepathy, clairvoyance, precognition . . . healing energies . . . the power of meditation, of transcendent forces. . . ."[22]

In the area of advancing technology, science fiction has proven to be remarkably prophetic. Are the incredible sci-fi portrayals of occult forces also prophetic of the new mind powers that mankind is about to develop? In Arthur C. Clarke's classic *Childhood's End*, the extraterrestrial Overlords (representing the Overmind of the universe), who have arrived in UFO's to rescue mankind from technological self-destruction, remind the earthlings:

> There are powers of the mind and powers beyond the mind, which your science could never have brought within its framework without shattering itself entirely.
>
> All down the ages there have been countless reports of strange phenomena—poltergeists, telepathy, precognition—which you had named but never explained. . . . But they exist, and . . . any [complete] theory of the universe must account for them.[23]

Shattering a Modern Myth

The view that science has disproved religion and that therefore no great scientist can be religious is one of the most widely believed yet humanly destructive misconceptions of the twentieth century. Most of the Nobel prizewinners and other brilliant theorists who have given us today's new physics are in agreement that in spite of any advancement science has made or may yet make, God and religion will always remain not only relevant to human life but beyond the scrutiny of science itself. As Max Planck, who is often called the father of modern quantum theory, has stated: "It is not by any accident that the greatest thinkers of all ages were also deeply religious souls."[24] When Einstein, who himself held religious beliefs, was asked what effect his theory of relativity would have upon religion, he bluntly replied: "None. Relativity is a purely scientific theory and has nothing to do with religion."[25] Nobel laureate Erwin Schroedinger, who also played a vital role in giving to the world the new physics, reminds us:

> The scientific picture of the real world around me is very deficient. It gives a lot of factual information, puts all our experience in a magnificently consistent order, but it is ghastly silent about all . . . that is really near to our heart, that really matters to us.
>
> . . . it knows nothing of beautiful and ugly, good or bad, God and eternity. Science sometimes pretends to answer questions in these domains, but the answers are very often so silly that we are not inclined to take them seriously. . . .
>
> Whence came I and whither go I? That is the great unfathomable question, the same for every one of us. Science has no answer to it.[26]

In *Quantum Questions: The Mystical Writings of the World's Great Physicists*, Ken Wilber has done a valuable service by presenting in one volume "virtually every major statement made" on the topic of the mystical and religious significance of science "by the founders and grand theorists of modern (quantum and relativity) physics: Einstein, Schroedinger, Heisenberg, Bohr, Eddington,

Pauli, de Broglie, Jeans and Planck." Together they dismantle the popular myth about science disproving religion. In fact, according to Wilber's perception, "*all* of these great physicists embrace mysticism of one sort or another." Driving this point home, he writes:

> You who—may I say so?—bow to physics as if it were a religion itself, to you I ask: what does it mean that the founders of your modern science, the theorists and researchers who pioneered the very concepts you now worship implicitly . . . were, *every one of them, mystics*? [emphasis his].[27]

By mysticism, Wilber means a religion that involves neither dogma nor organization, but is based entirely upon one's own subjective experience and transcends objective criteria as a basis of evaluation. While all these scientists speak of the experiencing of "God" by the human soul, they seem to have diverse ideas about who or what God might be. Why such differences—or does it even matter? What consequence might there be if such important beliefs proved to be false? Can experience really be trusted? Are all experiences, including those encountered while on drugs, under hypnosis, or in mystical trance, equally valid? By what criteria can mystical experiences be evaluated in order to eliminate self-delusion? Moreover, if Jastrow's or Strieber's nonphysical entities actually exist, might they not deceive Eccles's similarly nonmaterial "ghost" in the machine without being detected? Such questions are important enough to demand our attention.

An Awesome Perspective

Sir James Jeans put the new developments in physics in awesome perspective when he declared: "The outstanding achievement of twentieth-century physics is not the theory of relativity . . . or the theory of quanta . . . or the dissection of the atom . . . [but] it is the general recognition that we are not yet in contact with ultimate reality. . . ."[28] Putting this in layman's terms, Carl Rogers wrote: "The search for a basic material unit of the universe was fruitless. It did not exist. Our whole perception of reality vanished into unreality."

Einstein had earlier commented upon the inadequacy of science to explain ultimate reality. He had remarked that the study of physics leads inevitably to metaphysics by pointing beyond itself to some nonmaterial or spiritual source for the existence of the material universe. After studying the mystical writings of the world's greatest physicists, Ken Wilber wrote:

> There is no longer any major physical-theoretical objection to spiritual realities . . . this view—which is supported by virtually every theorist in this volume [Einstein, Sherrington, Heisenberg, Schroedinger, Planck, Eddington, et al]—is probably the strongest and most revolutionary conclusion vis-à-vis religion that has ever been "officially" advanced by theoretical science itself.
>
> It is a monumental and epochal turning point in science's stance toward religion . . . [and] in all likelihood marks final closure on that most nagging aspect of the age-old debate between the physical sciences and religion. . . .[29]

The fact that the greatest discoveries in physics point to a nonphysical (or spiritual) dimension of reality clearly encourages the exploration of this mysterious realm of "inner space." In fact, this new venture now seems far more significant for mankind's future than the vaunted exploration of outer space. And the fact that science cannot critique religion or mystical experiences would seem to leave the explorers of this realm in a precarious position.

Inner Space: The Mystical Journey

Edgar Mitchell, Commander of Apollo 14 and the sixth man to walk on the moon, is representative of the many scientists (including other astronauts such as Rusty Sweickart and Brian O'Leary) who are lending their prestige to the support of Eastern mysticism and the human-potential movement. It was on his moon mission, during which he engaged in telepathy experiments back to planet Earth, that Mitchell underwent a mystical experience of "cosmic consciousness" similar to what many people have encountered while under the influence of psychedelic drugs or in deep yogic trance. So profound was this experience that upon his return to earth this dedicated astronaut abandoned the outer-space program to join the exploration of "inner space," now considered by many to be the most promising and exciting frontier. To implement this new search, Mitchell founded the Institute of Noetic Sciences, a think tank of psychic research dedicated to recovering the "perennial philosophy" known to Yogis, gurus, and other ancient "spiritual masters."

A number of Soviet cosmonauts, among them Aleksey Leonov and Georgie Grechko, have reportedly experienced the same mystical transformation on space trips. It was Leonov and Grechko who worked with Sweickart of the U.S.A. to organize in 1985 the Association of Space Explorers. Along with the promotion of future cooperative space programs, ASE members hope to encourage peace and disarmament through spreading the new vision of the oneness of all life which they experienced in viewing earth from outer space. And to accomplish this goal, many of these astronauts/cosmonauts are convinced that it will be necessary to tap into an infinite but neglected human potential which can only be uncovered through the mystical exploration of "inner space." It is this non-physical dimension of mind and spirit upon which all New Age psychospiritual technologies depend.

In spite of their official materialist and antireligion stance, the Soviets are intrigued with the thought of paranormal mind powers and are working diligently to perfect mind-over-matter techniques. Soviet cosmonauts are already being trained "to control the autonomic nervous system through a unique blend of yoga, autosuggestion and other mind-over-body methods of self-control," which the Russian scientists call *psychical self-regulation* (PSR). Their common interest in the development of psychic powers and the sharing of mystical experiences in "higher states of consciousness" is a significant factor in bringing Soviet and Western scientists and astronauts together. This growing rapport is being implemented in unique ways, including global video conferences between the two nations over a satellite hookup called a space-bridge. Participants see this cooperative effort as an important step on the road to world peace.

The Soviet-American Exchange Program was spearheaded by Esalen, located on the California coast south of San Francisco and described as "the Harvard of the human potential movement . . . where science and mysticism have been wrestling with each other for 20 years." According to Soviet historian Paul Pozner, "No American group has ever penetrated as deeply into Soviet society as Esalen."[30] The common interest in the exploration of "inner space" has played a significant role in fostering grassroots cooperation between the two superpowers.

But just as the explorers of outer space cannot be certain of what they may find, so it is with inner space as well. That there could be grave dangers involved should be obvious. One critic wisely cautions:

> New Agers who are charging into the relatively un-mapped wildernesses of the psyche . . . should remember that strange beasts with unknown habits lie hidden in new territories. The uncleared and unfenced regions of the psyche contain a good many vipers, carnivores, freaks, and monsters. . . .
>
> The necessary weapons and instructions for confrontation have not yet been issued to the average person.[31]

Are We in Any Real Danger?

Something of great significance is occurring, and it must be taken seriously. The last revival of occultism played into Adolf Hitler's hands, and the eventual victims numbered in the millions. One can only wonder where the current and far more pervasive renaissance of such occultism will lead. One researcher and syndicated columnist has written:

> A whole generation has now assaulted the gates, using everything from the hallucinogenic drugs to tarot cards in their search for Godhead and unity with the super-mind. . . .
>
> The rapid growth of mind-expansion and consciousness-raising exercises is bringing about many psychological and sociological changes in our society. . . .

> Are we in any real danger? Is the phenomenon a threat
> to us as individuals? The answer to that is a simple yes.[32]

There is considerable evidence, much of which we will offer in the following pages, to indicate that the above statement is not overly sensational or alarmist. Even such a skeptic as Daniel Lawrence O'Keefe warns that man's "magical heritage . . . casts a threatening and possibly permanent shadow over all his other creations." And although O'Keefe (who has written what some consider to be an academic classic on the subject) sees no substantive reality in occultism but considers it to be a purely sociological/ psychological phenomenon, he nevertheless warns that man's "unshakeable occult heritage" could suddenly "overwhelm civilized cultures. . . ."[33]

The concerns of O'Keefe and other sociologists and psychologists are real enough. Suppose, however, that magic is not "all in the mind," a mere figment of man's fears and superstitions. It has been the consensus of mankind for thousands of years and in all cultures that "spirit" beings are behind sorcery. This idea is given little credence by today's materialistic society. Yet even scientific materialism, which was once looked upon as the sure way of escape from the "gods" or "spirits" of primitive religions, confronts us once again with these ancient entities in modern form. In declaring that the cosmos could have spawned creatures so far advanced in evolution that they would manifest godlike powers and might even exist without physical bodies, science has brought back, in perhaps more dangerous form, the "gods" and "demons" of ancient religions to haunt modern man.

We should remember that today's eager experimenters are mere apprentices in this new game of Westernized sorcery. The tale of the sorcerer's apprentice makes a sobering and instructive point: We too can lose control in a naive attempt to manipulate magical powers. In their desire to sell their techniques to a generation disillusioned with materialism and hungering for spiritual reality, thousands of self-proclaimed experts have with entrepreneurial zeal made available a worldwide mystical supermarket of staggering proportions. It is this fascinating world of exotic and potentially lethal products that we will explore.

2

Sorcery—The New Paradigm

Times of occult revival have come and gone through the centuries, leaving little trace upon the pages of history. Scholars who research and interpret the past have, since the much-vaunted days of the eighteenth-century Enlightenment, generally avoided referring to widespread mystical movements. Though occultism was publicly treated as nonsense, however, secretly it has continued to be practiced in various forms even in the highest academic and government circles. At long last there is a recent trend to candidly deal with this phenomenon. A new breed of historians who recognize the role it has played is now willing to confront the historic importance of occultism. [1]

The new sophistication that grew out of the Enlightenment also "demythologized" the miraculous from the Bible, thereby purging Judaism and Christianity of anything that suggested divine intrusion into a universe over which the ambitious inhabitants of planet Earth were seeking to take control. It was believed that *science*, as mankind's new hope, would eventually solve all problems and answer all questions. And as for God, there was no longer any "need of that hypothesis."

Such an egotistical and naive view is held by very few physical scientists today, although it is still the popular faith among so-called social scientists. Whatever one's view, however, there is no disputing Erwin Schroedinger's reminder that science is "ghastly silent" about all that "really matters to us." And as for mankind's "new hope," Sir Arthur Eddington, called by some the greatest of English astronomers, had this to say: "There was a time when the whole

27

combination of self and environment which makes up experience seemed likely to pass under the dominion of a physics much more ironbound than it is now. That overweening phase . . . is past."[2]

Arthur Koestler—editor, novelist, researcher, and one of the most celebrated writers of this century on both science and mysticism—put it in even stronger terms:

> The mechanistic and deterministic world-view which is still dominant in sociology and the behavioral sciences . . . has no longer a leg left to stand on; it has become a Victorian anachronism.
>
> The nineteenth-century clockwork model of the universe is in shambles and, since matter itself has been dematerialized, materialism can no longer claim to be a scientific philosophy.[3]

While we would not minimize the great strides that science has made, we must acknowledge that for every door it opens ten more unopened doors appear on the other side, like ever-receding images in a hall of mirrors. Moreover, while we have learned much *about* such things as energy, gravity, space, and time, we are no closer to knowing what any of these *is* than were the ancient Hindus or Egyptians 5000 years ago. Much less can science determine what love or truth or beauty *is*, or the real purpose of life. Eddington argues:

> When from the human heart, perplexed with the mystery of existence, the cry goes up, "What is it all about?" it is no true answer to . . . reply:
>
> "It is about atoms and chaos; it is about a universe of fiery globes rolling on to impending doom. . . ."[4]

Materialistic affluence and sensual pleasure may temporarily stifle the cry for meaning, but eventually the soul's thirst for waters from a deeper well becomes unbearable. Such was the longing which gave birth in the early 1960's to the flower-child rebellion against the monotonous tyranny of materialism. The fountain of financial success had polluted itself and turned bitter. Affluence satisfied a certain sensuality but left the spirit feeling strangely numb and empty. A disillusioned generation cried out for something more—and America's "demythologized religion" had nothing to offer. As Esalen's George Leonard put it: "The neighborhood Protestant church is the last place to have a mystical experience."[5] The same could be said for the local Catholic church, Jewish temple, or Moslem mosque.

A Question of Reality

The stage was set for the Pied Piper of Harvard to lead a parade of mesmerized youth to a new dimension of *spiritual* experience that science had told them did not exist. Timothy Leary's LSD (along with the other psychedelics) turned out to be the launching pad for *mind trips* beyond the physical universe of time, space, and matter to a strange dimension where intoxicating nectars were abundant and exotic adventures the norm. For millions it was a "mind-blowing" experience that forever changed their worldview.

The Beatles played a key role in leading a generation of youth into drugs. Leary, just back from India, called them "the four evangelists." Relaxing in his tepee and listening to the Beatles' album *Sergeant Pepper's Lonely Hearts Club Band*, Leary said, "The Beatles have taken my place. That latest album—a complete celebration of LSD."[6] The Rolling Stones and other big-time Rock groups were evangelists also. In 1969, *Life* magazine quoted Rock star Jimi Hendrix: ". . . through music, you can hypnotise people. . . . And when you get [them] at [their] weakest point, you can preach into the subconscious minds what we want to say." He was frank to admit, "Definitely I'm trying to change the world."[7] Lloyd Richards, dean of the Yale School of Drama, has said, "The arts define whatever [the] new society is that we're evolving. . . ."[8] The awesome power of music to mold the thinking of the masses (and particularly of its youth) has been demonstrated by those who unquestionably knew what they were doing. Crosby, of the Crosby, Stills & Nash group, boasted:

> I figured that the only thing to do was to steal their kids. I still think it's the only thing to do.

> . . . I'm not talking about kidnapping . . . [but] about
> changing young people's value systems. . . .⁹

Drug-users were initially intrigued with whether the vivid experiences on the drug high were *real* or merely a mental mirage somehow triggered by a chemical reaction in the brain. Was it all just a "head trip," or was it real? What *is* real? After enough trips such questions lost their meaning. *Experience* had become the sole and self-authenticating truth. Whether it was all merely imagined in the mind or not ceased to matter.

No argument could any longer convince those who had experienced the "altered state" that reality was limited to the physical world. The sights, tastes, smells, sounds, and feelings in this strange new land of the *mind* often seemed even more vivid and real than those in the so-called "real world," which to many of these adventuresome explorers now seemed drab and tasteless by comparison. The magical door to what Carlos Castaneda called the "sorcerer's world," [10] a realm surpassing even Alice's Wonderland, had swung open and America would never be the same.

Most dictionaries still categorize sorcery as an "evil" form of occultism in distinction to so-called "white magic." However, many of today's anthropologists, including best-selling authors such as Michael Harner and Carlos Castaneda, see sorcery (like all categories of occultism) as a neutral technique for manipulating reality for either good or evil—as with the dark and light side of the Force in *Star Wars*. There are others, however, who warn that it is as dangerous to become involved in white magic as it is in any other form of sorcery.

From Drugs to Eastern Mysticism

Drugs were only the first step into the world of mystical experiences. The real power was to be experienced through Eastern mysticism. Aware that the eager pursuit of "altered states of consciousness" while tripped out on psychedelics had rendered a generation vulnerable, the Eastern gurus lost no time invading the West with their cosmic gospel of reincarnation and Nirvana. Disciples flocked to them by the millions to learn techniques for achieving the same altered states through meditation which they had previously reached on drugs. Leary's Harvard colleague in drug experimentation, Richard Alpert, after spending a fortune in psychotherapy to no effect, went to India to "find himself" and came back as Ram Dass, one of the first Westerners to turn guru and lead others down the same path.[11]

After studying with Maharishi Mahesh Yogi at his ashram in India, the ever-popular and admired Beatles led multitudes of their worshipful followers into transcendental meditation and other forms of Yoga. Many other well-known Americans also began to practice and promote TM. In *The Relaxation Response*, which went to the top of the best-seller lists, Harvard Medical School associate professor Herbert Benson praised Maharishi and TM's results.[12] Unfortunately, Benson made no mention of the frightening spiritual side effects, of the suicides and insanity, or of the fact that the mantra (a secret word to be repeated while meditating) is not the meaningless sound which Maharishi represents it to be but instead is the name of a Hindu god. Moreover, according to the authoritative texts on Yoga, the repetition of this sound in meditation is a call to that entity to possess the meditator. Marilyn Ferguson would later rejoice that influential persons were using their talents to bring this "new consciousness" into every area of modern society.[13]

Others took a different view, but the voice of reason was drowned out in the clamor for instant bliss. One disillusioned former New Ager who was quoted in the *New York Times* insightfully complained: "The drug of the '60s was LSD and marijuana. I think the drug of the '80s is cosmic consciousness."[14] In his book *From Shaman to Psychotherapist*, Walter Bromberg writes:

> Whereas in previous generations "altered consciousness" was considered a mark of bohemian depravity if sought voluntarily or one of madness if involuntary, nowadays a "high" is the essence of psychologic sophistication.[15]

The Age of Aquarius had dawned, and with it came a new vocabulary that is all too familiar today. Instead of "freaking out," the new term was "enlightenment." And in place of "tripping out on drugs," one was now experiencing "higher states of consciousness." Only the labels had changed: The new "astral travel" brought the same experiences as the old "drug trip"; "enlightenment" simply reinforced in a more profound way the same Hindu pantheistic worldview that the drug movement had fostered. The weird and often frightening "spirit entities" (variously called *gods*, *masters*, *teachers*, or *guides*) which Eastern meditators claimed to meet in Yogic trance were unmistakably similar to those encountered on drugs. Although some of the masks they wore differed slightly, their personalities betrayed them, and the same basic "perennial philosophy" came through consistently.

Recognizing this rather remarkable fact, Leary used the *Bardo Thodol (Tibetan Book of the Dead)* in *The Psychedelic Experience*, his classic guide for drug-users. Some of those users even reported being initiated into transcendental meditation by "spirit entities" while on a drug trip. The connection could no longer be denied. Eventually the transition from drugs to Eastern mysticism became almost routine. East had met West in an encounter never dreamed of by Rudyard Kipling.

The Deepening Involvement in Eastern Mysticism

Since the early days when drugs and mysticism were a novelty, the influence of Eastern mysticism has spread to every area of Western culture. Organizational psychologist Marsha Sinetar declares that even the pragmatic corporate world will be transformed—by a new breed of "actualized" employees and executives who practice Yoga to relieve stress, have mystical experiences, follow an inner guidance, and place first priority upon personal spiritual growth.[16] This remarkable transformation is in fact already well underway. As only one of many examples that could be cited, the *New York Times* reported: "At Stanford University's well-regarded Graduate School of Business the syllabus for a seminar on 'Creativity in Business' includes meditation, chanting, 'dream work,' the use of tarot cards and discussion of the 'New Age Capitalist.' "[17]

The growing acceptance of New Age beliefs and practices by both hardheaded business executives and ivory-towered academicians is further proof of the surprising breadth of this exploding movement. Even venerable Harvard University in Cambridge, Massachusetts, has lent its immense prestige to New Age beliefs by hosting the 1987 Iyengar Yoga Convention. A few months earlier at highly regarded Claremont Graduate School in Southern California, a symposium of university professors seriously discussed out-of-body experiences, extrasensory perception, spirit survival of bodily death, and reincarnation. Commenting upon the new respect and openness toward what only a few years ago would have been written off as religious delusion, one of the participating professors remarked: "This kind of conference couldn't have been held in a university setting ten years ago."

Not everyone is attracted to the dazzling variety of today's spiritual merchandise. However, we all know someone who has been or will be involved. The issues raised are of immense importance and will eventually affect all of us. "Fad or movement," reported the *Los Angeles Times*, "New Age thinking is coursing through business, education, the arts, Madison Avenue, even politics."[18] University of Denver professor Carl A. Raschke, a critic of the New Age movement, calls it the "most powerful social force in the country today." It would be difficult to dispute that appraisal and irresponsible to overlook the hidden and oft-denied religious and occultic nature of what is occurring.

At the heart of this historic transformation is an undercurrent of revolutionary change that reaches the highest levels of religion and politics. Former California Governor Edmund G. Brown, Jr., for example, who spent four years in a Jesuit seminary before turning to politics, has committed himself seriously to the Eastern mysticism he had been dabbling in for some time. Brown has hopes that through embracing some of the spirituality which has been practiced in the East, the Western military powers can learn to coexist in peace. He recently spent about six months in Japan studying under Zen Buddhists as a means of meeting "his own spiritual needs." "Pope John Paul II's [surprising] admonition during [his] visit to India that the world—and Roman Catholics—ought to look to the East for inspiration"[19] played an important role in Brown's deepening involvement in Eastern mysticism.

The Aquarian Conspiracy

Why are highly educated Westerners turning back to ancient Eastern mystical practices in the midst of the greatest scientific/technological boom in history? How could it be that a world which is in mad pursuit of materialism is at the same time becoming increasingly enamored with spirituality and psychic powers? What is behind this obsession with occult forces, and where can it be taking us? These are legitimate questions that deserve a serious answer. In *The Aquarian Conspiracy*, a book that has been called "the New Age Bible," Marilyn Ferguson enthusiastically reports:

> A great, shuddering irrevocable shift is overtaking us. . . . It is a new mind, a turnabout in consciousness in critical numbers of individuals, a network powerful enough to bring about radical change in our culture.
>
> This network—the Aquarian Conspiracy—has already enlisted the minds, hearts and resources of some of our most advanced thinkers, including Nobel laureate scientists, philosophers, statesmen, celebrities . . . who are working to create a different kind of society. . . .
>
> The technologies for expanding and transforming personal consciousness, once the secret of an elite, are now generating massive change in every cultural institution—medicine, politics, business, education, religion and the family.[20]

Ferguson's triumphant declarations are based upon the peculiar belief that a revival of ancient occultism is the key to the salvation of today's modern world. It is remarkable how that questionable assumption is so readily adopted by otherwise cautious and intelligent leaders in their enthusiasm to welcome the dawning of a "New Age." Carl Rogers, who was one of the most influential psychologists of this century and impacted modern society as few others have since World War II, was in full agreement with Ferguson's appraisal. In an article for a South African New Age magazine, Rogers wrote:

> It is truly an "Aquarian conspiracy." Multitudes of congenial people the world over are "conspiring" together . . . discovering that they view life in this fundamentally new way. . . .
>
> We are facing a combination of paradigm shifts which

may be more powerful than anything the world has known before.[21]

Rogers neglects to tell us why this powerful "paradigm shift" will be beneficial. That seems to be taken for granted—but why? Nor is today's sweeping occult renaissance, with its dream of acquiring supernatural powers to attain both material prosperity and the spiritual transformation of our species, taking place only in the affluent and success-oriented West. One of the most convincing evidences of the power of New Age thinking is its amazing international scope. Reporting enthusiastically upon what it calls "a worldwide 'Aquarian Conspiracy,'" one popular New Age magazine (which offers video and audio self-hypnosis tapes for "programming the mind") recently declared:

> The strength of the New Age Movement lies in the fact that it grows in the consciousness of the world population . . . [and as this] thinking gains momentum, New Age influence becomes more obvious in every area of society.[22]

A Burgeoning Mystical Worldmart

To supply the skyrocketing demand, enterprising opportunists offer an almost-unlimited variety of exotic and well-packaged merchandise: everything from assorted subliminal self-hypnosis tapes to various techniques for contacting "spirit guides" in order to accomplish anything from improving one's tennis or golf to destroying cancer cells. Nearly every city of any size now has at least one if not several publications devoted entirely to New Age products and ongoing activities, usually distributed free wherever health foods and metaphysical books are sold. In Chicago one can pick up *New Age Chicago*, in Pittsburgh the *Three Rivers Network*, or in Los Angeles *L.A. Resources*; while periodicals such as *Whole Life Times* and *Common Ground* circulate nationwide, and similar magazines and newspapers (such as Australia's *New Age News*) can be found throughout the world.

To the astonishment of both hard-core materialists and the most astute economic forecasters, a burgeoning worldwide supermarket has appeared on the scene almost overnight—a conglomeration of business ventures for marketing spirituality that gives every indication of growing faster in the foreseeable future than any other segment of America's economy. In pursuit of the growing profits, a new generation of promoters and entrepreneurs of the mystical has arisen to take advantage of this exploding interest in psychic experiences and occult powers. And to make their services known nationwide, there is now the *National New Age Yellow Pages: A United States Guide to Consciousness-Raising Services, Products, and Organizations*, a publication which first appeared early in 1987.[23]

Literally thousands of organizations, most of which didn't exist 20 years ago, are now generating impressive profits as part of this fast-growing market for innovatively packaged occultism. The following is just a small but representative sampling of companies, organizations, and products listed in the Spring 1987 edition of *L.A. Resources*: "Spiritual Energy Consultant—The Soul Healing System"; "Rebirthing"; "Whole Brain Integration—Balance left/right and front/back brain for access to natural altered states"; "Laying on of Hands techniques to effect physical, emotional, mental and spiritual healing"; "A Meditative Approach to Colon Therapy"; "Ancient Tibetan science of Universal Energy"; "Aphrodisiacal Cooking for Rejuvenation"; "Collective Yoga of Integral Perfection"; "Gay Metaphysical Spiritual Association"; "Dharma Sah Zen Center"; "Deer Tribe Shamanic Lodge of Ceremonial Medicine"; "The Sorcerer's Shop"; and "Pyramid & Crystal Environment Systems."

The New Spirituality Doesn't Come Cheap

One of Mahatma Gandhi's intimate friends used to delight in saying that it took "a great deal of money" to keep him "living in poverty." Gandhi's obsession with denouncing all that was introduced by foreign interests and getting back to the simple and wholesome Indian lifestyle of pre-British times included damning railways as "a most dangerous institution." But that did not prevent him from using the railway system. It was only one of the many contradictions in Gandhi's life. To maintain his poverty stance, he always rode third-class. However, he had a special coach to himself, which of course cost far more than if he had ridden first-class.

Considerable money is also required when it comes to maintaining the allegedly simple, natural, and spiritual New Age lifestyle. Traditionally, spirituality has been offered freely or for voluntary contributions. The enticing gospel of the "new spirituality," however, most of which comes from Gandhi's India, is being packaged appealingly and sold for money, often at exorbitant prices. Beneath the seemingly sincere doublespeak about higher consciousness, enlightenment, astral travel, infinite psychic powers, and cosmic law, blatant bottom-line materialistic *profitability* plays a large part in the new spirituality. There is a new class of millionaires made up of gurus, psychics, "channelers," and promoters of assorted self-improvement techniques who have made very substantial fortunes selling ethereal ideas.

Those who scoff at what they call the impotent mysticism of the New Age need to remember that money is power, and that this movement is generating many *billions* of dollars in sales. *U.S. News & World Report* commented recently, "While skeptics cast doubts, psychics count dollars."[24] Early in 1987, *Newsweek* reported the staggering statistic: New Age self-improvement programs being pushed on employees by America's major corporations account for "about $4 billion in corporate spending each year."[25] And this is only one very small segment of the New Age movement.

Sales of occult books are expanding so rapidly (there was a 95 percent increase in sales for B. Dalton stores in the week that Shirley MacLaine's TV miniseries aired in January 1987) that *American Bookseller* magazine recently ran a feature article titled "A New Age for Metaphysical Books." To accommodate this change in values, B. Dalton (one of the nation's largest bookselling chains) has reorganized its merchandise: What used to be called "Astrology and Occult" is now included in a new section titled "New Age." At the 1987 American Booksellers Convention in Washington D.C., where among the more than 20,000 booksellers, exhibitors, and authors Shirley MacLaine drew the most attention, 52 publishers formed the New Age Publishing Alliance with the motto "A Consciousness Whose Time Has Come." As one New-Age-oriented journal recently observed, readers of the occult have become "more mainstream and affluent, with an increased number of professionals."

At the 1987 Awards Ceremony, a Grammy was presented for the first time for "New Age Music," a new category which was already generating over 100 million dollars in annual sales. United Airlines was quick to devote an entire channel to "New Age Music" for its passengers, and Lincoln-Mercury, BMW, and Honda were among the first auto manufacturers to jump on this skyrocketing bandwagon with the use of New Age music for promoting their products. By November 1987 the *Los Angeles Times* could report in its business section that "radio stations that play New Age music exclusively have suddenly sprung up in virtually every major U.S. city."[26] Much of this music is designed to help induce the altered state of consciousness that is essential to New Age spirituality, but seldom are purchasers advised of this fact.

A Vulnerable Population Ready for Magic?

Most astonishing is the acceptability and influence of this occult revival behind the Iron and Bamboo Curtains, in spite of Marxism's official rejection of all things "spiritual." Michael Murphy, the cofounder of Esalen, is one of the leading promoters of the human-potential movement (another alias for New Age). Commenting upon the growing worldwide receptivity to this new "spiritual awakening" (which he has enthusiastically observed in his promotional visits to many countries), Murphy declares: "Nowhere was this more evident than in my travels in the Soviet Union." He goes on to explain that shamanism (witchcraft) is on the rise in Russia, where it is being hailed even by leading scientists as the new hope of mankind.[27] Gorbachev's creeping capitalism also seems destined to partake of New Age magic: Werner Erhard has been given a three-year contract to enlighten Soviet managers with his psychologized mixture of Zen Buddhism and Scientology. In late 1986 the *Wall Street Journal* reported:

> The video recording that flickers on the television screen shows a startling scene: Werner Erhard, the founder of est and a guru of the Me Generation, is

> lecturing a group of Soviet bureaucrats . . . standing in a
> Moscow auditorium beneath a picture of Lenin. . . .
>   And so East meets est. The Kremlin thinks that Mr.
> Erhard's brand of instant self-help could motivate the
> sluggish Soviet bureaucracy. . . .
>   William Gaylin, a psychiatrist . . . [says] the Erhard
> nostrums appeal to a "vulnerable population ready for
> magic."
>   The Russians, apparently, are vulnerable.[28]

Western business and technology leaders are clearly vulnerable
also. In spite of the fact that Erhard abandoned his family and has
been less than successful in solving his own personal problems, his
clients in the West cover the spectrum from Ford Motor Company to
the National Aeronautics and Space Administration. One NASA
manager and est graduate, in fact, "persuaded the U.S. government
to spend $45,000 for a five-day workshop for 50 NASA engineers
and managers held by Mr. Erhard and his associates."[29] *California
Business* magazine reports that more than half of the 500 presidents
and company owners it surveyed have involved their employees in
New Age training seminars that make use of various "consciousness-raising" techniques taught in programs similar to Erhard's est
(now called the Forum).

There is perhaps no class of persons more vulnerable to this
worldwide "Aquarian Conspiracy" than employees who are required by their employers to take New Age courses. Ron Zemke,
senior editor of the prestigious business magazine *Training*, complains that "spiritual instruction" is now being "served up in
corporate ashrams."[30] Observing one such program in action caused
two reporters from another national magazine to ask facetiously, "Is
this the headquarters of a religious cult?" The answers they discovered after further investigation were extremely disturbing and
caused them to report:

> No, this is the *telephone* company. And its latest
> seminars . . . called Krone training . . . [are] required
> learning for the 67,000 employees of Pacific Bell, Cali-
> fornia's largest utility company. . . .

Besides Pacific Bell, such corporate giants as Proctor
& Gamble, TRW, Ford Motor Co. and Polaroid have all
signed on New Age consultants.[31]

Some employees of Pacific Bell "complained to the utilities
commission that the company's Kroning exercises [annual cost:
about 100 million dollars, ultimately paid for by phone subscrib-
ers][32] were in fact mind-control sessions based on the [mystical]
teachings of Georges Gurdjieff. . . ."[33] As a result of the commission's reprimand, those controversial workshops were suspended,
though PacBell insisted that they were beneficial. Employees of
many other corporations who are being required to participate in
similar New Age programs have added their voices to the growing
chorus of concern, but with little effect. In spite of the warnings
from numerous experts concerning the very real dangers that are
involved in such techniques, there is an expanding list of employees
(including those in management) who have been fired for refusing to
participate in New Age programs.[34]

The modern space age has been invaded by ancient occult beliefs.
There can be no doubt that Eastern mysticism has established a
strong and expanding beachhead in the Western world. The resulting blend of science and mysticism has become known as "the
consciousness revolution"—yet another alias for "New Age." A
generation not only of drug-users but of meditators and self-improvement enthusiasts from all walks of life and strata of society has
been initiated into sorcery. America has become the sorcerer's new
apprentice, and it may already be too late to turn back.

3

Caveat Emptor: Let the Buyer Beware

To all appearances, we are in the midst of an unprecedented and all-encompassing spiritual transformation that seems to be accelerating worldwide on all fronts. It cannot be explained away as an extremist movement of closet occultists suddenly crawling out of the woodwork to gather followers from the fringes of society. Nor can it be brushed aside as some weak ripple in the wake of the countercultural rebellion against Western materialism that seemed to come out of nowhere in the fifties and sixties to sweep away a generation of youth. It is true that many who were involved in the hippie movement became New Agers as part of a natural progression from drugs to Eastern mysticism; there is a close connection. Yet countless millions who never tuned in, turned on, and dropped out are now caught up in what can only be described as a sweeping *spiritual* metamorphosis of modern culture.

While no one has accused the New Age movement of being a cult, there are some disturbing similarities. Cult expert Reginald Alev warns that New Age groups tell participants "they're the master of their own destiny, sort of an Eastern version of Norman Vincent Peale, but they don't know they are being subjected to mind control."[1] The growing concern over mass manipulation seems valid enough when one considers the very claims of "transformational seminar" leaders such as John D. Adams, who boasts that "training for the technological age . . . is effective in aligning masses of people with a common cause."[2] According to the *New York Times*:

> Psychologists who have studied the process say that while participants are in this "altered state," leaders of the groups are able to implant new ideas and alter their thinking processes.[3]

The *Times* article declared: "Gurus hired to motivate workers are raising fears of 'mind control.' " This charge is so grave and has been made by so many experts that it has to be taken seriously. One of those experts is former University of Wisconsin psychology faculty member Edwin Morse, who warns that graduates of New Age courses now being required for employees of many businesses "are often psychically scarred." Now in private practice and specializing in helping such people, Dr. Morse declares: "These [mind control] groups are using hypnotic procedures and people are not being told about it."[4]

There are, according to Richard L. Watring, additional dangers inherent in the mind-control techniques at the heart of the New Age training programs. Watring, who is personnel director of Budget Rent-a-Car Corporation in Chicago, asserts that techniques are deliberately being introduced into employee training programs which "induce a trance-like state." He is concerned not only about the behavior modification similar to brainwashing which can result,[5] but also about the many reports from participants who are convinced that they have come under harmful influence from "spirit entities" as a result of these trance states.

Watring felt compelled to investigate after observing (with considerable surprise and alarm) the eagerness with which ordinarily cautious business leaders were buying into mysticism mislabeled as motivational psychology. Arguing that those exposed by employers to " 'New Age psychotechnologies' . . . [for] altering 'normal' consciousness . . . ought to [be told] up front" that inevitably their "fundamental worldviews and Judeo-Christian religious beliefs" are being tampered with,[6] Watring explains:

> For about the last three years, I have observed the introduction and growth of a new philosophy of human

potential and development. Lay people most often refer to it as the "New Age" movement.

Marilyn Ferguson chronicled the history and current development of this movement in her best-seller, *The Aquarian Conspiracy*. She lists a number of psychotechnologies . . . "for altering consciousness" such as Meditation, Self-hypnosis, Focusing, Centering, Guided Imagery, Visualization, Transcendental Meditation, Yoga, Biofeedback, Dianetics, Silva Mind Control, and many others.

I began noticing a number of consultants and corporate Human Resources Development practitioners who were promoting "higher creativity," "improved memory," "accelerated learning," "stress management." I found that most of these methods were somewhere on Ferguson's list of "means to altering consciousness."

I then began to wonder about the motives of the persons selling these concepts. Were they really out to improve human potential? Or had they had some profound experience on their spiritual journey and were really enlisting others to follow their path?

I recently had an opportunity to participate in a panel discussion at the Association of Humanistic Psychology Annual Meeting. The title of their conference was CHANGE AGENTS-85, and I accused them of trying to "change" the belief systems of their clients.

I suggested that some practitioners have a "hidden agenda," and that their clients are entitled to know how certain psychospiritual therapies will affect the client's employees.[7]

Evangelists of the "New Spirituality"

The mislabeling of Eastern religion as science is even affecting education. For example, the August 1987 annual convention of The Association for Humanistic Psychology included under the heading of Humanistic Education a workshop titled "Zen Buddhist Ethics and the Caring Classroom: The application of Zen Buddhism to educating children. . . ." A similar attempt to integrate Protestant,

Catholic, Jewish, or Islamic beliefs into the public classroom would quickly bring the ACLU on the scene to protest such flagrant state support of a religion. Yet Eastern mysticism and even various forms of witchcraft are regularly being taught and applied in public schools across America with government support. That growing trend will be addressed in more detail later.

Under the guidance of some state and federal officials, public schools have now become major centers for conditioning the present generation to be comfortable with the new paradigm of sorcery. This deliberate program (which has the full backing of the National Education Association)[8] to change *spiritual* values, which have traditionally been left to parents and church, has sparked a national home-schooling movement, resulting in the greatest flight from public education in the history of America.

The "change agents" may be very sincere in believing that their "hidden agenda" is the only hope for rescuing mankind from destruction. This does not justify, however, their use of deceit in peddling their products nor the suppression of information concerning the inherent dangers. Ron Zemke tells how appalled he was when, with "zealous excitement," he was told about a workshop that taught participants how "to sell a New Age agenda to management without them realizing what they were signing on for." Pointing out the contradiction of claiming that the New Age is concerned for "the rights and dignity of individuals" while at the same time denying "the right to be told the truth," Zemke writes:

> If the New Age is something we will have to be tricked into by an elite cadre of "enlightened" people certain that they know best what we ought to think and feel and value and believe, then I guess I'll have to stick with the old order.[9]

Yet such underhanded deception by elitists seems to be the accepted *modus operandi*. The editor of a New Age magazine boasts unashamedly of a gathering of professionals who "came from 11 states" to discuss how better to infiltrate New Age thinking into every area of society. As an example of how this was being accomplished, he mentioned "a Southern California Ph.D., director of a successful hypnosis center . . . employed by two of California's largest publicly held companies to teach 'success and positive thinking' to their employees." He explained that she carefully avoids using "the words 'metaphysics' or 'New Age,' but the ideas [she teaches] are nothing else." He went on to say enthusiastically:

> One of the biggest advantages we have as New Agers is, once the occult, metaphysical and New Age terminology is removed, we have concepts and techniques that are very acceptable to the general public. So we can change the names and demonstrate the power. In so doing, we open the New Age door to millions who normally would not be receptive.[10]

In spite of the dangers inherent in consciousness-altering techniques, New Age evangelists are convinced that the mystical supermart's gilded wares are essential not only for employees of major business concerns but for the well-being of society at large, whether it realizes it or not. They seem determined to convert the world with the gospel of their "consciousness revolution" even if it requires some subtle deceit.

A Web of Deception

The very term "New Age," however well-intentioned, is misleading. Its only claim to being *new* lies in the astonishing respectability, acceptability, and credibility now being granted in the space age to stone-age superstitious practices. Everything now known as "New Age" (herbal or traditional medicine, holistic health and vegetarian diets, self-hypnosis, reincarnation, spirit guides, pyramid power, color therapy, Yoga, and other forms of Eastern meditation) is simply a revival of ancient *religious* practices now being passed off as new advancements in *science*, *medicine*, and *psychology*.

There is little doubt that the promoters of this movement are aware of the irony of relabeling ancient occultism as something new. Edgar Mitchell and other leaders openly confess that they are promoting a revival of what they call the "*ancient* wisdom." "This stuff has been around for 5000 years," declares Shirley Mac-

Laine.[11] Then why call it *new*? As Timothy Leary (formerly ostracized as high priest of the drug movement, but now widely accepted in academia) defiantly declared in a speech, to the delight of his audience, at the 22nd Annual Convention of the Association for Humanistic Psychology:

> Our trip has always existed. . . . All through the dark ages there were the Sufis, the Kabbalists, the Brotherhoods and Sisterhoods and the witchcraft groups and the Knights of Malta, and the Masonic orders. . . .
>
> The spirit of humanism . . . the belief that it's all within and you're going to find God looking into the eyes of your lover, we didn't invent that. It didn't start in the '60s or even in the sacred '50s, it's been going on forever.[12]

In the process of calling "new" what is in fact extremely old, the *mystical* is being marketed as *technological*. In a classic flimflam, one of the world's most ancient *religious* practices is being sold as the "*science* of Yoga." The average Yoga student in the West is not aware that Yoga was introduced by Lord Krishna in the Baghavad-Gita as the sure way to the Hindu heaven, or that Shiva, "The Destroyer" (and one of the three most powerful and feared of Hindu deities) is addressed as Yogeshwara, or Lord of Yoga. In one of the most authoritative Yoga texts, the *Hathayoga-Pradipika*, dating back to the fifteenth century, Svatmarama lists Lord Shiva as the first in a long line of Hatha Yoga teachers. Nor does the average Yoga instructor mention or likely even know the many warnings contained in ancient Yoga texts that even "Hatha Yoga [the so-called *physical* Yoga] is a dangerous tool."[13]

The fact that Yoga is the very heart of Hinduism is usually suppressed and often denied. Hearing occasional references to Patanjali's second-century B.C. *Yoga Sutras*, the Westerner (who has been led to believe that Yoga is purely *physical*) erroneously assumes that Patanjali was an early Plato or Einstein and is unaware that Hindus regard him as one of their greatest *religious* leaders. Under the impression that they are buying *health*, millions of people are unwittingly getting involved in *Hinduism*. This type of deception is typical of most products in today's exploding mystical marketplace. Because of the flagrant misrepresentation and mislabeling, many purchasers of what they have been persuaded are *scientific* methods for developing their full potential are in fact being led into *religious* beliefs and practices.

That many of the practitioners of Yoga and other forms of Eastern mysticism do seem to reap benefits, at least for a time, cannot be denied. Nevertheless, their basic worldview and religious belief system are being tampered with in ways which they may not realize and which they are certainly not being alerted to by their instructors. Moreover, those engaging in consciousness-altering techniques involve themselves in potentially dangerous *spiritual* experiences, as we shall see.

Transcendental Trickery

Transcendental meditation (TM) is a typical example of New Age misrepresentation. When Maharishi Mahesh Yogi first introduced TM to the West, he openly taught that it was a Hindu religious practice and that its real purpose was to produce "a legendary substance called Soma in the meditator's body so the Gods of the Hindu pantheon could be fed and awakened!"[14] But when he was denied access to public schools and government funding on the grounds that he was promoting religious practices, Maharishi quickly deleted all reference to religion and began presenting TM as a *science*. Nothing was changed except the labels. This deception has been furthered by the many celebrities, athletes, psychiatrists, and other leaders who have practiced and promoted TM, some no doubt without recognizing that it is in fact pure Hinduism. Bob Kropinski, a former TM instructor, explains:

> I joined in '71. . . . in 1957 they [had] started an organization called Spiritual Regeneration Movement . . . for religious and educational purposes only.
> . . . in 1974 [Maharishi] . . . completely renamed all the corporations . . . [under] a new set of Articles of Incorporation deleting everything that said "spiritual" and "religious." . . .

> Using scientific terminology is his way to legitimize
> the teaching of Hinduism. For example, Maharishi . . .
> began calling God "the vacuum state."
> . . . He instructed people in the deception.[15]

Since that time advertisements have blatantly declared that TM is "not a religion, not a philosophy, not Yoga . . . it involves no change of belief system, is not thought control, mind control." In actuality it is all of these. According to Kropinski, who won a lawsuit against TM in January 1987, Maharishi made it clear to those on the inside:

> It doesn't matter if you lie teaching people . . . [be-
> cause] TM is the ultimate, absolute spiritual authority on
> the face of this Earth.
> [TMers] are the only teachers and upholders of genu-
> ine spiritual tradition on the face of the earth. They're
> running the universe.
> They are controlling the gods through the soma sacri-
> fice.[16]

TM is, in fact, one of many forms of Yoga, and is no less dangerous than the rest. Seven former TMers, for example, recently filed suit for nine million dollars each in Washington D.C., charging that Maharishi failed to teach them to "fly" as promised and that their practice of advanced TM had caused severe "negative emotional, psychological and physical effects." Kropinski relates that people were experiencing violent shaking, hallucinations, murderous impulses, and suicidal thoughts "as a result of the TM practice." At teacher-training sessions distraught TMers would tell of flying into an uncontrollable rage in the midst of meditation, smashing furniture, assaulting their roommates, and trying to commit suicide. In response Maharishi would tell them to "lie down on the floor and take it as it comes." Kropinski relates his own inner turmoil:

> When I left the movement I was filled with all sorts of
> wild superstitions; I believed that I was going to be struck
> down by the gods. . . .

[But then] I found out that . . . there were other victims of this process who also had to come to terms with the fact that they had been raped: spiritually and financially raped.[17]

Caveat Emptor

Most self-improvement techniques being adopted throughout society—by public educators, psychologists, psychiatrists, medical doctors, and success/motivation seminar leaders—employ varying forms of Eastern meditation and self-hypnosis similar to TM's variation on Yoga. It is these very "technologies for expanding and transforming personal consciousness" that Marilyn Ferguson lauds in *The Aquarian Conspiracy.* Yet in keeping with warnings expressed by Watring and others, there are many documented cases of persons involved not only in TM but in other forms of Yoga and autosuggestion having extremely frightening and uncontrollable spiritual experiences. As a result, some have been driven to insanity and even suicide—but these facts are deliberately suppressed.[18] The same problems often plague participants in assorted mind-dynamics and self-improvement courses, especially where the techniques involve contact with visualized "inner guides."

It is not uncommon for the practitioners of Eastern mysticism, even in its various Westernized self-help forms, to suddenly find themselves "out of body" or thrown across the room by some unknown force, or else encountering what seem to be very real alien entities who attempt "possession." In an unusually frank interview in *Yoga Journal,* Ken Wilber (practicing mystic and Yoga enthusiast who has been described as today's "Einstein of consciousness") warns that any form of Eastern meditation, even done "correctly," involves "a whole series of deaths and rebirths; extraordinary conflicts and stresses . . . some very rough and frightening times."[19]

In *Transcendental Misconceptions,* former TM instructor R. D. Scott tells of numerous "spirit manifestations" among meditators. Such experiences included: "visions of floating green eyes . . . creatures of light floating above the *puja* table [initiation ceremony altar]," as well as ghoulish creatures materializing periodically to stare with terrifying expressions at participants.[20] Scott gives a number of reasons for discounting the idea that these experiences could all be explained as hallucinations. Often more than one person saw "the same procession of spirit creatures simultaneously and without any advance warning. . . ."[21] Of course such possibilities are not mentioned in the ads and brochures promoting TM and other forms of Yoga.

There seems to be an alarming increase in the incidence of similar mystical or occult experiences among the general populace. The Durham, North Carolina, Foundation for Research on the Nature of Man (an institution founded by Duke University's famous parapsychologist J. B. Rhine) has lately reported a "greater number of callers seeking help." As a result, the Foundation "is compiling a directory of mental-health professionals with expertise in [counseling] those suffering from 'confusing or distressing effects of ostensibly paranormal experiences.' "[22]

"Normal" Spiritual Emergencies

Paradoxically, many psychologists and psychiatrists, whose function is presumably to identify and treat mental aberrations, now accept these "transpersonal crises" as *normal* for people "on the spiritual path." Nevertheless, mental-health professionals have found it necessary to organize support groups to help those overwhelmed by what they also categorize as "spiritual emergency." One such organization is called "Passages In" and offers "round-the-clock emotional and spiritual care and attention."[23] Passages In director David Pursglove, a therapist and transpersonal counselor for 25 years, lists some of the normal "transpersonal crises" as follows:

> There may be a striking number of frightening ESP and other parapsychological occurrences, such as out-of-body experiences or accurate precognitive "takes" [predictions].
> . . . [or] a profound psychological encounter with death and subsequent rebirth, often with an upsurge of special powers and strong impulses to heal.
> [Or] the awakening of the serpent power (Kundalini) . . . energy streaming up the spine, tremors, spasms and sometimes violent shaking and twisting movements.[24]

Researchers Flo Conway and Jim Siegelman note that the most startling effects of cult involvement are "bizarre disturbances of awareness, perception, memory and other basic information-processing capacities . . . floating in and out of altered states . . . unnerving 'psychic' phenomena. . . ."[25] Yet these are the very symptoms found among many people who are not members of a cult at all, but simply got involved with Yoga at the local YMCA or with self-hypnosis tapes or visualization through a self-improvement seminar, or with other Yoga-related consciousness-altering techniques required by an employer or taught as relaxation in public schools. Those who are drawn to the new spirituality because of the benefits it offers eventually discover that in order to reap these benefits it is necessary to cultivate altered states and psychic phenomena; "bad trips" seem to be a normal by-product.

"Such experiences," admits Marilyn Ferguson's *Brain/Mind Bulletin*, "are common among people involved in Yoga, meditation and other spiritual disciplines. . . ."[26] In fact, with the rapid spread of Eastern mysticism in the West, these "spiritual crises" have reached epidemic proportions. In order to deal with such problems, Johns Hopkins University School of Medicine professor Stanislav Grof (a leading LSD authority) and his wife Christina (a Hatha Yoga teacher) organized the "Spiritual Emergency Network" (SEN) in 1980. SEN was originally headquartered at Esalen, where psychologists such as Fritz Perls, Abraham Maslow, and Carl Rogers used to hold forth in the early days of the human-potential movement. Esalen had its share of "bad trips" leading to destroyed lives and suicide,[27] but again these were considered to be the normal casualties along the path to Nirvana. "We went too far," cofounder Michael Murphy admits. "I wish we hadn't made mistakes, but we were adventurists."[28]

The first words heard by those who call the SEN hotline are "Welcome to the club!" Of course those calling in desperation had no intention of joining such a club, and probably would never have gotten involved in New Age psychospiritual technologies had they been honestly told the dangers beforehand. Now located at the California Institute of Transpersonal Psychology in Menlo Park, California, SEN "coordinates 35 regional centers throughout the world"[29] involving about 1500 "professionals who understand the nature of spiritual awakening. . . ."[30] Ironically, Eastern mysticism's methods of "spiritual awakening" (the very methods that cause the "bad trips") continue to be promoted by the experts to whom the victims of such problems look for help.

"Tapping These Energies Is Fire"

Unfortunately, amid all the hype promoting questionable products in today's spiritual marketplace, there is seldom a *caveat* warning the buyer to beware. And when the rare warning is issued, it is all too often buried so deeply amid optimistic fluff that few people take it seriously. Consider, for example, the following from W. Brugh Joy, medical-doctor-turned-Eastern-guru, whom actor Richard Chamberlain credited with realigning his "psychic force":

> Not one person knows what [psychic power] is or all of its aspects, and no one has ever known, despite attempts over thousands of years to master this knowledge.
> Tapping these energies is fire, and the consequences . . . can be psychosis, aggravation of neuroses, acceleration of disease processes and suicide.[31]

Along with such a warning, one would expect the public to be urged at all cost to avoid any involvement with forces so lethal. Instead, like Shirley MacLaine and others of the new breed of Western gurus, Joy encourages cultivating the very "altered states of consciousness" that open the door to these admittedly dangerous "energies." As though enticed by a prize so dazzling that no risk is too great, Joy declares: "The awakening into certain states of consciousness can bestow gifts of such value that they are beyond price . . . powers not yet recognized by conventional Western science. . . ."[32] Appalled by such an attitude, astronomy magazine *Sky & Telescope* editor Alan M. MacRobert declared:

> The real significance of the paranormal boom is that so many of us take it so uncritically.
> It is as if the question "Is this so?" has become irrelevant—and has been replaced by the attitude, "If it

feels good, it must be right for me." . . .
I think this paradigm has served us poorly.[33]

That Was Zen and This Is Now

In a major article in *Training* magazine, Ron Zemke reminisces about his earlier involvement in the human-potential movement, when "be there or be square" was the way so many people regarded the perpetual round of New Age conventions and seminars. "We were regaled with Sufi wit and wisdom," recalls Zemke, "challenged to touch the spiritual in ourselves, encouraged to see the connectedness of all things and lectured on using the creative sides of our brains. We shared our most intimate insecurities with perfect strangers, challenged our paradigms, got real with our feelings, did a decent amount of illegal drugs and went home feeling we had indeed been transformed to another level of existence. Sort of." Noting that the lasting effects of Marilyn Ferguson's Aquarian Conspiracy "have been notable mostly for their modesty when compared to the promises," Zemke recalls:

> The sparkle and allure began to fade from the prospect of another marathon cosmic-consciousness seminar, another weekend encounter with my true self. Eventually it was impossible to deny that a pattern of predictable sameness had settled over these experiences.
>
> I shaved, cut my hair, slipped back into the straight world in a fairly straight job, and gradually lost touch with the human potential movement, with its lofty promises and peculiar avenues to truth, freedom, beauty and enlightenment. . . .
>
> For most of us, that was Zen and this is now. . . .[34]

While many people, like Zemke, have dropped out, the New Age movement has only grown stronger, picking up at least two new enthusiasts for each one lost. There is a desperate need for reliable criteria for evaluating the products being offered in today's exploding mystical marketplace. Yet it is doubtful that there will ever be an official watchdog agency making certain that New Age techniques meet established standards, because their *spiritual* and *religious* nature effectively places them off-limits to government regulation.

Unfortunately, all is not as upbeat as the smiling entrepreneurs of mysticism would have us believe. Like TM and other forms of Yoga, most psychospiritual technologies for "personal transformation" have hidden and dangerous defects. There is substantial evidence to indicate that some of the attractive New Age products should be clearly marked *Extremely Hazardous*. The role of sorcerer's apprentice can be a frightening and very dangerous game. University of California at Berkeley professor Jacob Needleman sounds this warning:

> [In the psychic market] there's no Better Business Bureau. Let the buyer beware. You should be open-minded, but not so open-minded that your brains fall out.[35]

Whatever other claims they make, entrepreneurs of the consciousness revolution must come clean and honestly admit to potential customers that what they are marketing is not modern medicine, psychology, or science at all, but is in fact ancient occultism and superstition. It is unconscionable not to make a full disclosure of the many grave dangers involved. Our intent in the following pages is to confront the major issues and to shed enough light to dispel the confusion that seems to be an integral part of today's burgeoning mystical marketplace.

4

Popularizing Spirituality

In his latest book, *Your Maximum Mind*, Herbert Benson reminds us that an ongoing project for many years "at the Harvard Medical School has been the exploration in the Indian Himalayas of the frontiers of the mind." Sponsored by major foundations, the research has centered on the psychic powers of Buddhist monks. In January 1985 a film crew sent by Benson (following an invitation from the Dalai Lama) documented some incredible events. In one test, the dressed-for-the-Arctic Harvard team set out in zero-degrees-Fahrenheit weather from a 17,000-foot-elevation monastery accompanying ten monks wearing only sandals and a light cotton wraparound cloth. At 19,000 feet on a rocky cliffside ledge "the monks took off their sandals and squatted down on their haunches . . . leaned forward, put their heads on the ground, and draped the light cotton wrappings over their bodies." Benson continues the account:

> In this position, being essentially naked, they spent the entire night practicing a special type of *gTum-mo* meditation called *Repeu* . . . a light snow drifted down over them during the early morning hours.
>
> No ordinary person could have endured these conditions. We're sure of that. Yet the monks . . . simply remained quietly in their meditative positions for about eight consecutive hours. . . .

55

> Finally, at the . . . sounding of a small horn, they stood up, shook the snow off their backs, put their sandals on and calmly walked back down the mountain again.[1]

Even more impressive accomplishments were witnessed by this same team and have been documented by other researchers around the world. Such extraordinary feats have been the common currency of Yogis, witch doctors, voodoo priests, and other shamans for thousands of years, of whom the vast majority have consistently attributed their unusual powers to spirit guides, gods, or demons contacted in altered states of consciousness. While still reluctant to consider spirit entities as its source, growing numbers of researchers are acknowledging the validity of occult power. With the increasing investigation of psychic phenomena, the prediction made by Shoshone medicine man Rolling Thunder seems to be in the process of fulfillment: "Scientists will eventually learn what pagans have always known." The key to this knowledge and power is acknowledged to be the ASC, or altered state of consciousness.

Whether experienced on drugs or in Eastern meditation, the allegedly "higher states" of consciousness seemed to confirm the existence of what religious mystics of all ages have called the "spiritual" dimension. Jon Klimo, former Rutgers University professor who has designed, administered, and taught in doctoral programs in education and psychology, provides an interesting example of those whose lives are being changed through recognizing the validity of a "spiritual" realm. In his book *Channeling*, an exhaustive study of that exploding phenomenon, Klimo candidly confesses:

> During the last five years I've continued my teaching, research, and administrative work at a small graduate school of integrative psychology. . . . Here my colleagues and I have attempted to add both "new science" and ancient psychospiritual tools to mainstream approaches to training counselors and clinical psychologists. . . .

I can no longer keep the spiritual part of the search separate from the creative or the scientific. They are all parts of an emerging unity. . . .

Yet I consider myself to be neither a mystic nor a psychic. Each week now, I meet more people who claim to be experiencing the same thing.[2]

Almost overnight the concept of "spirituality" began to find its way into the mindset of people who only a few short years before would have scoffed at the idea. In the process of this metamorphosis, however, such words as *spirit* and *spiritual* have been purged of objectionable religious dogma and now have a popular mystique. An avant garde journal for professional psychotherapists, which has published such articles as "The Therapist and the Medium: A Proper Marriage," declares: "The new frontier of psychotherapy is *spirituality*. There's a quiet revolution in the making . . . and professionals like you are the agents of this change."[3]

Promoting Spirituality as Science

The assumption that a spiritual dimension of reality exists underlies everything that the New Age offers. What is meant by spiritual, however, seems to be a matter of varying opinion. A Japanese scientist with doctorates in both physics and medicine is currently touring the world giving lectures on "A Medical Breakthrough from a Spiritual Viewpoint." He claims to "incorporate a *spiritual* dimension" into the treatment of disease through a "synthesis of medicine and religion," combining "present medical science with spiritual wisdom."

Promotion of spiritual practices in the name of science, however, creates confusion. Best-selling author and psychiatrist M. Scott Peck has called for "*spiritual* leadership" and a new American "revolution of the *spirit*."[4] Such an appeal is meaningless so long as "spiritual" is merely an inspiring euphemism to be flavored to individual taste.

The August 1987 annual conference of the Association for Transpersonal Psychology was titled "Spirit in Action." Pittsburgh psychologist Jon Spiegel, writing in the Association for Humanistic Psychology (AHP) *Newsletter*, declared: "AHP has always held spiritual concerns close to its heart . . . [remaining] open to spiritual practices both east and west. We have championed the return of spirit to therapy."[5] One might well ask what humanists mean by "*spiritual* concerns" and the "return of *spirit* to therapy." That question seems to be answered by the nature of the spirituality being promoted.

Scoffers who imagine that Shirley MacLaine is involved in something so bizarre that only a small fringe element takes it seriously need only attend a convention of the AHP to discover how widely the identical "spirituality" which MacLaine proclaims has been embraced. At the AHP's 24th Annual Meeting, for example, held at San Diego State University in August 1986, practicing shamans (witch doctors) were among the key speakers. Participants were given the opportunity to experience and learn to develop in other people the shamanic altered state conducive to contact with spirits. There were mediumistic seances for exploring communications with "spirit guides and other spiritual friends." In its report on the convention, the *Los Angeles Times* included a photo of Durchback Akuete, an African witch doctor, "inducing a trance in AHP co-president Lonnie Barbach."[6]

The AHP, which claims to be involved in the *science* of psychology, advertised its 1986 convention in *Shaman's Drum: A Journal of Experiential Shamanism.* (Shamanism is the most pervasive form of nature religion, or witch doctoring.) Clearly the AHP hoped to attract to its ranks practicing shamans by letting them know that much of today's psychotherapy involves adaptations of their ancient religion. The implication was also clear that psychologists may be able to teach shamans a few new tricks of the trade. The ad read in part:

> An unforgettable opportunity to learn from some of the most important healers and spiritual leaders in West Africa and Brazil—
>
> Journey into altered states of consciousness where one can meet one's higher spirit teachers and the "gods" themselves. . . .
>
> Topics Include: Ritual, Meditation . . . Altered States of Consciousness, Shamanism and Spirit Healing, Mediumship. . . .[7]

Clearly, to teach consciousness-altering techniques for the purpose of contacting "spirit teachers and the 'gods' themselves" is to engage in what has always been recognized as *religion*. Existential philosopher Maurice Friedman has stated, "I agree that humanistic psychology has mixed up psychology and religion. . . ."[8] The ad in *Shaman's Drum* would seem to leave little doubt as to what religion the highly respected AHP is promoting, though disguised beneath a layer of psychological jargon. The connection is an ancient one, for, as Herbert Benson has said, "Indeed, the shaman, or medicine man, can be viewed as an early psychotherapist."[9]

Psychology is only one area in which Hindu, Buddhist, and other shamanic beliefs and practices are gaining acceptance as science rather than religion. University of California at Berkeley physicist Fritjof Capra considers this to be a helpful trend, "part of a much larger movement," which he terms a "fundamental change of world views . . . a profound cultural transformation."[10] In *Science, Order, and Creativity*, physicists David Bohm and F. David Peat argue that for science to begin to answer life's most important questions, it must embrace a combination of Zen Buddhism and Hinduism.[11] We are well on the way to fulfillment of Stanford University brain researcher Karl Pribram's insightful prediction:

> There is no doubt in my mind that there will be a rapprochement between the spiritual values that New Age people hold so dear and what we are discovering in science.[12]

"It Works": Practical Applications of Sorcery

The endorsement of Eastern mysticism and shamanism by psychology has encouraged the man in the street to pursue mystical experiences and psychic powers. Multitudes are being drawn into Castaneda's "sorcerer's world." Although there is still much skepticism and opposition, the new paradigm is fast becoming the accepted view. While the psychic feats of Edgar Cayce were almost unique 40 years ago, there are literally millions of people today who can duplicate everything he was able to do. These mind-over-matter powers are being acquired through the many courses in "mind dynamics" or "alpha-level training" now being offered by scores of organizations. Many of these seminars guarantee to turn the student into an "Edgar Cayce" in a few sessions.

With over six million graduates in more than 70 countries, the Silva Method (formerly Silva Mind Control), developed by Jose Silva, is only one of many similar programs based upon psychic powers that are alleged to be available through attaining the 7-to-14-cycles-per-second alpha-brain-wave level of consciousness. This is not darkened-seance-room, closet-occultist stuff; it is taught out in the open in 32 hours over two weekends and is endorsed by business, political, and religious leaders. Lifespring, Actualizations, Direct Centering, Werner Erhard's Forum, and numerous other mind-dynamics courses had their genesis in the Silva Method. What it promises is incredible, and in many ways it seems to work. In order to graduate, each trainee is given a list of several names of persons whom he or she has never heard of, much less met. Based only upon the names and addresses, a psychic diagnosis (through techniques taught in the course) must be made of each person on the list. Anyone unable to do this at the end of the course to at least 80 percent accuracy (comparable to proven medical diagnoses) will be given a full refund of the course fee.

The story of one former Silva district director, who has left Silva Mind Control for reasons that will become clear later, provides a good example. A graduate engineer previously involved in nuclear research for the United States Navy, he was a promising young executive with United States Steel Corporation and manager of one of their plants. His involvement in the course came through the recommendation of a fellow executive who had found it tremendously helpful.

After the necessary level of training had been reached, the instructor paired off the students with partners to test each other's powers in real "cases." His first partner asked him to diagnose her 62-year-old uncle living in Pittsburgh, Pennsylvania. Going into the meditative state he had been taught, he called upon his two "inner guides." "To my surprise," he recalls, "a picture of a man appeared suddenly on my 'mental screen.' I was immediately able to describe his facial features (large nose, heavy eyebrows, gray hair and two days of unshaved beard) and general build (about 5'10", thin, with a stoop and a bad limp). He was wearing a bulky blue bathrobe and at the moment of my observance was sitting in a worn brown chair, drinking beer and intently watching a professional football game, to which he seemed addicted to the point of becoming very angry with anyone who disturbed him at such times. Other than the limp, which I determined had come from an industrial accident that seriously injured his right knee eight years previously, I found no physical ailments."

Coming out of his alpha levels, this neophyte Silva trainee opened his eyes to see his partner crying. Everything he had seen on the "mental screen" and described to her had been fully accurate! With his engineering background, he had been extremely skeptical about the psychic abilities which the instructor had claimed were universally resident in everyone and which the training was designed to develop. Yet now on his first attempt, these incredible powers had actually worked! There were too many details in what he had seen on his "mental screen" to be explained as the result of chance. It was a staggering and life-changing experience. In a very short time he became so enthusiastic about the seeming miracles which his two "inner guides" could perform that he left U. S. Steel, became a full-time instructor of the Silva technique, and rose rapidly in the ranks of that organization.

Guidance from a Mysterious Source

Most of the mind-dynamics groups similar to that of Silva are teaching methods very much like those which Napoleon Hill (patriarch of success-motivation and positive-mental-attitude training) first taught in the 1930's. Hill had at his disposal nine "inner guides," whom he visualized around a table sitting like a board of directors to advise him and his clients. And it worked. As a result of Hill's efforts, millions of other people (including many of America's leading business, professional, and political leaders) adopted, tested, and proved the astonishing power and practicality of this ancient sorcery technique in every area of their lives.

Still a perennial bestseller after 50 years, Hill's best-known book, *Think and Grow Rich*, has been credited with changing the lives and influencing the careers of a large percentage of America's top business executives. Its 1941 edition contains endorsements from United States Presidents Theodore Roosevelt, Harding, Wilson, and Taft; and from some of the world's greatest scientists and founders of America's leading corporations: Thomas A. Edison, Luther Burbank, John D. Rockefeller, F. W. Woolworth, William Wrigley, Jr., George Eastman (of Eastman Kodak), Robert Dollar (of Dollar Steamship Lines), and others.

Most astonishing was the source of the techniques which Hill taught. He believed in mysterious "guidance" from a spiritual dimension ("a region beyond the power of our five senses to know") from which "unseen, silent forces influence us constantly."[13] Although he spoke a great deal of "mind power" and "positive mental attitude" (a phrase he coined), Hill was convinced that behind these forces were "unseen watchers" guiding the destiny of those who were willing to submit to their leadership. There was no limit to the success and wealth which these allegedly higher beings would give in exchange for obedience to their principles. Hill claims to have gotten these secrets from contact with "The Great School of Masters," of which he wrote:

> Sometimes known as the Venerable Brotherhood of Ancient India, it is the great central reservoir of religious, philosophical, moral, physical, spiritual and psychical knowledge. Patiently this school strives to lift mankind from spiritual infancy to maturity of soul and final illumination.[14]

Hill claims that an emissary came in disembodied form across the astral plane and into his study. In a voice that "sounded like chimes of great music," this visitor from a world beyond declared: "I come from the Great School of Masters. I am one of the Council of Thirty-Three who serve the Great School and its initiates on the physical plane." Hill was informed that he had been "under the guidance of the Great School" for years and had been chosen by them to give the formula of success, the "Supreme Secret," to the world. And what is the "Supreme Secret"? That "whatever the human mind can believe, it can achieve." We are limited only by our lack of faith in our own infinite potential.

Though this may sound like science fiction, the "formula" received from this spiritual messenger nevertheless became the foundation for the entire spectrum of success/motivation, positive-mental-attitude (PMA) seminars that so heavily influence the entire Western world today. One can only wonder whether the many top leaders who credit their success with following the principles that Hill received from this astonishing source really believe in this spiritual "School of Masters" out there on the astral plane. If not, then what do they do with Hill's story? If he lied or was deluded, why would the techniques which he learned from that source bring such amazing success to millions of people?

Perhaps those who gain paranormal power are loath to question its source for fear of losing it. There is also the pragmatic attitude that if something works according to definite principles it is therefore "scientific" and the source of such power must be impersonal and is thus beside the point. This may account for the growing popularity of those "mind-over-matter" metaphysical religions originating in America (such as Religious Science, Science of Mind, and Christian Science) that claim to make a *science* out of *faith*.

Swami Vivekananda, who represented Hinduism at the 1893 Chicago World's Fair Parliament of Religions and created such a sensation there, maintained that it was the Hindus who first "made a science" of occultism. He resented the misrepresentation of Hinduism by what he termed the "third-rate magical powers" promoted by Madame Blavatsky's Theosophical Society.[15] Genuine psychic powers, according to Vivekananda (who founded the worldwide Vedanta Society), "can be systematically studied, practised, and acquired. . . ."[16] It is not surprising, therefore, that leading Hindus have made favorable mention of the similarities "between the fundamental principles of modern Christian Science and those of that ancient system of philosophy known in India as Vedanta."[17] Mary Baker Eddy, the founder of Christian Science, was confident that her particular system of occultism could be justified pragmatically. She wrote:

> Let the age that sits in judgment on the occult methods of [its] period sanction only such as are demonstrable on a scientific principle, and productive of the greatest good to the greatest number.[18]

The same "scientific power of belief" espoused by Hill and Eddy was taught in the charming tale that became a best-selling book and movie, *Jonathan Livingston Seagull*: "I can because I think I can!" Like Napoleon Hill, author Richard Bach claims that the entire story was dictated to him by a disembodied spirit on the astral plane. Likewise, Jose Silva tells us that his methods came from a similar source: a Chinese spirit guide sitting in Yoga position in the astral plane whom he met in the early days when he was learning how to have out-of-body-experiences. Hundreds of further examples could be given to show that similar initiations into classic sorcery have been a persistent phenomenon down through human history. In fact, this has happened so consistently and spontaneously to widely scattered persons of all cultures, without contact with one another, that it simply cannot be explained away as either hallucination or coincidence.

Making Sorcery "Scientific" and Respectable

Today there is an explosive revival of this historic phenomenon in every area of society. A major reason seems to be that psychology has given us an allegedly scientific explanation which removes any necessity of believing in "Masters" on the astral plane, gods, demons, or anything else except our own inner potential. The theory that the entities encountered on drugs, in Yogic trance, or through techniques such as taught in the Silva Method are simply archetypal images from the collective unconscious has made sorcery quite respectable. Consider the following from the prestigious Stanford Graduate School of Business *Creativity In Business* course, which has influenced thousands of top-level business leaders in the many years it has been taught:

> We look within to find our own individual and universal source. That source has been called the inner self, the Self, the hidden mind, the divine spark, the Divine Ego, the Great I AM, God, and Essence. [The latter is the term used in the course.]

Getting in Touch with Your Inner Guide:

In this exercise you will meet your wisdom-keeper or

spirit guide—an inner person who can be with you for
life, someone to whom you can turn for guidance.
[A relaxation exercise in preparation for visualization
is presented.]
Now surround your body with a white light. . . . Now
imagine that you're walking into some kind of situation
or favorite place. . . .
And now your inner guide comes to meet you here.
Focus on this figure as it walks toward you. Look at the
face. . . . You might have a brief dialogue [with your
guide]. . . . And now bring the conversation to a close.[19]

Much of the credit for giving the above occultic techniques a
scientific image goes to the renowned psychiatrist Carl Jung, who
like Silva, Hill, and Bach had a "spirit guide" also. It was in fact
Jung's "Philemon" who led him into discoveries that reinforced his
major theories, including the "collective unconscious" and "archetypal images." The insights that Jung acquired from this otherworldly source are gaining an increasingly wide influence in every
level of Western society today, while Freud, who rejected occultism
and spiritual experiences, is increasingly discredited. Elmer Green,
pioneer biofeedback researcher at the Menninger Foundation in
Topeka, Kansas, has said: "It is helpful that public and professional
interest is moving toward the Jungian view of humanity and the
cosmos.[20]

Although Philemon did not appear as his guide until after his
break with Freud, Jung had been deeply involved in occultism since
childhood, as had his parents, grandparents, and other relatives
before him. The home in which his mother was raised was so
infested with "ghosts" that as a girl she had to hold the "spirits" at
bay long enough for her father (who was himself a medium as well as
a Protestant minister) to write out his Sunday sermon. "Every
week, at a fixed hour, he used to hold intimate conversations with
his deceased first wife, very much to the chagrin of the second,"
who "could also see 'spirits'."

Jung described his mother as loving by day, "but at night she
seemed uncanny. Then she was like one of those seers . . . archaic
and ruthless."[21] After his maternal grandfather's death, his alleged

spirit spoke through a cousin of Jung's in seances which Jung avidly attended during his student days in Basel.[22] Jung's maternal grandmother once remained in trance for three days, during which she described with uncanny accuracy persons unknown to her but whose actual existence was later proved.[23] With this background, it should not be surprising that Jung himself (who confessed, "I too have this archaic nature") was deeply involved in occult experiences all his life. In his classic *Freud, Jung and Occultism*, psychiatrist and psychic investigator Nandor Fodor writes:

> The discussion of Jung's psychic participation must begin with taking a deep breath. It is a story so unbelievable, so fantastic that—ever since it was fully revealed—analytic psychologists have been staggering under the impact, psychoanalysts have ignored it as a fairy tale, and parapsychologists have found it a diet so rich that up to now they have not been able to digest it.
>
> The amazing thing is not only that Jung's psychic life was kept a secret most of his life but that his doctoral thesis of 1899 on *The Psychology and Pathology of So-Called Occult Phenomena* remained almost unknown [because] revelation of [this] skeleton in Jung's family closet . . . might have worked havoc with Jung's standing in the world of science. . . .[24]

In the 25 years since Jung's death there has been a dramatic increase in psychic belief and activity. No longer would his occult involvements tarnish his professional image as a psychiatrist. In fact, as we have seen, occultic techniques have now become an integral part of many psychotherapies.

A Coming New Pentecost?

Referring to the growing acceptance of mysticism, which is now influencing almost every area of society, a promotional mailer explains that the *New Age Journal* "was launched" in 1973 "because there was no publication that looked at this outpouring of consciousness as *one* trend—an awakening of all peoples on earth."

What could be the cause and why is it happening on such a grand scale at this particular time? Researcher and best-selling author Brad Steiger, himself a New Age leader and practicing occultist, makes this interesting statement:

> Nearly every observer of the contemporary spiritual scene seems to agree that there is some kind of new Pentecost going on at this time, some kind of spiritual awakening process at work. And a good many of these observers feel that this growing mystical consciousness may have something to do with the Last Days.[25]

This reference to "Pentecost" and the "Last Days" is interesting because these terms come from the Bible, most of which is incompatible with Steiger's convictions. In fact, the Bible records that shortly before his death Jesus Christ declared that an explosion of *false* religious beliefs involving unprecedented *spiritual deception* would be the primary sign of the "last days," indicating that his second coming was near. The nature of that deception is spelled out fairly clearly in the Bible and corresponds in remarkable detail to much that accompanies today's New Age mysticism.

The search for success, prosperity, and happiness through *power* has consistently proven to be a disappointment. Today's world suffers from a spiritual malaise that cannot be cured by "power," either physical or mystical. In fact, increasing power has always brought increasing problems. The more power we can command, the greater the danger that it will be misused. Power seems to breed only greater self-interest and its concomitant corruption. Human consciousness is capable of the extremes of both hate and love, selfishness and selflessness—and how to cure it of the former and limit it to the latter is the real issue.

That there may be powers accessible to the mind which are even greater than atomic power is staggering—but not necessarily the cause for great hope, particularly when the actual source and nature of this power is open to question. Yet that issue is being deliberately sidestepped. Writing in the *Journal of Defense and Diplomacy* on the subject of psychic warfare, Charles Wallach argues that in order to keep ahead of the Soviets in this field we must be willing to pursue with all speed the utilization of psychic power as a weapon even though as yet we have no scientific framework for explaining it. He writes:

> Just as man used fire long before he understood the principles of combustion, it would seem prudent to develop and utilize this [psychic] talent . . . rather than waste energy arguing . . . that it does not fit into the framework of our philosphy.[26]

Certainly it is relatively safe to burn wood without a full scientific understanding of combustion, but the same could not be said about releasing nuclear energy without a very sophisticated comprehension of the atom. And there are many serious researchers who are now convinced that psychic phenomena may well involve something potentially no less dangerous than atomic energy. Could it be possible that the Americans and Soviets (and all those who think they are tapping into psychic power) are already losing a war they don't even know is in progress, not against each other but against an "enemy" they don't even admit exists?

Toward the end of his life Carl Jung apparently began to suspect what he had long feared: that not only Philemon but the many other "spirit entities" which he and his close relatives had encountered repeatedly as an integral part of their lives were not "archetypes" at all. Rather than representing powers innate in the collective unconscious, these entities were in fact hostile beings independent of human consciousness.

What Jung tried mightily not to believe all his life is still unacceptable to the educated Western mind. Most psychologists today insist that "paranormal experiences" such as Jung, Hill, Silva, Bach, and many others have had involve nothing more than the powers of human imagination. There is increasing evidence, however, that this theory, while clearly inadequate to fully explain the phenomena, persists because the alternative is too dreadful to face.

A Pandora's Box?

It seems more than odd that those who promise a paradise through realizing "infinite human potential" seldom underscore the dangers that may lie hidden in the dark side of untapped powers of the mind. In this day of positivism most ears seem deaf to the voices of those few who warn that the development of mystical psychic powers might open a spiritual Pandora's box of inconceivable horror. In view of a mass of evidence now available, however, some of which we will consider in the following pages, such a possibility can hardly be discounted.

The present situation is reminiscent, but in an even more ominous way, of that faced by those scientists involved in the top-secret Manhattan Project. In numbing disbelief they began to realize the incredible potential for both good and evil which they were unleashing upon mankind from within the atom. As a result, the entire world now trembles under a nuclear Sword of Damocles. What unthinkable terrors might the unleashing of psychic powers bring? Mary Baker Eddy, who promised to those who followed Christian Science the occultic power to heal, also feared the dark side of this force. "Why we take so few students," she wrote, "is because of the great danger there is . . . [that] this developed mental power becomes the . . . extracts and essences of evil."[27]

It was with great enthusiasm and optimism that controversial Catholic priest and paleontologist Pierre Teilhard de Chardin, known as "the father of the New Age," wrote: "Daily the idea of awakening to a superconsciousness becomes better based scientifically and more necessary psychologically. . . ." Yet the possibility that unlimited psychic power might be at the independent and individual disposal of each person on this planet to use for his or her own selfish ends is even more frightening than having atomic weapons in the hands of a few governments. As one self-confessed "convert and fan" of the New Age movement nevertheless thoughtfully remarked in a recent nationally published interview:

> When you really look at it, we live in an apocalyptic time. It's very shaky and scary. . . .
> There are many gods afoot. There are many evil powers. . . . I *know* there is power in all of this stuff.[28]

5

Naturalism, Scientism, and Supernaturalism

It can hardly be denied that not only the lives of individuals but even the destiny of nations have at times been shaped by strange and seemingly inexplicable events. Although materialistic science continues to be the universally worshiped sacred cow, its explanation that these apparent quirks of fate are mere "coincidences" doesn't always ring true. Even in the space age the intuitive belief hangs on that somehow from behind the scenes a "higher power" is at work providing "guidance." Though it may be suppressed, the nagging suspicion persists that some unknown mind or minds possessing mysterious powers transcending the knowledge and capabilities of mere humans are influencing happenings here upon earth.

One such peculiar event played a significant role in shaping the human-potential movement. It happened on a fateful night in 1962, with long-term results that none of the parties involved suspected at the time. Lost in a dense fog along an isolated section of the California coast, famed psychologist Abraham Maslow and his wife, Bertha, were drawn to a dim light, just off the highway, of what they assumed to be a motel. Thus the "long relationship between the father of humanistic psychology and the Esalen Institute was forged." From this apparently "chance" partnership the human-potential movement erupted:

> "It's true! It's true!" [cofounder Michael] Murphy laughs as he describes this strange coincidence.
> "I took it as a sign from beyond. I saw my beliefs confirmed in these omens."[1]

71

This reference to "beyond" and "omens" is more than tongue-in-cheek. And Murphy apparently sees the same kind of intrusion "from beyond," but this time from the dark side of the force, in the stunning and macabre death of cofounder Richard Price in 1985. In the steep forest rising behind Esalen, where Price was making his way along one of the trails he loved so much, a huge chunk of rock, somehow loosened from the mountain above, seemed to hone in on him like a guided missile—or was it just a coincidence?

"We went up there and traced its path," Murphy reminisces. "A two-ton boulder exploded 10 feet below him. A 200-pound shard flew up and broke his spine. He was killed instantly. The boulder leaped 100 yards through a narrow opening in the redwoods. It partook of the occult."[2] In *The Tao of Psychology*, psychiatrist Jean Shinoda Bolen calls such an occurrence an "uncanny, meaningful coincidence," a "Tao experience" that causes the sudden mystical awareness that "we are not alone" in the universe.[3]

It was not only the manner of death but the ironic timing of the sudden end to Price's career that convinced Murphy of the "occult" connection. Enthusiastic about a recent reorganization and the stronger leadership role he would be playing in fulfilling Esalen's mission "to explore the mysteries" of mind, body, and spirit, Price had told Murphy: "We're finally doing it right!" The very next day he became the tragic victim of yet another of "those mysterious events that are intertwined with Esalen."[4] Yet if this was indeed another "sign from beyond," there is no indication that Murphy considers its message to be any different from the same "confirmation of his beliefs" that Maslow's stumbling upon Esalen 23 years before was understood to mean. Belief in "omens" has its problems of interpretation and carries its penalties intellectually if not in actuality.

Favorable "omens" are welcomed as supportive of programs in process. And when such an interpretation seems impossible, the "sign from beyond" can be neatly turned in one's favor by viewing it as opposition from the "dark side." Man has always been far more enthusiastic about using the "gods" to further his own plans than about submitting to their direction. And in that respect modern man is no different from his ancient ancestors.

Naturalism Versus Supernaturalism

In spite of the skepticism toward the supernatural fostered over the last 200 years by the growing dominance of scientific materialism, superstitious beliefs of every kind have persisted. Yale University professor Jon Butler documents occultism's significant role in the history of America. Its influence, while at times scarcely visible on the surface, has always been present,[5] not just among the poor and uneducated but in the highest strata of society as well. Like numerous other top stars, Daryl Hall of "Hall & Oates" fame ("the most popular duo in the history of the record charts") has been deeply involved in the occult for years—and even gives it credit for his success. In a recent interview, Hall reveals his high regard for sorcery's manipulation of the Force behind nature:

> This concept is called magic. Before Christianity, before paganism, before religion, before belief itself, it is said to have been the primary spiritual instrument of existence, a supernatural order of things more real than reality.[6]

Sorcery's promise of *magical* solutions to every conceivable problem makes it almost irresistible. The perpetual youth offered by Yoga, the miraculous curative powers attributed to crystals or herbal tea, and the eternal round of second chances guaranteed by reincarnation are typical examples of New Age promises which appeal to a universal human weakness. Beliefs that should be easily recognized as unwarranted superstitions persist nevertheless.

Top athletes and coaches have certain hats, or socks, or numbers, or days of the week which they are convinced bring "good luck," and no amount of evidence or reason can persuade them otherwise. Although many insist that they are not really "believers," about 70 million Americans consult their horoscopes daily, while the superstitious fears of modern, educated sophisticates dictate that the "unlucky" thirteenth floor of most high-rise hotels and office buildings will simply not exist. (Floor numbering progresses from 12 directly to 14.) Similar examples could be multiplied.

Most of those who indulge in such irrational behavior would protest that they don't really take these superstitions seriously. Yet their actions demonstrate that in spite of their professed skepticism, today's sophisticates have been unable to escape that universal intuitive sense of *something* behind the scenes mysteriously influencing the tragic or triumphant chain of events that molds human life and destiny. Varying techniques for attempting to manipulate this occult Force—techniques which are basically *religious*—find a ready market in secular society.

It is right here that the world's religions divide into two distinct camps: monotheism/supernaturalism versus polytheism/pantheism/ naturalism. In the Bible, honored by Christians, Jews, and Muslims, God is consistently depicted as the *transcendent Creator*, who is distinct and separate from creation (nature). It is a creation that is not part of him but which he has brought forth *out of nothing*. Unlike Hinduism and all other pantheistic/polytheistic religions, where the universe itself is God or an extension of God, the God of the Bible reaches into the cosmos from outside and overrides natural law to work *miracles*. This is the basis of what is called *supernaturalism*.

In contrast to *supernaturalism*, all other religions represent varying forms of *naturalism*. While the gods and spirits and higher powers of such religions may seem to vary, they have one thing in common: They are all part of the universe and work from within it in obedience to universal laws. In supernaturalism God is outside of nature and distinct from it. In naturalism, nature is all there is, and thus there can be no "miracles," but only natural events. Swami Vivekananda, known in India as "one of the foremost figures of the Hindu renaissance of the nineteenth century"[7] and remembered in the United States for his lasting effect upon American occultism, wrote:

> There is nothing supernatural. [Occult phenomena] are under laws just the same as any other physical phenomenon. . . .
>
> All these extraordinary powers are in the mind of man. . . . And each mind, wherever it is located, is in actual communication with the whole world.[8]

In naturalism, man as part of nature can hopefully "realize" his own godhood and create his own reality. As already mentioned, this is the purpose of Yoga (self-realization) and the goal of all Hinduism. This "realization," however, is impossible in supernaturalism, where only the one supreme God, who is not *bound* by laws, can create or perform miracles. These are not "mind powers" innate within the human psyche or collective unconscious and thus subject to human manipulation, but come only by sovereign intervention of the God who is totally other (transcendent), and as he alone wills. He may be petitioned in prayer, but he cannot be compelled to respond in a certain way by ritual, formula, or affirmations.

Astrology—Matter Over Mind?

Dating back thousands of years at least to the time of early Babylon, astrology declares man to be the victim of forces beyond his control and presents a strange contradiction to nature religion's basic goal of manipulating reality through sorcery. There are other contradictions as well. Since *mind* is nonphysical, it must exist in a different dimension from the space-matter-time continuum of cosmic rays and intergalactic forces and atomic rhythms. Consequently, mind and consciousness must be independent of planetary force fields. If this is indeed the case, then it cannot be true, as astrology claims, that the positions of certain planets in relation to the place and date of one's birth determine personality and destiny. Astrology must be a myth—yet it has consistently maintained an almost unbreakable hold over hundreds of millions of the world's population.

Strangely enough, most psychics believe strongly in both "mind power" and astrology. Yet the whole idea of "mind-over-matter" (psychokinesis or PK) is destructive of the basic tenets of astrology (that physical forces exerted by planets and stars determine human destiny), which actually represents "matter-over-mind." Beginning with Professor J. B. Rhine's work at Duke University in the 1930's, numerous PK experiments repeated in laboratories around the world seem to have indicated that *mind* is able to influence physical forces and objects. Jeane Dixon's astrology columns appear in hundreds of newspapers along with her psychic predictions, yet the two concepts are mutually exclusive: *Mind* cannot create its own reality and control its own circumstances while at the same time human destiny is determined by physical planetary forces. Both cannot be true.

ιst astrology buffs recognize what Carl Sagan has sarcastically ιed out: that at the time of birth the gravitational influence of thε obstetrician's body is greater than that of any heavenly body. Moreover, we can demonstrate that any correlation between astrological predictions and actual personalities or events is caused by *belief* in astrology rather than by the positions of stars or planets. From the very beginning, astrologers have failed to take into account a wobble in the earth's axis that has changed the positions of the stars relative to the earth, moving the zodiacal signs almost a full position since the second century, when Claudius Ptolemaeus first arranged them. The constellation Aries is now in the position assigned by the zodiac to the sign of Taurus, and so on.

Of course the zodiac could be adjusted to conform to present planetary positions, but most astrologers fear tampering with it or are unable to perform the necessary mathematics. Nor does it really matter when we understand that astrology and the zodiacal symbols have no more to do with the existence and actual locations in space of heavenly bodies than does a Ouija board. These symbols are related to the archetypes which Jung's spirit guide Philemon encouraged him to believe haunted the collective unconscious. Consequently Jung had great respect for astrology and used it in his analysis. "In cases of difficult diagnosis I usually get a horoscope," wrote Jung. According to *Wholemind* newsletter, "A surprising number of today's psychotherapists are following Jung's advice." New York City therapist Susan LeMak, for example, finds "the symbols and archetypes of astrology" helpful in giving clients a new perspective on their problems.[9]

Fear of a Different Sort

Regardless of cultural differences, all religions since the dawn of history have been based upon the common belief that some "higher power" controls the universe and human affairs. They vary only in their conception of this "power" and in the means which they adopt to influence it (or him or her) to act on their behalf. In the nature religions, the "higher power" was seen as innate within the universe and was generally associated with "spirits" believed to inhabit elements of nature such as the earth, sun, moon, or sky. The Findhorn community in Northern Scotland, founded by Eileen and

Peter Caddy, provides one of the best examples of the recent resurgence of these beliefs in the Western world.

As Esalen is the Mecca of the human-potential movement, so Findhorn is the Vatican of the New Age movement. Findhornians claim to be in visual and verbal contact with the "nature spirits" that inhabit and maintain the plant world. The unexpectedly magnificent produce (in quantity, quality, and size) that grows out of Findhorn's sandy soil on a windswept North Atlantic coastland is offered as evidence of help from the "devas." And numerous visitors of more than ordinary credentials, such as former MIT professor and author William Irwin Thompson, to name only one, have come away thoroughly convinced that the "nature spirits" are indeed running Findhorn and the universe.[10]

In clear-cut terms, the Bible indicts those who, like popular astronomer Carl Sagan, worship the creation instead of its Creator.[11] While Sagan would ridicule the suggestion that "spirits" inhabit elements of nature and guide its development, he attributes the same spiritual qualities of intelligence and purpose to matter. This neopantheism of academia is called *ecotheology*. One of its advocates, Georgetown University professor Victor Ferkiss, says it "starts with the premise that the Universe *is* God." Ferkiss seems convinced that this belief will "prevent the environmental exploitation of the Universe."[12] Of course this is not science, but *scientism*, a religious faith unsupported by evidence. Unfortunately, it is often mistaken for science when authoritatively proclaimed by scientists.

"If we must worship a power greater than ourselves," says Carl Sagan, the high priest of cosmos worship, "does it not make sense to revere the Sun and stars?"[13] A native bowing before a stick or stone which he credits with some mysterious power, a witch worshiping "Nature, O mighty Mother of us all," and a university professor worshiping the atom as the universal father offer obvious similarities. There is, however, one significant difference: Although they are all involved in nature worship, the native and witch remain true to a basic human instinct which Sagan's scientism seeks to deny. And eventually the worship of a purely *physical* cosmos proves to be unsatisfying. A deeper sense of awe is demanded by the common conviction of mankind that *something* of fearful power exists in a dimension beyond the material realm.

And if there is no such dimension, then how can we explain the unshakable conviction shared by all cultures in every period of history that a spiritual realm does in fact exist? The skeptics who bravely deny the spiritual realm are like those who protest their disbelief in astrology yet continue to consult their horoscopes. This universal sense of the *noumenal* (a reality beyond the senses) can be easily demonstrated. For example, a suspenseful mystery or a realistic war movie can stimulate a certain fear in an audience; however, horror films are much more frightening. Why?

It is not so much the *amount* of fear that makes the difference as it is the *quality*. Facing a gun is one thing; facing an unseen "ghost" brings terror of a different sort, even to the dogmatic materialist who denies the existence of such entities. And it is out of this sense of awesome fear of something or someone *unearthly* that the universal impulse to worship is born. As philosopher A. E. Taylor argues:

> As far back as we can trace the beginnings of religion, the "holy," even if it is no more than an oddly shaped stone, does not simply mean the strange or the formidable; it means, at the lowest, the "uncanny," and the "uncanny" is precisely that which does not simply belong to "this" everyday world, but directly impresses us as manifesting in some special way the presence of "the other" world. . . .
>
> It is as doubtful whether there is really any man who has never worshipped anything as it is doubtful whether there is any man who has never feared or never loved. . . . It is hard to believe that the most skeptical among us does not know the experience. . . .
>
> The experience moreover seems to be specially characteristic of man: as the Greeks said, "Man is the only animal who has gods."[14]

Marxism insists that religion is without validity—an opiate for the foolish masses. Like Freud's related thesis that religion is "the obsessional neurosis of humanity," Marxism's claim does not ring true to human experience. That sense of the "uncanny" to which Taylor refers is normal, not abnormal; it may be repressed, but it remains, no matter how deeply buried. According to his biographer, Ernest Jones, even Freud (who made a rejection of God the foundation for his system of psychoanalysis) could not entirely escape what he termed the universal neurosis. His own nagging occult beliefs persisted in spite of his proposed psychological explanations and scathing ridicule of the religious fantasies held by others.[15]

Far from resulting from insidious lies manufactured by religious charlatans, belief in the supernatural is so much a part of human consciousness that it persists in spite of all the arguments that skepticism can marshal. The Soviet Union and China present two classic examples. Although atheism has for decades been the official state religion, and totalitarian governments in complete control of education, the arts, and media have used every power available to wipe out religion, belief in the supernatural remains firmly entrenched.

The Way of the Shaman

Never content to be a pawn of "higher powers," mankind has sought ways to bargain with the unseen "masters" of fate. The ultimate goal, of course, has always been to manipulate these forces and eventually to take control. It was out of this desire that nature religions were born. Thus within the seemingly rich variety of such religions there is an underlying unity. Each differs only in its description of the gods and in the details of the rituals or other techniques it offers as the means of manipulating the "higher powers" for the benefit of its followers.

In every culture those who spent their lives learning the secrets of occult power were honored as the priests, priestesses, witches, witch doctors, medicine men, sorcerers, magicians, gurus, and masters. All of these functions are so basically similar that they are now included by anthropologists under the one term "shaman," the title given by the Tungus tribe in Siberia to its witch doctors or medicine men. Siberian shamans practice the same sorcery that Castaneda calls "a religious and philosophical experience that flourished [in America] long before the white man came to this continent, and flourishes still." The shamans were held in awe by the rest of mankind as those who mediated with the spirit world and had at their disposal the mysterious force necessary in order to bless or to curse. They were honored, placated, bribed, and flattered in exchange for arranging favors from the spirit world; but at the same time they were hated and feared for their secret knowledge and the power they wielded over other people.

Materialism sought to liberate mankind from the hold of what it perceived as mere unfounded superstition. With the demise of materialism, however, occultism is once again exploding worldwide. As a result, the pendulum is swinging sharply back to classic nature religion. Because of its concern for the earth, the ecological movement has been heavily influenced by this occult revival.

Physicist/mystic Fritjof Capra argues that "deep ecological awareness" is of necessity a *spiritual* consciousness "in harmony with . . . the texts of Hindus, Buddhists, and Taoists . . . in which the individual feels . . . embedded in nature and the cosmos."[16] Similarly, anthropologist Michael Harner, founder of the Norwalk, Connecticut, Center for Shamanic Studies (who has been called "not just an anthropologist who has studied shamanism, [but] an authentic white shaman"), describes shamanism's current resurgence as awakening "forgotten connections with the powers of nature."[17] Carl Jung, who played a key role in laying the foundation for today's New Age movement, believed that "a balance had to be restored between people and the earth . . . a balance to which his psychology could contribute" through fostering a *spiritual* awakening.[18] What we have is more than an ecological movement; it is a revival of nature religion. In the catalog of a Theosophy-related New Age center, the description of a two-week retreat titled "COUNCIL OF THE KEEPERS OF THE EARTH: The Way of the Shaman" contains the following interesting commentary:

> At the root of all the world's great spiritual traditions lies the aboriginal pulse of shamanism, the archaic spiritual heritage of humankind stretching back 40,000 years or more into the mists of pre-history.
>
> The shamanic tradition draws its tremendous healing power and wisdom from direct contact with the earth, the plants, the animals, the spirit realms of underworld and sky, and the sacred teachers of death and change.

This ancient wisdom is still preserved and practiced by shamans in native cultures throughout the world, cultures which have not succumbed to the advance of industrial civilization. It is precisely this ancient wisdom, which has been lost within our own Western culture, that we so urgently need at this time in order to correct the condition of extreme imbalance, disease, and destruction we find on the planet today.[19]

The essence of the New Age movement can be described as a return to the "nature religion" that has dominated all cultures and against which the Bible, representing supernaturalism, stands alone in unrelenting opposition. This dichotomy between supernaturalism and naturalism (shamanism) can be traced back thousands of years. In fact, the worldwide consistency in shamanism down through history is remarkable. As Harner points out in *The Way of the Shaman*, one can visit tribes which have been isolated for thousands of years by thousands of miles of ocean with no known contact and many cultural distinctives—yet their shamanism is consistently the same.[20] Apparently there has been a common source of continuing paranormal inspiration for all shamanism regardless of historical era or geographical location. While fetishes and rituals may differ, the underlying belief structure is as unvaried as the Bible's opposition to it.

Shamanism and Science

Shamanism in its varying forms was spawned by mankind's ambitious and desperate prescientific attempts to understand and control the mysterious forces of nature; and it was out of this womb that science later emerged. Here again we find the same division as in religion: between the naturalist and the supernaturalist. The supernaturalist scientist studies the universe to discover the awesome order built into it by its Creator. He argues that there could be no science without the confidence that a personal God of infinite wisdom and power had designed the physical universe to work according to consistent laws. On the other hand, the naturalist/materialist scientist limits himself to studying the material universe as if it were all there is, and he attributes its incredibly intricate and magnificent order and design to chance plus time.

While the supernaturalist scientist seeks to know and worship the God who created the universe, the naturalist scientist seeks to know himself, his "connectedness" to the universe, and the cosmic powers that consequently reside within him as human potential. As the goal of Eastern mysticism is to awaken man to his true but "forgotten" identity as a god, so the goal of materialistic science (through conquering the atom, space, and disease) is to establish man at last as ruler of the universe and in technological control of nature. The magician and the naturalistic scientist are thus partners in the same enterprise, often without knowing it. In *Millennium*, Harvard theologian Harvey Cox writes: "The magical impulse is the desire to control and direct nature, to use it for human ends, to tame its sometimes malevolent side." Cox goes on to explain:

> This impulse developed through the centuries not into religion but into empirical science. The true successors of the sorcerers and the alchemists are not the priests and theologians but the physicists and the computer engineers.[21]

In this sense, naturalistic science is simply an academic attempt to explain and control cosmic forces within a materialistic/mechanistic framework. It is the same old sorcery, now demythologized of its miraculous and transcendent elements. Thus it has been said that today's science is yesterday's magic explained. Science fiction writer Arthur C. Clarke points out that for those in less developed societies, "any scientifically advanced technology is indistinguishable from magic."

There are many similarities between magic (shamanism/naturalism) and naturalistic science that result from their common roots and goals. For example, in both sorcery and science the "power" is beyond the comprehension of the unenlightened and can only be activated by those privy to its secrets. Both function according to natural laws, both reject the supernatural, and both deny the possibility of "miracles" in the biblical sense. Carlos Castaneda "entered the world of the sorcerer" and returned to earn his Ph.D. from UCLA by writing about his initiation under Indian sorcerer don Juan Matus. From firsthand experience, Castaneda argues that sorcery is just as exacting as science:

The same criteria [as for science] apply to the sorcerer's world: their schooling, which relies on oral instruction and the manipulation of awareness, although different from ours, is just as rigorous, because their knowledge is as, or perhaps *more*, complex.[22]

Fought largely in the West, the struggle between magic and materialism saw the scientists emerge as the new shamans. They became the high priests of a substitute secularized sorcery designed to free a skeptical and materialistic culture from its fear of the gods and spirits of its ancestors. Like Marxism's great experiment, however, the venture was a failure. Centuries of scientific and technological advances culminating in the space age have provided no new answers to ultimate questions and have not freed mankind from either its long-standing attraction to or its fear of magic. That instinctive awareness of some "higher power" remains unshaken. Apparently there is no escaping this universal conviction. And now materialism is dead. As Arthur Koestler so aptly put it, physics has gotten so "far out" that it can no longer support materialism.[23] It never could support esthetics or morals. Sir Arthur Eddington wrote:

For if those who hold that there must be a physical basis for everything hold that these mystical views are nonsense, we may ask: What, then, is the physical basis of nonsense? . . .

"Ought" takes us outside chemistry and physics.[24]

In the final analysis, science has been able to explain nothing that really matters. It has left the ultimate questions unanswered, while materialism has only accentuated the spiritual hunger of the soul. As William Irwin Thompson has pointed out, for materialists such as Von Daniken, "Gods are astronauts . . . a halo about the head of a figure carved on the rock at Tasili N'ajjer is . . . a space helmet."[25] Such "gods" lack the otherworldly quality that mankind senses they must have, a quality which materialism lacks and mysticism seems to supply.

The Merger of Science and Sorcery

What we seem to be heading for now is a rapprochement between what have until recently appeared to be two rival religions: science and sorcery. There is a growing hope that a new worldwide religion formed by the merger of science and Eastern mysticism will at last bring the unity and peace so desperately needed if humanity is to survive. Recalling the insights he derived, not from logic or scientific discovery but from a powerful mystical experience, Fritjof Capra says: "I *knew* with absolute certainty that the parallels between modern physics and Eastern mysticism would someday be common knowledge . . . as part of a much larger movement [involving] . . . a profound cultural transformation."[26] Influential psychologist Carl Rogers was a leader in this movement. He saw a new science emerging, "resembling the views of the Eastern mystic, rather than Newtonian mechanics."[27]

Many top scientists have shared this same view. Now it seems to be capturing the hearts and minds of increasing millions of people. As early as 1979, at the second annual "Open Conference for Mystics and Scientists" meeting near London, Sir George Trevelyan reminded conferees that "materialism is no longer a scientifically-based philosophy."[28] The purpose of such gatherings (prestigious institutions such as MIT have hosted similar conferences of scientists and theologians) is to lay the foundation for a new "religious science." Presenting their version of this same message, 100 musicians representing *His Holiness* Maharishi and *the science* of Transcendental Meditation completed a tour in 1987 in which they presented Gandharva, "the eternal music of nature," to appreciative audiences in 300 cities worldwide. While one of the groups was performing in Los Angeles, a spokesperson explained:

> This is not entertainment. We are on a mission . . . to correct the imbalances of nature . . . to bring about world peace.[29]

Thirty years ago such an idea would have been laughed out of existence. Yet in December 1987 the *Los Angeles Times* found it newsworthy enough to give it a bold four-column heading, a large picture, and a serious account that went the entire width of a page.

The "reconciliation-with-nature-is-our-hope" religion seems to hold an increasing attraction for the masses.

Varying estimates indicate that the December 31, 1986, "World Instant of Cooperation" involved 100-500 million persons meeting in thousands of locations around the world to "meditate" for peace. This unprecedented event was based upon the ancient nature-religion belief that everything in the cosmos (animate and inanimate) is part of a Universal Mind. Therefore, if enough people meditating together held the thought of peace in their minds, a "critical mass" could be reached that would tip the balance in cosmic consciousness and thus infuse the world with peace. The August 16/17, 1987, "Harmonic Convergence" similarly involved millions around the world in Eastern meditation, chanting, and other shamanic activities. Its principal organizer, Jose Arguelles, explained the purpose as a symbolic "surrender to Mother Earth," which would bring international peace.

What we are seeing is the revival on a very large and growing scale of ancient paganism and a rejection of scientism. There is no more reason, however, to believe that personal fulfillment or international peace will be accomplished by somehow getting back in touch with "Mother Nature" than by the conquest of nature. Can it really be a "quantum leap forward" to revive ancient pagan earth rituals in a vain attempt to placate the wrath of the nature gods? It would seem just as sensible to pray to a bolt of lightning or to a hurricane as to petition the earth.

In spite of the accelerating return to shamanism, the past few decades have seen unusual growth among the Christian and Islamic fundamentalists in tandem with the rising wave of conservatism. This movement may soon be submerged, however, and even to a surprising extent absorbed, by the inrushing tidal wave of sorcery. In fact, a penchant for occultism has always survived beneath the surface even within those biblical traditions which outwardly were opposed to naturalism/shamanism. There was cabalism in Judaism; Sufism in Islam; and Gnosticism, mysticism, spiritualism, and more recently New Thought (Religious Science) in Christianity. And now for the first time in decades those churches which present New Age ideas under the banner of Christianity are beginning to experience explosive growth. Consider, for example, Seattle's Unity

Church, which has mushroomed from a modest 600 members to more than 2000 in just three years and is still growing. Early in 1987 *U.S. News & World Report* noted:

> Accompanying the interest in psychics is a steady growth in mystic religion. The Unity School of Christianity, a mystic organization in Kansas City, MO, reports a 34 percent increase in its ministries and study groups in the past five years.[30]

Whether the New Age movement in its present form will continue to be the primary expression of shamanism's revival or not, one thing seems clear: No matter what form the "new consciousness" now sweeping the West may take, if current trends hold, neither scientism nor the increasingly aggressive fundamentalist movements within Islam, Judaism, and Christianity can any longer hold it back. In a recent issue published to define the movement, the editors of *New Age Journal* declared: "Society is now in the midst of a change potentially as sweeping as the Renaissance or the Protestant Reformation . . . as more and more people begin to question traditional assumptions about life, the future of the planet, and the nature of reality."[31] Whether this surprising development ultimately proves to be for better or for worse, one thing is certain: The winds spreading the seeds of sorcery have reached gale proportions.

A Haunting Sense of *Déjà Vu*

Esalen has been at the center of that gale. Its purpose from the very beginning has been to bring about a merger of Eastern mysticism with Western culture. It has played that role to the hilt, serving as the major think tank of the human-potential movement, where "men of letters and science" could preach a modern revival of sorcery. Its success as a consciousness-revolution catalyst infusing occultism into the American psyche has been astonishing. As the *Los Angeles Times* in a front page article noted: "Many of the concepts pioneered at Esalen—considered experimental and outrageous at the time—are now accepted elements of suburban living" to be found at YMCA's, churches, and universities.[32] As another chronicler of Esalen's success has written:

Ideas dismissed as crackpot in crackpot New England or as occult in the born-again heartland have been explored at Esalen by some of the best publicized minds of our century. Not only Joan Baez and Simon and Garfunkel and some of the Beatles, but every celebrity intellectual of the past 25 years has been there.

The Carl Saganicity is astounding. Participants have ranged from Henry Miller to Aldous Huxley to Paul Tillich to Arnold Toynbee to Susan Sontag to Herman Kahn to Buckminster Fuller to B. F. Skinner to Linus Pauling to Jerry Brown to Fritjof Capra. We're talking weight.

It's as if someone with land, money, free time and relentless curiosity (an apt description of Esalen's leadership) decided to hold a party and everyone came.[33]

A civil rights reporter and *Look* magazine editor when he came to Esalen in 1965 to interview Mike Murphy, George Leonard has been a fixture there ever since. Like the rest of its leadership, he persistently tries to distinguish Esalen from what they call "the schlock" invariably associated with so much of the human-potential scene. But while Leonard, who became president of the AHP, writes off "Shirley MacLaineism as 'end-of-the-millennium behavior,' " he also affirms, "there is a spiritual side of life." And in spite of Leonard's criticism of her, Esalen's view of "spiritual" happens to coincide very nicely with Shirley MacLaine's.[34]

Esalen was into "channeling" long before MacLaine and others made it so popular. In fact, beginning around 1980, Esalen had its own resident "channeler," a young English woman named Jenny O'Connor, who was more or less a permanent fixture for years. By means of automatic writing, a group of nonhuman entities allegedly based on the star Sirius delivered regular messages through Jenny that were at times quite remarkable for their uncanny wisdom and precognitive accuracy. Richard Price was so impressed that he began to involve the Nine, as they were called, in his gestalt sessions. In fact the Esalen Catalog for several years offered a course in gestalt which it promised would be facilitated by "The NINE, a paranormal intelligence. . . ."[35]

There was even a biographical entry in the catalog for the Nine, which described them as "giant reflectors of your selves, gestalt practitioners, marriage counselors—pure energy of emergence quality available to all." Price expressed the opinion that it didn't matter whether the material channeled through Jenny from the Nine "came from Sirius or from Jenny's unconscious." The Nine were even consulted by Esalen's senior directors in a famous meeting that resulted in a shake-up of the top leadership apparently as prescribed by these mysterious intelligences.[36]

Here again we have the same naturalistic idea that some "higher power," of which all things are a part, is influencing human destiny. This idea is foundational to all occultism. While it takes many forms, there is an unmistakable consistency beneath the surface differences. This pantheistic belief that is so deeply rooted in human consciousness is experiencing a worldwide revival. Having played a powerful role in shaping past history, it seems to be poised to do so once again in our time.

To any student of the past, the current scene has a haunting sense of *déjà vu* about it. More than one analyst has pointed out the role which this perverse mixture of science and religion has played in the fall of previous civilizations. Referring to the decline and fall of Greek and Roman Empires, Franz Cumont observes:

> In the declining days of antiquity the common creed of all pagans came to be a scientific pantheism, in which the infinite power of the divinity that pervaded the universe was revealed by all the elements of nature. . . .
>
> Preached on the one hand by men of letters and by men of science in centers of culture, diffused on the other hand among the bulk of the people . . . it is finally patronized by the emperors. . . .[37]

6

The Resurgence of Nature Religion

"Tonight, the startling, sobering results of a 20/20 investigation. Satanism—devil worship—is being practiced all across the country." It was the voice of Hugh Downs, who was cohosting with Barbara Walters an ABC Newsmagazine television special on May 16, 1985, titled "The Devil Worshipers." What had caused ABC's investigative team to take on this unmentionable topic? The voice of Hugh Downs continued: ". . . it's affecting America . . . perverse, hideous acts that defy belief. Suicides, murders, and the ritualistic slaughter of children and animals. Yet so far police have been helpless . . . there is no question that something is going on out there, and that's sufficient reason for 20/20 to look into it."

Detectives and judges have tended to shy away from evidence pointing to satanic involvement in crimes ("Don't come into court blaming the *devil!*" comments an investigator). According to Sandra Gallant of the San Francisco Police Department, that attitude is changing, however, because of the accumulation of substantial evidence. All over America police and sheriff departments have formed special ritualistic and occult crimes investigations task forces to deal with the growing incidence of such occurrences. Chicago psychotherapist Kathy Snowden "estimates that about 250 therapists nationwide are working with satanist ritual abuse cases. Satanists "include doctors, lawyers, professors, university presidents and military officers," says detective Robert Simandl of the Chicago Police Department.[1]

In their disillusionment with technology, millions of Westerners are turning back to witchcraft or various other forms of shamanism/nature religion. There is, of course, cause to be disillusioned with modern science because of the destruction it has brought to our environment and to our personal lives. The fault is not with science itself, however, or with the power it produces, but with man's abuse of it. We have been described as a generation of nuclear giants but moral midgets. Until that fatal flaw is somehow mended, the acquisition of occult power would only worsen a situation that is already out of control.

Among the religious groups pursuing occultic powers is Santeria. It is one of the fastest growing witchcraft cults in America, with an estimated 100 million adherents worldwide. While most of its practitioners would deny any involvement in human sacrifices, that side of Santeria was depicted in *The Believers*, one of the most horrifying feature films to come out of Hollywood in 1987. In the movie, the "believers" were highly respected community leaders who in secret banded together to practice ritual sacrifice of children in order to appease higher powers and thereby "save the world."

Santeria mixes African native rituals with veneration of Catholic saints. "The first symptom is the animals killed in a ritualistic way," Sergeant Richard Valdemar, a sheriff's deputy in Los Angeles, explained in an interview. "Then it's the [human] bodies." An undercover detective with the Richmond, Virginia, Bureau of Police says he would send agents to infiltrate any group—the Mafia, drug dealers— "but not this; the danger is too great of being killed or turned around." Los Angeles police department detective Frank Adair warned:

> I have a brother who is a [Catholic] priest and when I asked him about Santeria, he said, "Don't mess with it."
> When you start tampering with a religion like this, you don't know what you may unleash.[2]

"A lot of people—maybe most—confuse witches with Satanists," complains James Johnson. The slender and boyish 18-year-old is a student at Southern California's prestigious Pomona College, where he also teaches witchcraft in a noncredit course sponsored by Mortar Board, an honor society for seniors. A practicing witch himself, Johnson insists that "witches, real ones, don't believe in Satan, or practice black magic . . . at least not Wiccans."

Nevertheless, in spite of variations in the rituals, from the Satanists on one end of the witchcraft spectrum to the practitioners of "white magic" on the other, the underlying belief remains the same: It is all *nature religion*. All of the rituals share a common purpose: to invoke and/or manipulate a *natural* force innate within the cosmos in order to achieve health, wealth, or success, or to bring a curse upon one's enemies. Whether the "power" believed in is called Satan or the goddess does not affect the basic philosophy. Trying to sound broad-minded, but at the same time distinguishing nature religion from supernaturalism, James Johnson declares:

> You can call it occult if you want, even supernatural. I prefer to think that we witches just find the super in the natural.[3]

The Dark and Light Sides of the "Force"

With the rise of relativism, a large segment of American sociey seems to be losing the capacity to make moral distinctions, leaving people vulnerable to the amoral philosophy of witchcraft with its promises of self-fulfillment and personal power. While some witches would confess that they are involved in *black* magic, most Wiccans, like Johnson, claim to practice only the *white* variety. Anton Lavey, founder of San Francisco's First Church of Satan, insists that there is no difference between "black" and "white" magic. And if pressed, most occultists would admit that every form of magic comes from the same source and that the difference depends upon whether the force is used for good or evil.

Supernaturalists would argue, however, that there is no basis in nature religion for arriving at morals that apply either to the "higher power" itself or to its usage. There are no ethics or morals in nature; therefore, every kind of nature religion (whether called Satanism, Wicca, Hinduism, or whatever) is by very definition amoral. "Good" and "evil" do not apply to atoms or galaxies or natural forces such as gravity or electricity or psychic power. Historian/philosopher Herbert Schlossberg reminds us, "Animals do not act morally or immorally; they only act naturally. A system of ethics that says human beings ought to base their behavior on nature therefore justifies any behavior, because nature knows no ethic."[4]

Nobelist Sir John Eccles points out in *The Wonder of Being Human—Our Brain and Our Mind*:

> The concepts of injustice, unfairness, and perverse-
> ness—like the obligations to honor, to respect and to
> permit—are intelligible only within a *moral* context and
> to moral beings.
>
> In the mindless universe of mere nature . . . there is
> neither justice nor mercy, neither liberty nor fairness.
> There are only facts, and no fact—as a fact—seeks or
> requires a justification.[5]

Some practicing witches claim that the power they draw upon can
only be used in benevolent ways, a claim which seems to attribute
morals to an impersonal force. However, morality is clearly not a
"power," nor is any power either moral or immoral. Thus to speak
of a "higher power" or the "dark" and "light" sides of a force is
misleading. Morals imply responsibility to an ultimate *authority*—
something which is entirely lacking in nature and cosmic energy. No
one can say that atomic power has authority, much less that it is a
"higher power" than electricity. Biblical supernaturalism argues
that moral authority cannot derive from molecular structure or
evolutionary forces (or an occult force with "dark" and "light"
sides), but only from an intelligent personal Creator. As Eccles
pointedly observes:

> [It is] not at all clear how "natural selection" has
> somehow selected for Bach's Partitas . . . or for a sys-
> tem of justice that will let a thousand guilty men go free
> lest one innocent man be constrained of his liberties.[6]

The fallacious concept of a force innate in the cosmos, with a
"light" and "dark" side producing "white" and "black" magic, has
caused much confusion. For example, at the same time that the early
American colonists were stamping out what they perceived as
witchcraft, they were practicing it themselves in its unrecognized
"white" form of "Renaissance esotericism . . . [such as] astrology, palmistry, and magical healing."[7] In Salem, Massachusetts,
toward the end of the seventeenth century, 20 persons found guilty
of practicing witchcraft were put to death and another 150 were
imprisoned. Those regrettable events have since been universally

condemned, and rightly so. In reaction against that extremism, however, has the pendulum swung too far the other way?

A New Respectability for Witchcraft

Today Salem has its own official witch, Laurie Cabot; and best-selling author Lynn Andrews has been called the "Medicine Woman of Beverly Hills." Active participants in witchcraft/shamanism in the United States far outnumber the membership of some Christian denominations. Even the United Nation's World Health Organization has given its approval to a revival of witchcraft under the popular euphemism of "traditional medicine" or "native cures." It's just a matter of getting back to our pagan roots, a very acceptable goal in today's society. One Church of Wicca in the Los Angeles area, with more than 8000 members, boasts of its infiltration of nearby Protestant and Catholic churches, of its many converts from mainstream Christianity, of its well-attended classes for children who are released an hour each week from public school for religious instruction, of its summer camps for youth, and of its funding from international bankers. In a cover story, a Southern California weekly newspaper recently reported:

> Maybe you don't think that you know any witches. . . . They do exist . . . [and] they don't look any different from you or me or the people you see at the bus stop.
> Witches are in Altadena, in Sierra Madre, in Woodland Hills, in Carson—all over Los Angeles County and all over the country. . . . They're computer technicians, electrical engineers, and the folks next door. But they're witches, too. . . .
> When the Covenant of the Goddess, a witchcraft umbrella organization, held a meeting in the mountains north of L.A. last year, 3500 witches showed up.[8]

Sorcery in various forms is moving steadily into the mainstream of today's American culture. One recent volume, a symposium by a number of experts on the occult, refers to this revival as "a simultaneous restaging of impulses that have never been quiescent on the

American scene."[9] This "simultaneous restaging" has become an explosion with ever-widening repercussions. Witchcraft is an important factor not only in ecological activism, as already mentioned, but in other influential movements as well. "Feminist spirituality," for example, which prominent leaders in the Women's Movement identify as the "oldest spirituality on earth" (i.e. Wicca),[10] is now recognized as one of the largest submovements within the feminist camp. According to one of its leading spokespersons:

> It's [feminist spirituality] amorphous, blending in a surprisingly smooth amalgam radical feminism, pacifism, witchcraft, Eastern mysticism, goddess worship, animism, psychic healing, and a variety of practices normally associated with "fortune-telling."
>
> It exists nationwide and takes the form of large, daylong workshops, small meditation groups, and even covens that meet to work spells and do rituals under the full moon. . . .
>
> To the women in feminist spirituality, witchcraft . . . is a women's religion, a religion of the earth, vilified by patriarchal Christianity, and now, finally, reclaimed.[11]

Even the United States armed services are being pressured into accommodating witchcraft. Acknowledging that witches among U.S. forces in Europe are demanding official recognition, the U.S. military's unofficial daily newspaper, *Stars and Stripes*, recently explained that "Wiccans, like other pagans, believe in multiple deities as well as the oneness of all with nature."[12] The *Army Times* carried a story titled "Witches, Pagans in Military Demand Rights." It sympathetically reported that those who practice Wicca need "chaplains who understand pre-Christian beliefs and who can help them form worship groups at remote duty locations." The *Times* article referred to the Army's chaplain handbook for an authorized perspective:

> Wiccans are considered pagans because they worship several nature gods instead of a single god. . . . They also believe in psychic powers and hold rituals according

to lunar cycles. Other pagan groups include Druids, who base their rituals on solar cycles, and those who worship the Norse gods of the ancient vikings.

Their religion, Wicca, is the tribal worship of ancient peoples based in "magick," herbology, healing and the worship . . . of the Mother Goddess and her consort, the Horned God.[13]

The Movement Back to "Nature"

One of the most respectable paths leading into witchcraft is today's back-to-nature movement. It is a paradox that the Western world is eagerly embracing the notion that "natural" is somehow more beneficial, more benign, and more pure in content and intent than all the technological enhancements which science has thus far been able to bestow upon us. Little reflection is required, however, to realize that this theory contains a number of basic flaws. There is nothing more natural than disease, pain, death, and those calamities categorized by insurance companies as "natural disasters" (hurricanes, earthquakes, lightning, drought, and famine, to name a few). In fact it is against such offspring of nature that humanity has desperately struggled to protect itself, and in so doing has arrived at the present stage of civilization. As Francis Bacon declared in the seventeenth century:

> Nature has to be hounded in her wanderings, bound into service and made a slave . . . [and] put in constraint.

It seems ironic that after mankind has courageously fought for thousands of years to conquer the often antagonistic and sometimes deadly forces of nature, there is a popular and growing movement calling for surrender to these same forces. As a "basic principle," the authors of *Rebirthing In The New Age* recommend "forming a conscious relationship to the planet."[14] Sympathetic to this cause, Carl Rogers advocated living "in a comfortable relationship to nature, a responsible kinship," with the very thought of "the conquest of nature" being "abhorrent."[15] While on the surface this might sound reasonable, "nature" is not so constituted as to offer a benign and dependable kinship. It is absurd to speak of living in a "comfortable relationship" with an erupting volcano or a cholera epidemic. Before we all surrender to nature as divine, we ought to recognize that to do so is a repudiation of all that mankind has called progress since the dawn of history. It is a quantum leap from respecting and protecting our environment (which we ought to do), to worshiping "Mother Earth."

It was the unnatural act of reason opposing the natural processes of nature that brought under control a host of formerly fatal diseases (such as polio, tuberculosis, and malaria), that lowered the death rate in infants, and that has steadily increased the average life expectancy. Medical science is far from perfect, but it is the repeated unnatural act of taking out an appendix, of transplanting a kidney, or of removing a tumor that has saved millions of lives. Such realities ought not to be forgotten in our rush to "surrender to Mother Earth." Moreover, we do well to remember that it was Western science that brought these benefits to mankind. These blessings would never result from the pantheistic philosophy produced by altered states of consciousness induced in Yoga or other forms of Eastern meditation. Nor would medical science ever have blossomed from the mystical beliefs that the West is now embracing in its pursuit of "natural health."

It has been through the continuing battle to overcome the elements of nature that the many comforts and benefits unknown in earlier times and taken for granted in today's highly advanced civilization have been produced. None is a product of nature. There is nothing *natural* about computers, television, space travel, dams, bridges, books, or even such basic necessities of human life as weaving, food processing, plowing, weeding, or cooking. Such obvious considerations seem to be overlooked by those who so loudly trumpet the praises of the "natural." This is not to deny that ecological destruction has been unnecessarily wrought by human folly. At the same time, however, complaints against the intrusion of science and technology must be made on reasonable grounds, and not on the assumption that the earth is a goddess to be worshiped, held in awe, and left untouched.

From Instinct to Reason

Such a "hands-off" mentality is more pervasive and influential than most people realize. For example, a family of beavers builds a dam, leaving many trees unnecessarily felled helter-skelter, some partially gnawed and still standing but now dead, with a meadow flooded and other plants and trees dead as a result—but this is part of *nature*, and as such it is the delight of environmentalists. A group of highly educated engineers, on the other hand, carefully plans a dam to minimize damage and maximize benefits for millions of people for generations to come—and the ecologist lobby hires attorneys and succeeds in getting the project stopped because it may bring extinction to an obscure species of fish and "spoil the natural beauty."

What is the distinction between the two dams? Why is one "natural" and the other "unnatural"? Why is it that mankind's actions always interfere with nature, while those of all other living creatures enhance nature? Why does a bird nest or beehive blend into the environment, but a human structure (be it skyscraper or log hut) stands out as clearly not part of nature? And why does the animal world, in its reactions to humans, so obviously recognize that mankind is an alien species in a unique category of its own? Does it not seem ironic in the extreme that evolution itself, in presumably its highest form on planet earth (if that is really what our species represents), has produced a being who is alienated from and destructive of the very "Mother Nature" which supposedly spawned him?

If mankind was developed by the same evolutionary forces as the beaver, bird, or bee and is thus equally a product of "natural selection," then why are human activities condemned as *unnatural*, while the most vicious behavior of animals (which are supposedly related to man through the process of evolution) goes unchallenged as simply *natural*? Is it because humans *reason* but lower creatures act by *instinct*? Bees instinctively construct containers in a shape that maximizes strength while minimizing material, a structure which modern engineering with its mathematics and computers has not been able to improve upon and which is still copied in our most advanced designs. A single cell, the smallest living unit, is more complex in structure and function than the largest city—so complex that it is presently inconceivable that human ingenuity will ever be able to fully understand, much less duplicate, a cell. Confronted by the awesome genius of design and construction displayed throughout the cosmos, from atoms to stars, the supernaturalist seeks to know the Creator in order to worship and obey him. The naturalist, however, insists that it all came about by some impersonal force, and seeks to learn the secret of controlling and using it for his own ends.

Literally millions of examples could be given to show that instinct provides animals and even the tiniest insects with survival capabilities beyond the capacity of our most advanced technology. And even if technology caught up with nature, it would not be available to the average person. That fact raises huge questions. A baby chick pecks its way out of its shell and is able to walk about and forage for food, but human offspring are helpless for years. Even as adults we have to study and draw upon centuries of laboriously accumulated knowledge, but we are still behind the animal or insect world in crucial survival capabilities. This fact doesn't seem to square with the theory that our species, as the "highest form" produced by the same evolutionary forces, has been given reason as a replacement for instinct.

If mankind is the end product of billions of years of natural selection through survival of the fittest, then why in the process of reaching this pinnacle of evolution did that "highest" species lose the entire armory of essential survival mechanisms possessed by its alleged "ancestors" and which is still so common throughout nature? The arctic tern can unerringly navigate across thousands of miles of ocean, even in a storm; yet for a human to do the same thing requires years of schooling, advanced training, and sophisticated instruments. Without any education at all a tiny gnat can survive in jungles or on a glacier and accomplish feats that are far beyond the capabilities of the toughest and best-trained Marine or Green Beret.

The capacity to reason could more readily be looked upon as an advantage if instinct supposedly accumulated over billions of years had not been the price that evolution exacted in bestowing it. There is no way to explain mankind's rational faculties in terms of "natural selection." It is reason, in fact, which places mankind in an *unnatural* class by itself.

The Capacity to Reason and the Difference It Makes

It is the ability to reason that has brought mankind into conflict with nature. Either this capacity must be admitted as evidence that man is not the product of *natural* selection and therefore does not belong to nature, or else what this capacity produces cannot be dismissed as *unnatural* but must be considered as natural as the functions and activities of every other life form. If man is the product of nature, then everything he does (whether it be the building of dams or nuclear power plants or the waging of wars) must be a natural act and as devoid of blame as the eating of insects by birds or the destruction of a forest by blight. Yet the understanding that mankind differs from all other creatures on this planet, not just in degree but in kind (as Mortimer J. Adler has so well pointed out in *The Difference of Man and the Difference It Makes*), separated by a chasm that cannot be bridged by any evolutionary process, is recognized intuitively by humans and instinctively by animals. It is strange indeed that what the world of academia has attempted to educate us to believe for the past hundred years, the entire human species (and animal world as well) continues to contradict by its behavior.

In contrast to the animal world, mankind's ability to reason made science possible. This difference is of tremendous significance, as C. S. Lewis argues so well in *Miracles*. The mere fact that we can reason about our circumstances and speculate about purpose and meaning is proof that our thoughts are not themselves programmed and determined by the stimulus of natural events. We are thus faced with a major weakness in the theory of evolution, a weakness which Darwin himself recognized.[16] If everything is determined by natural selection and the survival of the fittest, then his theory itself must have resulted from the same forces at work. Evolution would therefore be meaningless, having nothing to do with truth or reasonable deductions from facts, but would be purely the result of a natural process, with no more relationship to logic than a chemical reaction in a test tube. Sir Karl Popper explains that if Darwinism is right, then any theory (such as evolution, for example):

> . . . is held because of a certain physical structure of the holder—perhaps of his brain.

> Accordingly, we are deceiving ourselves and are phys-
> ically so determined as to deceive ourselves whenever we
> believe that there are such things as *arguments or rea-
> sons* [for accepting a theory].
>
> Purely physical conditions, including our physical en-
> vironment, make us say or accept whatever we say or
> accept.[17]

Every attempt to find evidence to *prove* that evolution is *true* is a
denial of the theory itself. Reason, then, not only makes it possible
to argue against Darwin's theory (and caused Darwin himself to
doubt its validity), but this unique human capacity is itself evidence
that mankind is not part of nature but reflects a higher origin and
possesses capabilities that transcend anything found in nature. This
human capacity to resist nature did not fit into Carl Jung's naturalistic scheme of the collective unconscious. In perplexity he wrote:

> One asks oneself where our consciousness gets its
> ability to be so contrary to nature and what such arbi-
> trariness might signify.[18]

The Harsh Amorality of Nature

Hinduism provides the most comprehensive representation of
witchcraft's "nature-is-God" beliefs and occultic practices. Nazism, in turn, was closely related to both Hinduism and today's New
Age movement—a connection which we will explore later. It is
more than coincidence that so many Hindu gurus demand, as Hitler
did, absolute obedience and worship from their followers. And,
strangely enough, in spite of the horrifying lessons from the Third
Reich, there are still millions of people who are willing to abdicate
reason and blindly follow a leader. The attitude toward Hitler still
widely held in influential circles in India today is summarized in the
following remarks made by Swami Svatantrananda to a learned
Hindu audience:

> Whatever you may say against him, Hitler was a ma-
> hatma, almost like an avatar. . . . he was the visual in-
> carnation of Aryan polity.[19]

That so many leading Hindus have praised the ideals of Nazi Germany is quite consistent with Hinduism, from which Hitler borrowed the swastika. Compassion is contrary to nature religion, a revival of which was a key element in the Third Reich. Those who hold to the same naturalism today must adopt Hitler's pragmatic willingness to eliminate "undesirable elements" if they would be consistent with their professed beliefs. Maharishi Mahesh Yogi exemplifies that consistency when he writes of the new society that TM is intended to usher in:

> There has not been and there will not be a place for the unfit. The fit will lead, and if the unfit are not coming along there is no place for them. . . . In the Age of Enlightenment there is no place for ignorant people. . . .
> Non-existence of the unfit has been the law of nature.[20]

Maharishi is expressing the logic of naturalism: Nature is not kind; it is harsh. In actual fact, however, nature is neither of these. Such terms no more apply to "nature" than to a rock or cloud. Nor would love or compassion have any more meaning for humans than for an amoeba if we were in fact the products of impersonal natural laws and evolutionary forces. If those were indeed our origins, then the establishment of hospitals and every act of mercy and self-sacrifice for the benefit of others ought to be banned by ecologists as destructive of the natural order, and the law of tooth and fang ought to prevail as the only reasonable alternative.

Giving insulin to diabetics, for example, should not be allowed because it increases the hereditary pool of diabetes and thereby weakens the race. It is thus an unnatural interference with the evolutionary process. Every vaccine also works against nature's process of weeding out the weak. Such unnatural extensions of life for the sick or handicapped (who otherwise would be eliminated by natural forces) should therefore be opposed by all convinced evolutionists. Yet Jonas Salk, developer of polio vaccine, is a confessed "evangelist" for evolution. And he admits the glaring contradiction.

He also admits that the Salk Institute, with its dedicated staff of medical scientists battling to conquer disease, is worsening the problems of an exploding population. Caught red-handed undermining the very evolutionary forces in which he claims to implicitly trust, Salk, like all proponents of Sagan's scientism, is left without moral arguments to justify his behavior. As a convinced evolutionist, he has no basis for valuing medicine above murder, and can only paint himself further into the corner by suggesting that his desire to save lives is "genetically programmed":

> We are impelled to extend the human life span. I think that we are genetically programmed to behave that way.[21]

Salk believes that *ideas* (there are no *morals*) are as much the product of blind evolutionary forces as a leaf or a gene.[22] We are left to wonder why evolution would produce so many brilliant ideas and the compassionate behavior which undermines it. Of course even our speculations about such contradictions have been programmed into our genes and are therefore not really speculations at all! Evolution does make countless mistakes along the way, so the compassion that has been programmed into us could be the result of one of those unfortunate harmful mutations that will lead to the extinction of our species. This theory, which does away with all purpose, brings to mind the words of Alfred North Whitehead: "Scientists who spend their lives with the purpose of proving that it is purposeless constitute an interesting field of study."

Expendable Experiments of Nature

The hopeless contradiction which Whitehead identified results from trying to explain human behavior by the laws of physical science. It can't be done without dehumanizing us into stimulus/response mechanisms. In *Walden Two*, psychologist/novelist B. F. Skinner has his alter ego Frazier explain to his guest that the purpose of the "controllers" is to develop "a science of human behavior." Of course it is impossible to develop a science when the subject of the experiment is hopping about capriciously with a free will and one never quite knows what he is going to do next. Five years later, in *Science and Human Behavior*, Skinner writes: "The hypothesis that man is *not free* is essential to the application of scientific method to the study of human behaviour."[23] Concerned at the demoralizing result of such a philosophy being widely taught in American universities, Allan Bloom points out in his classic *The Closing of the American Mind*:

> This contradiction runs throughout the natural and social sciences. They [purport to] give an account of things that cannot possibly explain the conduct of their practitioners. . . . [For example] the physicist who signs petitions in favor of freedom while recognizing only unfreedom—mathematical law governing moved matter—in the universe. . . .[24]

Nor is the dilemma helped by Salk's assertion that evolutionary forces have prepared us now to guide our further evolution into higher states of consciousness. He has already claimed that we have been programmed to work against evolution. Moreover, "higher" is a statement of values for which naturalism provides no basis. Yet the "new paradigm," writes Marilyn Ferguson, "sees humankind embedded in nature."[25] Ramtha, through J. Z. Knight, "channels" the same message of harmony with nature. It is the common message of the entities that communicate through channelers, mediums, Ouija boards, and other occult means.

The basic contradiction between human compassion and the impersonal harshness of nature remains unresolved. Again Eccles points out: "The facts of human morality and ethics are clearly at variance with a theory that explains all behavior in terms of self-preservation and the preservation of the species."[26] Recognizing that he was holding irreconcilable beliefs, but unwilling to resolve his inner conflict by choosing between them, the illustrious German poet Goethe wrote:

> As a moralist I am a monotheist; as an artist I am a polytheist; as a naturalist I am a pantheist.[27]

Of course it is impossible to be a monotheist and polytheist/pantheist at the same time. In tacit admission that Goethe's (and his own) naturalism/pantheism provides no basis for moral values, Salk clearly states that the survival not only of any individual human but of our entire species is of no significance; only evolution itself matters. Nor can we even enjoy the dubious satisfaction of knowing that our race will prove to be the ancestor of some ultimate species that may be worth saving. Although he claims that evolution seems to have something "guiding" it, Salk insists that neither he nor evolution itself can predict the final outcome. He does suggest that "we may evolve into something better." Not "better" from our point of view, however, but for the "good" of the evolutionary process:

> We do not have to survive as a species. What is important is that we keep evolving.[28]

We are simply expendable "experiments" of nature along the path toward some future superspecies. This philosophy would seem to justify Hitler's experiments to produce the "master race." Nor can we blame Hitler or his underlings who ran the extermination camps for simply carrying out what had been "programmed into their genes." After all, Hitler's determination to eliminate the weak is more in line with the evolutionary process than Salk's desire to save them.

The completely amoral, self-centered creature that was the ultimate mechanism of survival (and thus of destruction for all others) so fearfully depicted in the movie *Alien* represents the "morality" of nature. Could anyone trust a goddess "Mother" whose ultimate fulfillment would lie in producing such an offspring? No wonder Salk declares, "Our faith must be in *ourselves*."[29] Yet if we are the products of "natural selection" (and not the end product, but an intermediate species not worth saving), to trust ourselves would seem to be the height of folly. That too has apparently been programmed into our genes. Such a belief may be held theoretically, but to practice it in daily life would be to reject common sense and to deny our very humanity.

The Unfathomable Source of Creativity

What reasonable person could live as though love, joy, appreciation of beauty or poetry, fear of the unknown, desire for meaning, and concepts of truth, justice, ethics, and respect for the rights of others were simply survival reflexes programmed into one's genes? If that were so, then all of life would be one huge charade. The Declaration of Independence attributes the right of "life, liberty, and the pursuit of happiness" not to nature but to nature's *God*. Equality is nowhere found in nature; and if it were, "survival of the fittest" would come to an immediate halt. America's Founding Fathers seemed to be of the opinion that if there were to be equality among men it had to be the result of being *"created* equal." Before throwing this valuable heritage away, we ought to weigh the alternatives more carefully.

We are something more than highly-evolved complex clusters of protein molecules wired with nerves and programmed by trial and error to respond to various stimuli in certain scientifically explicable ways. It is inconceivable that a sense of guilt or shame could be explained in terms of the flow of electrical current in certain patterns in the brain, or by mere glandular chemical reactions. There is a profound mystery to human life underlying each individual's sense of personal identity. Personality may indeed be affected by the parade of experience, but something more than that is involved. Each individual has his or her own mysterious autonomy that defies scientific analysis.

In attempting to accept these realities of human experience, Salk at times comes close to compromising his scientism. His allusions to "spirit" in his writings and speeches indicate that, like so many other committed materialists, he understands that there must be a nonphysical reality beyond the universe and inaccessible to our senses. And, like other evolutionists, he inevitably contradicts his reductionist theories by speaking of the human *spirit*. Eccles, however, points out the impossibility of reconciling mankind's unique spiritual values and experiences with Darwinism:

> Since materialist [evolutionary] solutions fail to account for our experienced uniqueness, we are constrained to attribute the uniqueness of the psyche or soul to a supernatural spiritual creation. . . .
>
> We submit that no other explanation is tenable; neither the genetic uniqueness with its fantastically impossible lottery nor the environmental differentiations, which do not *determine* one's uniqueness but merely modify it.[30]

Of course Salk recognizes the problem Eccles addresses. However, unlike Eccles, he is unwilling to transfer his allegiance from nature to nature's Creator. In *The Survival of the Wisest*, Salk writes of what he calls an "unfathomable source of creativity" at work behind the scenes directing "Nature's 'game'." He must attribute this "unfathomable creativity" either to nature itself or to the Creator of nature. He opts for the former.

Salk cannot escape making religious pronouncements, but, like Sagan and the other priests of scientism, he is now forced to attribute godlike intelligence and powers to impersonal cosmic forces. These are pronouncements of *faith* that cannot be substantiated by science. The deification of nature and of mankind as its offspring, though expressed in the erudite language of academia, is the same religious science espoused by witches and other worshipers of the mysterious force they believe to be innate in the cosmos.

For those impressed by rhetoric this may sound inspiring. It should be remembered, however, that in turning back to nature religion, Western society cannot pick and choose the aspects of shamanism which it finds appealing (or has demythologized and psychologized) and discard the rest. There are gods and spirits that not only come with the package, but which have traditionally played the key role. The "spiritual entity" is a major part of the program and cannot be separated, distilled, twisted, bent, mythologized, or simply ignored in order to make sorcery academically respectable. It is the deliberate cultivation of a relationship with these entities (though called by modern names) that has become the major concern of many critics of the New Age movement.

7

Freud, Jung, and the Occult

Any attempt to understand the current worldwide revival of sorcery must candidly face the issue of "spirit manifestations." Since the dawn of history, a belief in the existence of nonphysical beings who interact with mankind has been basic to all religions and occultism. It is not surprising, then, that a belief in these mysterious entities (whether they are real or imagined), is also playing a key role in today's New Age movement. As we have already noted, an uncanny sense of the behind-the-scenes existence of the spirit world is so deeply embedded in the consciousness of every human being that nothing can uproot it. This is just as true of modern, sophisticated Westerners, who consider themselves too scientifically oriented to be religious and who reject the possibility of psychic experiences.

Take for example Carl Rogers, who, while studying for the ministry, renounced the conservative Protestant Christianity of his youth, left seminary, and went on to become one of the most influential and highly respected psychologists of the postwar period and a leader in the rise of humanistic psychology. Toward the end of his life, however, Rogers became convinced, in spite of his earlier rejection of the supernatural, of the reality of the spirit world and the soul's survival after death. This remarkable change came about as the result of his attending a series of seances, in one of which his wife, Helen, allegedly made contact with her dead sister's discarnate spirit. Explaining that the voice speaking through the medium revealed intimate facts "that the medium could not possibly have known," Rogers declared:

> The messages were extraordinarily convincing. Three years ago I would have thought this was stupid . . . I never used to believe in immortality, but now all the evidence shows that there's something to it.[1]

Just prior to her death, according to Rogers, Helen (who had also been "a great skeptic about psychic phenomena and immortality") nevertheless " 'saw' evil figures and the devil by her hospital bed . . . [and] had visions of an inspiring white light which came closer, lifted her from the bed, and then deposited her back on the bed."[2] In writing about his wife's experiences, Rogers mentions "Robert Monroe, a hard-headed businessman and engineer" who found himself suddenly out of his body and, after recovering from the initial fright, eventually learned to enjoy astral travel and even formed a company to initiate others into its pleasures. He also mentions Carlos Castaneda and his initiation into the sorcerer's world "where the 'man of knowledge' has a spirit ally, where the impossible is experienced." He also alludes to Carl Jung's psychic experiences and those of others. Then Rogers comments:

> These and other accounts cannot simply be dismissed with contempt or ridicule. The witnesses are too honest, their experiences too real.
> All these accounts indicate that a vast and mysterious universe—perhaps an inner reality, or perhaps a spirit world of which we are all unknowingly a part—seems to exist.[3]

An Epidemic of Surprise Visitations

Rogers also claimed that after Helen's death he was contacted by her spirit. Psychologist William Kirk Kilpatrick was present when Rogers related this experience to a small group. The father of "client-centered" therapy confessed that as Helen lay dying he felt "heavily burdened by . . . her need for care" and decided (true to his selfist philosophy) to put his own survival first and "lead his own life" separate from her. In the process he "formed a new relationship" coincident with Helen's death. Hounded by guilt, Rogers consulted a Ouija board. "Now he never believed in Ouija boards before, mind you," writes Kilpatrick, paraphrasing Rogers, "and he knows this will sound strange . . . [but] suddenly letters began to form . . .":

> It is Helen, and her message is one of complete absolution: "Enjoy, Carl, enjoy! Be free! Be free!"
> "Well by gosh!" says Rogers, and he wipes his hand upward across his brow. "What a wave of relief swept over me when I heard that."
> From the group, exclamations of awe can be heard: "That's incredible!" "Fantastic!"
> And now it seems everyone in the group has had their mystical and quasi-mystical experiences: . . . premonitional dreams, poltergeists, and encounters with something known as "the white light." Whenever the latter is mentioned there are nods of familiarity, as though the white light were an old friend or a new G.E. product.[4]

Such experiences, fairly rare only a few years ago (or at least seldom admitted), are now almost commonplace. This is not because so many more people are attending seances. Rather, the "dead" are seemingly coming to the living, surprising them when they "appear" or "communicate" from the spirit world. University of North Carolina associate professor of family medicine P. Richard Olson "found that nearly two-thirds (64%) of widows at two Asheville nursing homes had at least 'once or twice' felt as though they were in touch with someone who had died" and a startling 78 percent of those reporting these experiences "said they *saw* the dead one." Moreover, Dr. Olson reported in *Geriatrics Today*, "even psychoactive drugs didn't end the 'visits.' "[5]

Supporting this surprising trend, a recent nationwide survey found that "nearly half of American adults (42%) now believe they have been in contact with someone who has died. . . ." Millions of Americans have had such experiences, so that our nation is now "living with a split between scientific belief and personal reality." And instead of declining with the advance of education and technology, as one might expect, that split is growing rather rapidly. The figure of 42 percent represents nearly a 60 percent increase from the previous poll 11 years earlier.[6] Any disease showing statistics like that would be recognized as epidemic.

One of the most convincing indications that the "spirit world," though inaccessible to our five physical senses, does in fact exist is found in the startling frequency with which it intrudes spontaneously into the lives of those who neither believe in nor have sought such contact. Many of those to whom "ghosts" have unexpectedly "appeared" had previously vehemently denied their existence and, oddly enough, continued to do so even after their experience. According to the latest national poll, "30% of the Americans who do *not* believe in life after death still say they've been in personal contact with the dead."[7] These are not gullibles searching for mystical experiences but a skeptical cross section of intellectual sophisticates to whom these appearances came as unbelievable surprises.

Even cadets at the Military Academy at West Point—the last place one would expect such phenomena to surface—have reported seeing ghosts. A number of plebes swear that they witnessed several appearances, beginning on October 21, 1972, of a ghostly soldier about five-feet-three-inches tall dressed in full Jackson-era regalia. The "ghost" repeatedly appeared and dematerialized in room 4714 of the 4th Division barracks. This was nothing new at West Point, where a number of such "appearances" have been reported.[8]

The consistent nature of such experiences down through history, even among vastly different and widely scattered cultures around the world, is a strong indication that something more than hallucination or superstition is involved. Philosopher Immanuel Kant perceptively observed over 200 years ago that "ghost" stories are believed secretly but rejected publicly because unbelief is fashionable among the educated. As for himself, he confessed that he was skeptical about any one story, but had "a certain faith in the whole of them taken together."[9] After devoting his life to the investigation of the psychic world, Carl Jung observed that while intellectuals publicly scorn belief in such things, nevertheless:

The same primitive fear of ghosts is still deep in our bones, but it is unconscious.

. . . things are continually happening that have accompanied human life from time immemorial: premonitions . . . hauntings, ghosts, return of the dead, bewitchings, sorcery, magic spells, etc. [10]

Rationalization and Confusion

Jung himself grew up in an atmosphere of seances and persistent poltergeist activity. He had his first psychic vision at the age of three. And at an even earlier age than Rogers, he too renounced the austere and formal Protestant Christianity in which he was raised. The occult, however, was an obsession which Jung could never escape. And the odyssey which he took from firm believer to skeptic to reluctant believer once again (with its many twists and turns in between) is a fascinating study. In a series of lectures in 1897 to a student organization at Basel University while an undergraduate there, the 22-year-old Jung said that "the soul does exist, it is intelligent and immortal, not subject to time and space." He also affirmed "the reality of spirits and spiritualism, on the evidence of telekinesis, messages of dying people, hypnotism, clairvoyance . . . and prophetic dreams." [11]

As he progressed in his studies of psychology, however, it became academically embarrassing to Jung to admit his psychic experiences and convictions to his rationalistic colleagues. Then came the shattering disillusionment of catching his favorite cousin and medium in fraud. For many years thereafter, as Nandor Fodor so well points out, Jung engaged in "masking his [occult] involvement and passions behind words and phrases that will not be too startling to the academic ear . . . quick to contradict himself whenever he feels . . . he may have indicated his personal involvement too strongly." [12]

Jung struggled to find the answers to life's ultimate questions through the exploration of the "psyche." After a lifetime of advising others on this subject, however, and making authoritative pronouncements about it that are still cherished and quoted by millions, Jung admitted that "no one knows what 'psyche' is." [13] He was also recognized worldwide as one of the foremost experts on an alleged extension of the psyche which he called the "collective unconscious" of the race. The latter became Jung's "God," encompassing both the source and solution of all problems. It was not until he neared the end of his life that Jung would candidly admit that, far from being the science he had represented them to be, everything ("all my works, all my creative activity") derived from horrendous experiences with haunting spirit entities that nearly drove him insane.

Hiding these facts during most of his life, Jung "demythologized" his continuing spiritual experiences, no matter how "real" they seemed, by identifying them as "exteriorizations" of suppressed wishes, fears, memories, and archetypal images dredged up from the mythical "collective unconscious." Such explanations allowed Jung to rationalize away, at least for a time, the dread implications of the incredibly persistent visitations from all manner of "spirit entities" that continued to haunt him throughout his life. These horrifying experiences, which led him to the brink of suicide, reached a crescendo during a six-year period of near-psychotic-collapse following Jung's traumatic break with his mentor Freud in 1912. It was during this time that "Philemon" became his "spirit guide."

A Delusion of the Senses?

So real were the "spirits of the dead" that Jung felt he was at times traveling with them and had become their "parson." It was an awesome experience, with his house seemingly filled with "spirits," under whose urging and inspiration Jung says his *Septem Sermones ad Mortuos* (*Seven Sermons to the Dead*) "began to flow out of me, and in the course of three evenings the thing was written." This was one of Jung's key works. His answers to the crucial questions demanded of him by the "spirits of the dead" concerning the nature of God, the universe, and man carried the seeds of all of his future work in psychology. When the story of Jung's life was finally told, more than 40 years later, the American publisher of *Memories, Dreams, Reflections* left out the *Seven Sermons*, apparently considering this part of Jung's life too unbelievable, in spite of the crucial role that it had played in the formulation of his theories.

Struggling to explain psychologically this apparent reality (if demons existed, then perhaps so did the despised God of Protestantism), Jung wrote: "Even spirits appear to be psychic phenomena whose origins lie in the unconscious. . . . They are, so far as my experience goes, the exteriorized effects of unconscious complexes." Could such statements be anything more than desperate rationalizations from the man who, in 1916, had been inspired by a screeching chorus of ghosts to write one of his most important works? Jung's guarded and often-contradictory pronouncements on this subject betrayed an ambiguous uncertainty. "I shall not commit the fashionable stupidity of regarding everything I cannot explain as a fraud," he wrote in 1919; and in 1948 he cautioned: "Those who are not convinced should beware of naively assuming that the whole question of spirits and ghosts has been settled and that all manifestations of this kind are meaningless swindles."

This did not mean that Jung was ready to admit that psychic phenomena had an objective reality, but only that they were "real" to the unconscious—though he could never quite define what that meant. His stubborn attempts to explain all such experiences (even those so vivid that they thoroughly frightened him) as the "exteriorizations" of the contents of his unconscious, which had "somehow or other . . . manifest[ed] themselves outwardly," always lacked the ring of full conviction.[14] While he never could explain "somehow or other," this theory persisted in spite of such frightening experiences as the following, which took place in 1920 during the several weekends he spent with a friend at a cottage in England. In recounting it years later Jung wrote:

> The next weekend . . . hardly had I been in bed for half an hour than everything was there as before: the torpor, the repulsive smell, the dripping . . . something brushed along the walls, the furniture creaked . . . there were rustlings in the corners. . . .
>
> The phenomena grew still more intense during the following weekend. . . . I cautiously suggested to my host that the house might be haunted, and that this might explain the surprisingly low rent. . . .
>
> The fifth weekend was . . . unbearable . . . there were rustlings, creakings, and bangings; from outside,

blows rained on the walls. I had the feeling there was something near me, and opened my eyes.

There, beside me on the pillow, I saw the head of an old woman, and the right eye, wide open, glared at me. . . . I leapt out of bed with one bound, lit the candle, and spent the rest of the night in an armchair.

. . . my health had suffered under these experiences.

. . . I consider it out of the question that it was a delusion of the senses. [15]

Contradictions and Reluctant Admissions

Eventually no one would rent or buy the house, and it was torn down. "I have observed a sufficient number of such phenomena," Jung would later write, "to be completely convinced of their reality. To me they are inexplicable, and I am therefore unable to decide in favor of any of the usual interpretations . . . there is not a single argument that could prove that spirits do not exist." Yet mixed in with such cautious comments were more dogmatic pronouncements such as: "I see no proof whatever of the existence of real spirits, and until such proof is forthcoming I must regard this whole territory as an appendix of psychology." [16] Toward the end of his life, however, Jung footnoted that statement in "The Psychological Foundations of Belief in Spirits" with the following amendment—not an easy admission for a man as proud as Carl Jung:

> After collecting psychological experiences from many people and many countries for fifty years, I no longer feel as certain as I did in 1919, when I wrote this sentence.
>
> To put it bluntly, I doubt whether an exclusively psychological approach can do justice to the phenomena in question. [17]

That conclusion must have trembled on the tip of his pen for years before he finally put it down on paper. From about 1946 onward, according to Aniela Jaffe, his private secretary of long standing, "Jung was no longer able to maintain with certainty his original thesis that spirits are exteriorizations or projections of autonomous

psychic complexes. What they really are, where they come from
. . . remained for him . . . a baffling question . . . ."[18] While he
still clung to his theory of a collective unconscious inhabited by
archetypes that were largely symbolic, he became convinced that
underlying it all were "psychoid" archetypes. By this Jung meant
entities which, though they were *psychic*, could manifest themselves in apparent *physical* form.

Logically the admission that psychic phenomena involved at
times physical manifestation had been demanded by common sense
all along. The fact that Jung waited so long to admit the obvious is
indicative of deep inner turmoil. Though he had bravely preached
"exteriorizations" of unconscious impulses for years, Jung must
have been aware of the incurable flaws in that theory long before he
openly abandoned it. One can only wonder why he waited more
than 40 years before publishing the following:

> Philemon represented a force which was not myself.
> . . . It was he who taught me psychic objectivity, the
> reality of the psyche. . . . He was a mysterious figure to
> me.
> At times he seemed to me quite real, as if he were a
> living personality. I went walking up and down the gar-
> den with him, and to me he was what the Indians call a
> guru.[19]

Such admissions hardly ring true to the current "scientific"
insistence (to which Jung himself clung desperately for years) that
psychic phenomena are somehow caused by eruptions in the psyche
and thus are little more than vivid hallucinations. In telling of the
poltergeist phenomena which he caused in Freud's presence when
they first met, Jung writes reproachfully: "It was some years before
he [Freud] recognized the seriousness of parapsychology and acknowledged the factuality of 'occult' phenomena."[20] Strange complaint, considering the fact that Jung himself kept his true convictions on the subject secret for much of his life. Reportedly Freud said
that "if he had it to do over again, he would devote his life to
psychical research."[21] We have from Freud's own pen in his later
years the admission that he had at last abandoned his earlier skepticism on the subject:

It no longer seems possible to brush aside the study of
so-called occult facts; of things which seem to vouchsafe
the real existence of psychic forces . . . or which reveal
mental faculties in which, until now, we did not believe.[22]

Choking on a Gnat While Swallowing a Camel

Yet today most psychologists and parapsychologists still cling to
the theory which the two founders of modern psychology, Freud and
Jung, both considered untenable and which they abandoned. In his
new best-seller on psychic phenomena, Bernard Gittelson ("Mr.
Biorhythm") echoes the popular view which attributes poltergeist
activity to "pent-up stress" or "severe mental disturbance," usually
in an adolescent person, and "somehow" manifesting itself in the
mysterious moving or even flying about of physical objects.[23] Parapsychologists spend years painstakingly designing laboratory psychokinesis experiments and meticulously documenting the modest
results produced by trained psychics attempting to move physical
objects solely with mind power. Yet those same researchers, oddly
enough, seem to see no inconsistency in declaring that flying
objects in a poltergeist situation, some of them huge and following
elaborate patterns, are being thrown about by "psychic energy"
emanating from the "unconscious" of some unknown person who is
totally unaware of accomplishing this amazing feat.

This myth born of "spiritual" skepticism dies hard. The well-
known "Philip Experiment" is a most incredible case in point.
Several members of the Canadian Toronto Society of Psychical
Research made up the history of a "ghost" named "Philip," who
eventually "communicated" with them through table rappings.
(Similar effects have been duplicated by other experimenters.)
Eventually the table around which they sat with their hands resting
upon it began to levitate and could not be held down by their weight.
It even sailed around the room with the members of the group having
to run to keep up with it.

It sounds incredible. Most incredible of all, however, was the
continued insistence of these skeptics that such amazing physical
phenomena were caused by the subconscious release of a mental
force innate within themselves—and all without their being aware

of what their minds were doing or how! Confessing that no one knows how it works, the experimenters are now diligently trying to understand the mysterious "force" allegedly created by their pooled subconscious minds. Even supposing that such a "force" could be measured, a mystery would still remain. How could this "mind power" be transmitted to physical objects, causing them not only to move but to do so as though under intelligent direction, without the "minds" which are supposedly causing this activity even being aware of it?[24]

It would make more sense to assume that some "spirit"—allowing that such exist—willingly adopted the fictitious identity of "Philip" and was purposely causing the phenomena. The only reason for rejecting such a hypothesis would be the very prejudice against the existence of spirits which the experimenters admit was their motivation. It would seem that these scientists have not heeded Jung's warning to "beware of naively assuming that the whole question of ghosts and spirits has been settled."

In spite of the debunking of such widely publicized "haunted houses" as that depicted in the book and movie *The Amityville Horror*, the fully documented cases of poltergeist activity observed by numerous witnesses simultaneously, including police who have been called to the scene, are too numerous and too well-known to need further comment here. Teams of scientists have even set up their instruments and meticulously recorded and measured intensity of sounds and trajectories of flying objects and then read their reports to gatherings of experts.[25] To seek to explain all of this as a projection of telekinetic force from the unconscious mind, which is subconsciously directed by some unknown person without his or her comprehension of what is happening, strains credulity. The evidence, as Carl Jung himself had to admit (though reluctantly), points strongly to the involvement of nonphysical intelligences in poltergeist activity. To dismiss that possibility out of hand and cling to the "unconsciously-directed-mind-power" hypothesis would seem to be choking on a gnat while swallowing a camel. Lawrence LeShan, recognized as one of the world's leading parapsychologists, writes in his latest book, *The Science of the Paranormal*:

> The feeling one gets when a good medium is in trance
> and talking as though she were the spirit of someone

biologically dead is frequently very convincing. It can feel so real that it curls your hair.

However, since the scientific view today is that a belief in spirits is, at best, rank superstition, and since parapsychologists want very much to be thought of as scientists, the problem [of whether "spirits" might be involved] has been abandoned.[26]

The Deep Silk Hat of the Magicians of the Mind

That is a sorry admission. And most tragic is the fact that LeShan, who has been a tireless crusader for truth in parapsychology, lets the subject drop there with the further lame admission, "We have simply accepted the solution most in line with the popular metaphysics of our time." So the band of materialism continues to play the same old tune, and too many researchers dance in step like robots. In his recently published *ESP, Hauntings, and Poltergeists: A Parapsychologist's Handbook*, Loyd Auerbach (who was Public Information and Media Consultant to the American Society for Psychical Research and now teaches parapsychology at John F. Kennedy University) declares as though it were scientific fact:

> Poltergeist experiences . . . are, by the currently held model, related to the subconscious mind of a person . . . in a stress-related tense, and frustrating situation. . . .
>
> For some reason, the reaction to the stress is a subconsciously directed psychokinetic outburst . . . the apparent reaction of the subconscious mind takes place on a psychokinetic channel.[27]

Here we have the parapsychologist's application of the modern myth of the all-powerful and all-knowing Unconscious. Freud and Jung share most of the credit for popularizing this Westernized form of Eastern religion's "All-is-One" philosophy by cloaking it in scientific terminology. Yet the theory of the "unconscious" solves no problems and only raises more unanswerable questions. At best it is a cop-out and at worst a piece of sophistry designed to cover up ignorance with the language of academia. As Allan Bloom so aptly put it:

Biologists can't even account for consciousness within their science, let alone the unconscious. So psychologists like Freud are in an impossible halfway house between science, which does not admit the existence of the phenomena he wishes to explain, and the unconscious, which is outside the jurisdiction of science.[28]

No one could calculate the billions of hours and the prodigious effort and fortunes spent around the world in consulting psychologists and psychiatrists by the untold millions of faithful believers in this highly promoted myth. Those honored high priests and mediators of the omnipotent/omniscient unconscious have undergone the esoteric initiation that qualifies them to interpret the symbolic language of this "God within" through ink blots, dreams, Freudian slips of the tongue, hypnotic "regression," and an almost endless list of other ingenious techniques invented by leaders of the craft for consulting this inner oracle. Behold the deep silk hat from which the magicians of the mind pull out all their cures and rationalizations! As investigative journalist Martin L. Gross perceptively observes in *The Psychological Society:*

> *One of the most powerful religious ideas of the second half of the twentieth century is the Great Unconscious* . . . [emphasis his].
>
> In this religion of the Unconscious, our conscious mind is a second-class being . . . a mere puppet of the unknown true self. . . .
>
> Is there an Unconscious? . . . From a scientific point of view, it is a theological device which fills the gap in man's biological ignorance. . . .[29]

The Materialists' Paranoia About Spirits

While Gross accurately argues that there is in fact not a shred of scientific evidence to support the mythical powers attributed to the unconscious, he betrays his own materialistic bias. No amount of *biological* insight will ever explain *psychic* phenomena. Sir Arthur Eddington pointed out that demanding a physical explanation for mental or spiritual events made no more sense than attempting "to extract the square root of a sonnet." And to imagine that consciousness is ruled by the laws of physics and chemistry, added Eddington, "is as preposterous as the suggestion that a nation could be ruled by . . . the laws of grammar."[30]

What Eddington so justly scorns was widely taken for granted 40 years ago, but not today. At the Hixon symposium in 1948, for example, biologist K. S. Lashley declared "as the common belief of all the participants" the notion that "all manifestations of life can ultimately be explained by the laws governing inanimate matter." Philosopher Michael Polanyi indignantly called that assumption "patent nonsense." Complaining that Lashley had made this remark "without even consulting his distinguished colleagues," Polanyi later wrote:

> The most striking feature of our own existence is our sentience [consciousness]. The laws of physics and chemistry include no conception of sentience, and any system wholly determined by these [physical laws] must be insentient [i.e. without consciousness].
>
> It may be to the interests of science to turn a blind eye on this central fact of the universe, but it is certainly not in the interest of truth.[31]

In full agreement with Polanyi, Sir John Eccles writes: ". . . nowhere in the laws of physics or in the laws of the derivative sciences, chemistry and biology, is there any reference to consciousness or mind . . . its emergence is not reconcilable with the natural laws as at present understood."[32] If consciousness cannot be explained in physical terms, then it must involve something nonphysical. That is, of course, why there is such reluctance to abandon a materialistic explanation in spite of its incurable flaws. The motivation may, however, involve more than academic pride and prejudice. Could it be that the real skeleton in the closet is the very "fear of ghosts" that Jung claimed is still in the bones of even the most highly educated and skeptical among us?

The denial of the existence of spirit beings could have serious consequences. Richard Watring's major concern over techniques for altering consciousness being introduced into the business world is the fact that they often, even when not so intended, lead to contact with "spirit entities" who in fact may have evil intentions. "Consciousness researchers," writes Watring, "report that subjects who reach certain states of altered consciousness often encounter 'other' entities . . . regardless of the method used to reach the state."[33] Moreover, the contact with "spirit guides" is no longer incidental, but is being deliberately cultivated.

Is it the uncanny feeling that nonphysical intelligences of some kind might in fact exist that causes the scientific community to strain so hard to find an explanation that will eliminate this possibility? In fact its designers admit that the entire motivation behind the famous "Philip Experiment" was to "prove" that spirits are not involved at all in psychic phenomena. Consequently, everything that happened was interpreted in harmony with the original prejudice. As a member of one group declared: "We clearly understand and have proved that there is no 'spirit' [involved]." Of course they hadn't proved that at all; but why was this "proof" so important that the entire experiment was designed to produce it?

As we have seen, Carl Jung spent much of his life trying to escape his earlier conviction that spirits do in fact exist. It is undoubtedly the inevitable implications which would follow that make this possibility so distasteful that almost any other theory, no matter how absurd, is considered more acceptable. Revealing his own inner turmoil and unscientific reluctance to face the clear but academically demeaning evidence, Jung confided:

> I once discussed the proof of identity [of "channeled" entities] for a long time with a friend of William James, Professor Hyslop, in New York. He admitted that, all things considered, all these metapsychic phenomena could be explained better by the hypothesis of spirits than by the qualities and pecularities of the unconscious.
>
> And here, on the basis of my own experience, I am bound to concede he is right. In each individual case I must of necessity be skeptical, but in the long run I have to admit that the spirit hypothesis yields better results in practice than any other.[34]

Yet psychologist Jean Houston, who claims to follow the Jungian tradition, nevertheless cannot accept what Jung himself felt he was driven by the evidence to acknowledge. She insists that the entities that speak through channels or mediums are somehow (no explanation offered) "projections and creations of the immensity that is the personal and collective unconscious . . . 'goddings' of the depths of the psyche . . . personae of the self that take on acceptable form so that we can have relationship to them and thus dialogue [with ourselves]." Why the God of the Bible is outdated superstition and " 'goddings' of the depths of the psyche" (whatever that may be) is modern science is not explained by Houston. Consulting someone wiser and more experienced than oneself used to be the way to acquire wisdom, but now the ultimate is to take counsel from oneself—the so-called "Higher Self" (though no one can explain what this actually means).

Faced with a Cruel Dilemma

Why this insistence upon insupportable theories? One senses a deeper motivation than mere stubbornness or pride: something more akin to fear, but a fear masked either with considerable bluster or with sophisticated denials that claim to have the support of science. It would be too terrifying to admit the existence of a spirit dimension over which science has no control. Consequently there is an attempt to explain spiritual experience within a materialistic framework. The result is a mythologized science.

In his classic *The Screwtape Letters*, Cambridge and Oxford Universities scholar C. S. Lewis, who earlier in his life derided a belief in demons, presented hypothetically what their strategy toward humans might be if demons did in fact exist. Lewis depicts an interesting character named Screwtape (a senior devil) advising his nephew Wormwood (a junior devil) how to deal with his human "patients." "If any faint suspicion of your existence begins to arise in his [your patient's] mind," explains Screwtape, "suggest to him a picture of something in red tights, and persuade him that since he cannot believe in that (it is an old textbook method of confusing them) he therefore cannot believe in you." A bit later, divulging the long-range plans of the powers of darkness, Screwtape confides in Wormwood:

> We [demons] are really faced with a cruel dilemma.
> When the humans disbelieve in our existence we lose all the

pleasing results of direct terrorism and we make no magicians.

On the other hand, when they believe in us, we cannot make them materialists and skeptics. At least not yet.

I have hopes that we shall learn in due time how to emotionalise and mythologise their science to such an extent that what is, in effect, a belief in us (though not under that name), will creep in while the human mind remains closed to belief in the Enemy [God].

The "Life Force," the worship of sex and some aspects of Psychoanalysis, may here prove useful. If once we can produce our perfect work—the Materialist Magician, the man, not using, but veritably worshipping, what he vaguely calls "Forces" while denying the existence of "spirits"— then the end of our war will be in sight. [35]

Lewis was presenting in parable what he had come to believe after an agonizing reassessment of his former atheism. The possibility that "spirit entities," even evil ones, may exist independent of mankind and capable of influencing human minds, can no longer be relegated to primitive superstition. In addition to the psychologists and scientists already mentioned, many more could be quoted who have come to similar conclusions. Surely the concern expressed by James Hyslop, Columbia University professor of logic and ethics with whom Jung had that important discussion, warrants serious consideration:

If we believe in telepathy, we believe in a process which makes possible the invasion of a personality by someone at a distance.

It is not at all likely . . . that sane and intelligent spirits are the only ones to exert [such] influence . . . there is no reason why others cannot do so as well. [36]

8

Psychotherapy: The Religious "Science"

Strange though it may seem, the unscientific theory of the "unconscious" has provided the major "scientifically acceptable" explanation for New Age occult phenomena—an explanation that it was hoped would take the place of the belief in spirits that has been the common understanding in all cultures for thousands of years. This theory that Martin L. Gross calls "one of the most powerful religious ideas of the second half of the twentieth century" has been used by the high priests of psychology to suppress all religions other than their own. Upon this shaky foundation psychologists have built what Gross calls "an international colossus whose professional minions number in the hundreds of thousands . . . [and whose] experimental animals are an obliging, even grateful human race."[1] In short, what Freud and Jung started is today a multi-billion-dollar international industry with a record of growth that few blue chip stocks on Wall Street have matched.

There is something insidious, however, about this spectacular growth. Psychology has changed the world's thinking, lifestyles, and standards through what Gross again points out is a "new truth [which] is fed to us continuously from birth to the grave"—a "truth" that is composed of unproven and contradictory theories. In *The Myth of Neurosis*, British psychiatrist Garth Wood bluntly charges that "what has become big business is in fact fraud. The evidence does not support the claims of psychoanalysis and psychotherapy."[2]

The Unscientific "Science"

A lengthy study appointed by the American Psychological Association (subsidized by the National Science Foundation and involving 80 eminent scholars) concluded that psychology is not and cannot be a science. This is the case in spite of decades spent in "ritualistic endeavor to emulate the forms of science in order to sustain the delusion that it already *is* a science."[3] Karl Popper, considered to be one of the greatest philosophers of science, has concluded that psychological theories have "more in common with primitive myths than with science. . . ."[4]

Psychiatrist Lee Coleman titled his exposé of psychiatry *The Reign of Error*. Having testified in more than 130 criminal and civil trials, Coleman explained that his task was "to educate the judge or jury about why the opinions produced by these professionals [psychologists/psychiatrists] have no scientific merit."[5] Unfortunately, few of Coleman's and Wood's colleagues are willing to be as forthright—it would mean the dismantling of a worldwide empire that grosses 15 billion dollars or more annually in the United States alone. Any facts that would endanger the future of this huge industry are kept as professional secrets among its members.

It would be too harsh to accuse the average psychotherapist of deliberately perpetrating a hoax, and that is certainly not our intention. Nevertheless, what Gross, Coleman, Wood and some others are saying is that the methods being practiced on the public are of dubious value at best, are harmful at worst, and are based upon contradictory and changing theories for which there is no proof but which must be accepted by faith.

In an article titled "Psychology Goes Insane, Botches Role as Science," psychologist Roger Mills writes: "I have personally seen therapists convince their clients that all of their problems come from their mothers, the stars, their biochemical make-up, their diet, their life-style and even the 'kharma' from their past lives."[6] How can such unscientific diagnoses be made and accepted in the name of science? Unfortunately, with the greatest of ease.

The Antireligious Religion

Psychology was envisioned by Freud and many of his successors as the means of delivering the world from religion—that stubborn human derivative which Freud termed "the obsessional neurosis of humanity" and Marx called "the opiate of the masses." Instead, psychology has enslaved the world to the priesthood and dogmas of psychotherapy. Far from being selfless crusaders for freedom, Freud and Jung each had their ulterior motives, which became the passion also of their disciples. One psychologist has written, "It appears that certain of the most influential pioneers in American psychology found in it an ideal vehicle for renouncing their own Christian upbringing in the name of science."[7] Professor of psychiatry Thomas Szasz declares:

> The popular image of Freud as an enlightened, emancipated, irreligious person who, with the aid of psychoanalysis, "discovered" that religion is a mental illness is pure fiction. . . .
> One of Freud's most powerful motives in life was the desire to inflict vengeance on Christianity. . . .[8]

That desire, of course, necessarily involved what Szasz called "the clever and cynical destruction of the spirituality of man, and its replacement by a positivistic 'science of mind.' "[9] Clinical psychologist Bernie Zilbergeld agrees: "Those whose ancestors took comfort from the words of God and worshiped at the altars of Christ and Yahweh now take solace from and worship at the altars of Freud, Jung, Carl Rogers . . . and a host of similar authorities."[10] Rogers himself, who had turned sharply against his former Christian beliefs, admitted: "Yes, it is true, psychotherapy is subversive. . . . Therapy, theories and techniques promote a new model of man contrary to that which has been traditionally acceptable."[11] Only upon the ruins of traditional religion could the theologians of psychology build their new secular faith. As another writer points out:

> *Psychology Today* has, from the very first, taken its religious responsibilities seriously. Already in its second year (1969) they were observing that psychology must help man "face our own inner experiences without the guidance of traditional . . . foundation stones of Judeo-Christian experience.

"Left without collectively sanctioned God-values and moral absolutes, we are compelled to erect our own morality, arrive at our own faith and belief, and discover the meaning of our own existence."

In . . . the same year in *PT*, Rollo May declared that "we have bid goodbye to the theologians at the wake for our dead God."[12]

Viennese journalist Karl Kraus has called psychoanalysis "the faith of a generation incapable of any other."[13] Jean Houston makes no apology for presenting psychology as a "scientific" religion and is highly acclaimed for doing so. Integrating ancient occult theories and practices into modern psychotherapy, Houston presents an extremely popular workshop called "Therapeia," which she explains is literally "doing the work of the gods . . . *restoring 'sacrality' to psyche*." Thomas Szasz titled one of his books, written to debunk his own profession, *The Myth of Psychotherapy*. In it he called psychotherapy "not merely a religion that pretends to be a science . . . [but] a fake religion that seeks to destroy true religion."[14]

In the place of traditional theologies, a new "scientific" religion was offered, mediated by a new class of priests. Human behavior would be explained without resorting to soul, spirit, God, Satan, angels, demons, sin, or guilt. Paradise would be restored by pointing men and women to their own inherent goodness and infinite inner potential. It was made perfectly clear, however, that the road to Utopia involved submitting every area of society to the mandate of the new priesthood.

The New Ideology of Intervention

That priesthood considers itself competent to extend to the entire populace the control it now exercises over patients in psychiatric wards. For example, in 1973 *Psychology Today* published the proposal that "parents be licensed to have children only upon demonstrating a sound understanding of 'behavior development,' 'principles of reinforcement,' 'stimulus-control generalization,' and other truths dispensed by psychologists. It was recommended that non-licensed couples would be subject to 'mandatory birth-control.' "[15]

Already in 1971 the president of the American Psychological Association had "proposed that psychologists be permitted to administer behavior modification drugs to the nation's elected and military leaders to reverse their 'nonadaptive primitive aggression impulses.' " Although that proposal may not yet have been implemented, drugs now play a major role in psychiatry, but few voices are raised in protest. Yet as Maryland psychiatrist Peter Breggin reminds us, the drugs used "to 'torture' Russian political dissidents are exactly the same drugs used to 'treat' mental patients throughout the Western world." "We are appalled," Breggin adds, "to hear that Russian dissidents are having their minds blunted and bodies tortured by major tranquilizers, but we tolerate the same treatment of those of our citizens who have been labeled mentally ill by the psychiatric establishment."[16] It is frightening to consider future society controlled by psychiatrists and psychologists who determine by their own inquisitorial religious standards what behavior is "normal" and dictate the fate of those who fail to measure up.

In 1984, Stanford University's Alumni Association published an interesting collection of papers by experts examining the question of whether we had arrived at the year 1984 ahead of or behind George Orwell's scenario. The conclusions of some of the writers were devastating. Reference was made to the abuse of psychiatry in the Soviet Union; and it was pointed out that equally frightening possibilities exist even in a so-called free society. Remarking that "Orwell deserves credit for seeing the potential power of professionals whom society sanctions to intervene into the lives of its citizens 'for their own good,' " Philip G. Zimbardo pointed out that Orwell had nevertheless "barely hinted at the extent and depth of that power which is so evident in our 1984." Zimbardo continued:

> [In] the new ideology of intervention . . . instead of punishment, torture, exile, and other tricks of the tyrant trade, we are seeing such tricks of the treatment trade: intervention as therapy, education, social service, reform, retraining, and rehabilitation.
>
> In a critical attack on the role of the mental health establishment as the new Party of our 1984, investigative journalist Peter Schrag warns us of the insidious danger

inherent in the unquestioning acceptance of its seemingly benign ideology.[17]

"The Olympian Glibness of Psychoanalytic Thought"

In spite of the messianic hopes with which it was originally greeted—hopes for the redemption of the world through scientific behavior-modification of the masses—the new panacea of psychotherapy proved to be a dismal failure. The attempts to deal with human problems on the basis of Freudian/Jungian theories of the unconscious have spawned more than 250 contradictory therapies and 10,000 competing techniques. Take your pick, from sex with your psychologist as "therapy" to a variety of "Primal Screams." In the latter, a patient gets into an adult-size crib, sucks a bottle, cuddles a doll, and screams, "Mommy, Daddy, I hate you!" in order to get back to that "primal pool of pain," which allegedly holds the key to present problems.

The "analysis" of human behavior through the alleged exploration of the unconscious has involved some of the most incredible methods imaginable. Take, for example, the Rorschach inkblot test, which has been in use for about 60 years. To call this means of exploring the psyche "scientific" would be a macabre joke. Yet the official "interpretation" is explained confidently, and the anti-religious bias is presented as a matter of fact. The Rorschach instruction manual declares that if anyone taking the test should happen to see some religious symbolism in one of the odd-shaped inkblots on the ten cards presented, it is a sign of schizophrenia or sexual preoccupation. In the *Mental Measurements Yearbook*, Arthur Jensen writes: "Put frankly, the consensus of qualified judgment is that the Rorschach . . . has no practical worth for any of the purposes for which it is recommended by its devotees."[18] Yet this absurd "test," so costly from both a monetary and emotional standpoint, is still being administered to about one million persons annually.

Long before Shirley MacLaine saw the light, psychologist Jean Houston was already established as one of the brightest stars on the higher-consciousness seminar circuit. This high priestess of "sacred psychology" dazzles her audiences with esoteric Jungian abracadabra about such imponderables as "archetypal dimensions of the psyche" and "the constellation of psycho-physical potentials and psycho-spiritual patterns. . . ."[19] As though she were representing an established science, Houston invokes the "*physics* of consciousness" and expounds upon "the *ecology* of inner space" [emphasis ours]. Referring to such arrogance (so typical of the entire psychology/psychiatry profession), Garth Wood writes: "The effrontery of these brazen pseudoscientific poseurs takes away the breath."

Analyzing a cross section of ideas presented at the 23rd International Psychoanalytic Congress in Stockholm, Sir Peter Medawar found "the self-satisfied self-confidence in the importance of their insights . . . [to be] sinister." After presenting examples of the unsupportable and wildly imaginative "interpretations" of dreams and behavior, which rivaled their patients' most bizarre fantasies, Sir Peter concludes:

> I have not chosen these examples to poke fun at them, ridiculous though I believe them to be, but simply to illustrate the Olympian glibness of psychoanalytic thought. The contributors to this Congress were concerned with . . . *difficult* problems . . . far less easy to grapple with or make sense of than anything that confronts us in the laboratory.
>
> But where shall we find the evidence of hesitancy . . . that is commonplace in an international congress of, say, physiologists or biochemists? A lava-flow of *ad hoc* explanation pours over and around all difficulties, leaving only a few smoothly rounded prominences to mark where they might have lain.[20]

An Unparalleled International Scandal

The evidence that psychotherapies are harmful is mounting. Unfortunately, the damning truth has been (and still is) systematically covered up in what amounts to an international scandal unparalleled in history. In a valiant attempt to alert his readers, Garth Wood points out that a new prescription drug must be thoroughly and repeatedly tested (not only on its own merits but in relation to competing pills) and must meet strict standards before the Food and Drug Administration will approve it for public consumption. Yet psychotherapy has been licensed with an abandon that is nothing short of criminal, in spite of the fact that a drug producing the same results would be quickly banned by the FDA. Likening psychoanalysis to a new drug, Psychiatrist Wood asks us "to dream the nightmare":

> What if nobody bothered to test my pill . . . [and] an army of smooth-tongued salespeople . . . travel the . . . world flogging my pill unscrupulously to the sad and afflicted . . . a band of dedicated men, possessed of an almost messianic belief in my pill's efficacy, wearing the cloak of science . . . peddling it to those whose judgment the disease had weakened in the desperation of their desire to be made whole.
>
> Live through the nightmare and experience a whole industry profiting from and preying on the gullible, the disappointed, the weak, as they sell shamelessly their snake oil equivalent, their "guaranteed" restorer. . . .
>
> Now, as you wake in a cold sweat . . . consider Freudian psychoanalysis. It is now well over eighty years since the psychoanalytic "pill" was invented, and yet in 1985, Arnold Cooper, a past president of the American Psychoanalytic Association, was quoted in the *New York Times* as saying, ". . . the time has come to recast psychoanalytic assumptions so that they can be tested scientifically." . . .
>
> The situation is mind-boggling . . . psychoanalysis [has] . . . never been validated by the scientific method. . . . Of course, many of us have known all along that psychoanalysis was scientifically bankrupt. . . .
>
> Why should the doctors who dispense this "therapy" be immune from the attentions of the government watchdogs who protect us from other scientifically disreputable "cures"? For theirs, I am afraid, is the "pill" of the nightmare. Untested and unproved, it is dispensed by the unscientific for the consumption of the unhappy.[21]

Lawrence LeShan, past president of the Association for Humanistic Psychology, has suggested that psychotherapy will probably be known as the hoax of the twentieth century. Yet its popularity and influence in society continue to grow almost exponentially and its mushrooming army of unabashed missionaries persists in foisting upon the public its messianic myths, which Lance Lee calls "religion hidden beneath scientific verbiage."[22] After investigating his own profession for more than 15 years, clinical psychologist Bernie Zilbergeld wrote *The Shrinking of America: Myths of Psychological Change*. In a later interview he explained:

> One of the most consistent and important effects of [psychological] counseling is a desire for more counseling . . . it is no longer unusual to meet people who are looking for . . . a therapist to resolve problems caused in a previous therapy. . . . There is absolutely no evidence that professional therapists have any special knowledge of how to change behavior, or that they obtain better results—with any type of client or problem—than those with little or no formal training.[23]

In their best-selling book *Psychoheresy*, educational psychologist Martin Bobgan and his wife, Deidre, point out that the Cambridge-Somerville Youth Study of 1935 "is well-known to researchers but little known to the public," having been suppressed for obvious reasons. It began with the selection of 650 boys aged six to ten who were considered likely to develop delinquent behavior. The subjects were divided into two groups as equal in every respect as possible. One group received no treatment, while each boy in the other group was provided all of the benefits available: academic tutoring, Boy Scouts, YMCA, summer camps, and about five years of either psychoanalysis or Rogerian therapy. About two-thirds of the participants (both counselors and boys) agreed that great benefits had resulted. It appeared certain that this huge project would conclusively demonstrate the efficacy of psychotherapy.

Imagine the surprise when the first follow-up studies in 1948 revealed slightly more delinquent behavior in the group that had received the treatment than among those who had received none. The 30-year follow-up in 1978 [24] revealed an even greater disparity between the treatment and nontreatment groups. The incidence of criminal behavior, mental and work problems, and alcoholism was far greater among those who had received the psychotherapy than those who had not. Instead of demonstrating, as had been anticipated, the benefits of psychotherapy, the Cambridge-Somerville Youth Study actually demonstrated its harmfulness. There are many other skeletons in the psychotherapy closet—a closet that is kept tightly shut lest an unsuspecting public learn the truth.

Bridge to the East

Rather than abandon their obviously bankrupt profession, many psychologists and psychiatrists have compounded their error by trying to shore up their collapsing house of cards with Eastern mysticism of one form or another. Having failed miserably to change their clients' behavior, the psychotherapists reached deeper into their silk hat and pulled out *altered states of consciousness*, the same magic long used by the "traditional psychologists from the East"—the gurus, Yogis, and shamans. A *change* of consciousness became the key to everything, even though no one yet knew what it was that was being changed.

Increasing numbers of psychologists and psychiatrists are being drawn into Eastern mysticism because of their discovery that it offers the very transformation of consciousness which psychotherapy seeks to effect. At the 25th Annual Meeting of The Association for Humanistic Psychology, held on August 5-9, 1987, participants shared "channeling, rebirthing, energy healing, metaphysical counseling" as well as "consciousness group work." The "traditional morning meditation, yoga and aerobics programs" were enhanced with "some of the new high-tech, whole-brain synchronization techniques."

Representative of this growing trend, Psychiatrist Rudolph Ballentine and clinical psychologist Allan Weinstock have both studied under gurus in India. Weinstock is now known as Swami Ajaya after his ordination as a Hindu monk. Ballentine and Ajaya joined Swami Rama of Chicago's Himalayan Institute in coauthoring *Yoga and Psychotherapy: The Evolution of Consciousness*. In it they explained that Yoga "has offered for thousands of years" what Western psychotherapists "are seeking."[25] As University of California professor Jacob Needleman has said:

A large and growing number of psychotherapists are now convinced that the Eastern religions offer an understanding of the mind far more complete than anything yet envisaged by Western science.

At the same time, the leaders of the new religions themselves—the numerous gurus and spiritual teachers now in the West—are reformulating and adapting the traditional systems according to the language and atmosphere of modern psychology.[26]

Eastern religion and various forms of occultism are now packaged in psychological terminology for twentieth-century public consumption. Abraham Maslow's "self-actualization" should have been easily recognized as a Westernized version of Yoga's "self-realization," but that connection was slow in being acknowledged. Psychologist Daniel Goleman was among the first to point out that Eastern philosophies "seem to be making gradual headway [in the West] as psychologies, not as religions."[27] That transmutation should have surprised no one, for as LeShan explains, "The basic model of man that led to the development of [Eastern] meditational techniques is the same model that led to humanistic psychotherapy."[28] "The Medicine Woman of Beverly Hills," Lynn Andrews, recently told the *Los Angeles Times*:

> Shamanism is really like gestalt therapy. It's like primal therapy, and it has a lot of Jungian in it.[29]

According to research psychiatrist E. Fuller Torrey, "The techniques used by Western psychiatrists are, with few exceptions, on exactly the same scientific plane as the techniques used by witch doctors."[30] A recent test measuring psychotherapists against witch doctors ended in a dead heat, the major difference being that the witch doctors charged less and released their patients sooner. Nobelist Richard Feynman describes psychotherapy as "not a science . . . [but] more like witchdoctoring."[31]

Having ridiculed and debunked for nearly 80 years mankind's universal and long-standing belief in things spiritual, psychologists have begun to reintroduce ancient occult beliefs and practices, but with the new labels of their own secular "spirituality." The same occult powers are being sought through basically the same altered states, but now as "human potential" instead of as coming from independent spirit entities. Many of the same words and rituals are used, but with altered meanings that fit the new religion of psychology. God is now "the collective unconscious" and spirits have become "splits of the psyche."

Witchcraft is out of the cocoon and flying, having metamorphosed into a socially and academically acceptable "therapy." And the followers of this new religion are vulnerable to a horror they have been promised is only a myth. The bait on the hook is the promise that within the psyche an infinite potential awaits discovery and exploration—but the treasure is dispensed by "spirits."

The Revolution in Higher Consciousness

In the process of subjecting his patients to "dream analysis" and hypnotic trance in pursuit of childhood memories, Freud "discovered" that there was an *unconscious* side to consciousness, and he concluded that it was in fact the most important part. He also suspected that it might be greater in scope than the individual's own experience. Jung decided (with encouragement from his spirit guide, Philemon) that at this unconscious level all minds were a part of something which he called the *collective unconscious* and described as the source of mystical powers. Without any scientific basis, these twin beliefs were accepted by faith by the disciples of Freud and Jung and became the foundation for the many psychologies and therapies that followed. As a result, nearly everyone now accepts as scientific fact the religious belief that this vast unexplored region of "inner space" is a reservoir of magical powers which exceed even the wildest science fiction fantasy.

On the less-than-solid foundation of such theories—and the mystical experiences that seemed to confirm them—the human-potential movement was built. Self-improvement seminar leaders assure us that by simply looking within ourselves we can discover all truth, all knowledge, and all power. In order to mine this presumably unlimited human potential, psychologists have attempted to explore consciousness through Eastern mysticism's *altered states*—states of consciousness that were first explored through hypnosis, then LSD. Oddly enough, it was decided that the further one re-treated from normal consciousness the more "enlightened" one became.

The lowest level was assigned to ordinary states of awareness, while "higher consciousness" required losing touch with what is generally considered to be normal perception. Thus any basis for objective evaluation of the experience must be relinquished in order to reach "enlightenment," which in itself should make that state highly suspect. Suspicions should also arise on another count. As MacLaine and so many others tell us, one amazingly discovers in this "higher state of consciousness" that one is actually "God." Interestingly enough, our alleged oneness with "God," or Jung's "collective unconscious," has been the constant refrain of the channeled entities down through history. In *Channeling* Jon Klimo reminds us:

> Virtually all of the sources above the lower astral levels tell us that . . . we are evolving . . . toward an eventual reunion with the one God, which is the under-lying identity of All That Is. . . .
>
> The various occult, esoteric, and mystery school teachings repeat the theme. . . .
>
> Enlightenment involves realizing [the] illusory state of our daily entranced experience, and awakening to the . . . oneness of all.[32]

Stephen Williamson, director of the Institute for Bio-Acoustics Research, warns against techniques whose goal is to bypass the conscious, rational mind where information is accepted or re-jected.[33] Yet this is precisely one's condition in the "altered state" being sought by millions for "enlightenment." And Herbert Ben-son, despite some ambivalent warnings, even recommends his "Relaxation Response" technique as a means of "pass[ing] into the so-called hypnotic state" precisely because, as he says, ". . . in this state of enhanced left-right hemispheric communication . . . 'cognitive receptivity' or 'plasticity of cognition' occurs, in which you actually change the way you view the world."[34] It hardly seems advisable to make a major change in one's thinking in such a fluid mental state. Such active promotion of delusionary altered states by leading members of the medical and psychological professions has given the New Age consciousness revolution an undeserved aura of "scientific" credibility that has persuaded millions of people to get involved.

Truth or Lie—Be "Positive" About It

Personnel director Richard L. Watring makes clear his reason for objecting to New Age training techniques involving "a state of altered consciousness." According to Watring, "self-hypnosis and other consciousness-altering techniques induce a mental state that denies trainees an opportunity to make reasoned decisions about the information they are asked to accept as true."[35] Herbert Benson realized this also and warned that his "Principle of the Maximum Mind" could be "employed in what has been called a demonic fashion . . . we must always be aware of the possible dangers."[36] By "demonic" he simply means that the high suggestability of the meditative state may also open one to being influenced to an evil or destructive end.

One of Watring's major concerns is that in altered states, basic belief systems can be manipulated. Benson issues a similar warning, but not out of concern for the *validity* of a belief. He apparently sees no relevance in whether a value statement is *true* or *false*. In fact, those concepts seem to have no meaning for him. His only concern is that his readers remain "positive" about whatever it is they already believe, whether truth or lie, because this attitude enhances what he calls the "faith factor," which in turn elicits the placebo effect that releases potentials for health and happiness allegedly hidden within the brain.

The issue, according to Benson, is not whether Jesus, for example, was a self-deluded maniac, deliberate impostor, or who he claimed to be (the only three possibilities). Nor does it concern Benson that likening the monotheistic and personal Judeo-Christian God to an impersonal pantheistic *force* may involve a complete contradiction. The only real value in religious dogmas or symbols, as Benson portrays them, is to arouse *faith* in the same manner as a placebo does. This arousal will then allegedly trigger the release of chemicals in the brain, will initiate glandular reactions, and will unleash a variety of latent human powers. Consequently, we don't actually need "God," "Buddha," "Jesus," or the "Star Wars Force," and whether they really exist or not is immaterial, since their only value is as placebos to trigger faith in our own innate powers.

Getting in Touch with Oneself

With understanding out and experience in, happiness (or almost anything else) became simply a state of consciousness to be sought as an end in itself. By turning the focus inward, the Freudian/ Jungian obsession with the unconscious spawned a menagerie of selfisms: self-love, self-acceptance, self-improvement, self-worth, self-confidence, self-esteem, self-ad nauseam. Only 40 years ago, self-centeredness was considered a human failing, and an ugly one. Today self is the center of most psychotherapies, the god at whose altar nearly everyone bows to beg favors—for self is now considered to be the hope of humanity, the inexhaustible source of man's salvation. "*Everything* you need is inside of you!" is the bold promise of the modern hucksters of innumerable ingenious techniques for tapping into the infinite You.

Looking inside oneself to get in touch with one's feelings, however, only intensifies the loneliness and alienation which couples feel who are trying to learn to live with each other while at the same time *Looking Out for Number One*, as that best-selling book instructed. "Dealing with stress" has become a national pastime, and the old methods of self-denial, self-control, and counting to ten are now too laborious. Everyone wants a quick fix, a magical formula—and there are experts by the thousands who claim to have the ultimate technique.

Here is just one more form taken by the ancient nature religion versus the Bible scenario. It is the same old polytheism/pantheism/ scientism resurrected with a new twist and an even more overt opposition to supernaturalism. The new way of getting in touch with and worshiping nature is getting in touch with and worshiping self as nature's most highly evolved form. The demeaning biblical myth of man's rebellious separation from God has been replaced with psychology's more positive myth of alienation from the self. *Sin* is no longer the root of mankind's troubles; the problem as now perceived is simply *ignorance* of one's true identity and worth. There is no explanation, however, of how perfect beings could have "forgotten" who they were—nor any guarantee that this mysterious ignorance, once dispelled through reaching a "higher" state of consciousness, will not arise again.

Subjective feelings (and how to manufacture and manipulate them) have inevitably become all-important. How one *feels* is now the only criterion, while how one *ought* to feel or act has lost all meaning. Since consciousness is susceptible to control by each individual, there are no longer any moral restraints involved. In justification of psychology's encouragement of hedonism, Esalen has offered techniques for "recognizing that *your* feelings—*your* discoveries—are *your truth*, without needing outside validation." It was this revolutionary gospel, preached by psychologists, sociologists, and educators, that created the "do-your-own-thing" Me Generation.

The basic theories that built Haight-Ashbury and Woodstock (and were finely tuned at Esalen) are still being promoted by humanistic psychologists as the gospel truth. The once-upon-a-time "flower children" of the fifties and sixties are the highly respected doctors, lawyers, politicians, schoolteachers, university professors, psychologists, social workers, and scientists who have become our leaders. The drug-spawned consciousness revolution that failed in the fifties and sixties is now being fed to us from the top down, recycled and wrapped in the bright ribbons of thousands of psychotherapies and self-improvement techniques.

More Powerful than Drugs

The "liberating effects" of the drugs that united the hippie movement, Aldous Huxley believed, had to be experienced by everyone in order to deliver educated Westerners from what William Blake called the "confident insolence sprouting from systematic reasoning."[37]

That type of thinking has a long history that ought to serve as a warning to us today. Freud was convinced that cocaine was the wonder drug of his day, and some of his theories were no doubt conjured up while under its influence. In addition to using it himself, he prescribed it for others, resulting in the death of one of his friends. Even Bayer, the highly regarded German pharmaceutical company, offered heroin to the world as a promising new cough medicine in 1888, one year before it introduced aspirin. It would be foolish to think we have gotten beyond such delusions. In *Psychiatric Drugs: Hazards to the Brain*, Breggin points out:

> All the major psychiatric drugs are highly neurotoxic (poisonous to nerve cells), all frequently produce widespread brain disfunction in their routine therapeutic dose range; and all achieve their primary overriding effect on the patient by producing some degree of brain disfunction.[38]

As we have already noted, however, Eastern meditation, transcendental meditation, and other forms of Yoga, including postures and breathing, produce a similar (but potentially even more powerful) altered state of consciousness than that caused by drugs. "Buddha reportedly recognized only one miracle—the transformation of human consciousness." That transformation is the major goal of virtually all psychotherapies today.

Increasing numbers of researchers and ex-meditators are warning the world that the various techniques for altering consciousness are far more lethal than cocaine or heroin. Yet hardly anyone seems to be listening. No government regulatory agency has required warning labels on Yoga, TM, or the many psychotherapies which are based upon dangerous consciousness-altering methodologies. Some of these techniques are specifically designed to mimic drug-induced states. The situation is staggering.

After using LSD on about 4000 patients, Czech-born psychiatrist Stanislav Grof (for a number of years scholar-in-residence at Esalen) developed his "holotropic breathing" technique. Grof made the discovery that "the [holotropic] breathing itself had psychedelic effects, triggering a mind trip that ran the gamut from waking dreams and flashbacks to birth memories, past life memories, and encounters with spiritual beings." One observant of a weekend workshop utilizing the Grof method and conducted by UCLA psychiatrist Curt Batiste at Sky High Ranch in Palmdale, California, reported:

>   The breathers lay on the gray pile carpet breathing
> with pranayamic gusto. Within minutes the room was
> transformed into the bowels of a madhouse a la Hiero-
> nymous Bosch . . . bloodcurdling screams and deep
> moans emerged from many of the breathers. . . .
>   [One woman] had a vision of herself in the body of a
> man walking down a street a hundred years ago, prepar-
> ing to rape a series of women.
>   "I was him," she gasped. . . .[39]

Those engaged in such occultic practices sometimes seem to
come out of the bedlam with "deeper insights" and to experience
"positive" changes in their lives. However, the benefits generally do
not last, and all too often new problems arise to replace those
originally dealt with. Nevertheless, the game goes on. There seems
to be no limit to the faith placed in this magical but unexplained
realm of *consciousness* or to the godlike powers its devotees hope to
acquire through entering altered states and thereby tapping into the
collective *unconscious*. It is astonishing that this faith persists in
spite of the obvious absurdities, contradictions, dangers, and disasters.

Playing Cosmic Russian Roulette with the Mind

Even the most enthusiastic promoters of the consciousness revolution admit that there are bad trips. It takes only one disaster—and
there have been thousands—to contradict the basic New Age teaching that we're tapping into a benevolent and good "Higher Self"
through "altered states of consciousness." Why the evil and destructive forces that suddenly break out as though a mask has
inadvertently slipped off? Why did Paramahansa Yogananda, for
example, founder of the Self-Realization Society and one of the
greatest Yogis of all, "fall apart" toward the end of his life?

"He was taking on the evil karma of others," was the explanation
given. However, what Yogananda's close assistant, Charya Bernard, observed disillusioned him completely. It caused Bernard to
finally admit to himself that of the 40,000 people he had counseled
during his years at Yogananda's side, only a handful had received

any lasting benefit while thousands had actually been harmed by Yoga.[40]

Carl Jung laid the foundation for the consciousness revolution with his own psychic adventures. In the process he encountered "the stuff of psychosis . . . found in the insane." Jung called this analytical journey under altered states of consciousness "a risky experiment" and he considered it "a questionable adventure to entrust oneself to the uncertain path that leads into the depths of the unconscious." Yet like a man who is torn between the dread of a great danger and a prize he covets, Jung complained that our "rational age" failed to see the value in his "voyage of discovery." Yet since Jung's death, and despite disastrous results that are seldom admitted, this voyage has become extremely popular.

There was something almost sinister in Jung's desire to see other people involved in what he confessed was an "uncertain, risky and dangerous" path that could well become "the quintessence of horror." The fact that Jung, in order to retain his sanity, had to fight his own altered consciousness by clinging desperately to "ordinary consciousness" should be a warning to others. Describing those years when he teetered on the brink of what he called "total psychotic breakdown," Jung wrote:

> I needed a point of support in "this world," and I may say that my family and my professional work . . . remained the base to which I could always return . . . [or] the unconscious contents could have driven me out of my wits. . . .
> "I have a medical diploma from a Swiss university, I must help my patients, I have a wife and five children, I live at 228 Seestrasse in Kusnacht"—these were actualities which made demands upon me and proved to me again and again that I really existed, that I was not a blank page whirling about in the winds of the spirit, like Nietzsche [who died insane].[41]

Here we have a strange paradox: The man primarily responsible, if not for today's consciousness revolution itself, then certainly for the aura of respectability which it bears, had to cling desperately to ordinary consciousness in order to retain his sanity. Yet he suggests that salvation comes through attaining the very altered state that nearly destroyed him. We dare not ignore the fact that altered states of consciousness have traditionally been cultivated in order to experience "spirit possession." If any man was ever "possessed," surely it was Jung himself.

Possession: Myth, Mania, or Demonic?

In *Hostage to the Devil*, Malachi Martin relates a number of examples of demonic possession that go beyond the dangers of "negative thinking" that Herbert Benson and other popularizers of psychology's religious "science" consider to be the great evil. There are thousands of such well-documented tragedies, which demonstrate that psychological explanations involving the "unconscious" for the phenomenon long known as "possession" are pitifully inadequate. Many of these cases involve intelligent and apparently well-meaning persons who believed and followed the latest psychological theories, only to find themselves "possessed" by an evil spirit—in spite of the fact that they had until then considered "possession" to be a religious delusion.

With undergraduate degrees in biology and anthropology from Harvard University and a Ph.D. in ethnobotany, Wade Davis is representative of today's highly educated Westerner. His participation in numerous expeditions to the jungles of Central and South America and elsewhere, however, and his exposure to spiritualist societies have given him another perspective. With his background it was difficult for Davis to lay aside the superiority that scientists exude when analyzing "primitive" cultures, but the numerous cases of "spirit possession" which he witnessed forced a reevaluation of his thinking. Davis wrote:

> For the nonbeliever, there is something profoundly disturbing about spirit possession. Its power is raw, immediate, and undeniably real. . . .
>
> The psychologists who have attempted to understand possession from a scientific perspective . . . [avoid] issues that cannot be approached by their calculus—the existence or nonexistence of spirits, for example . . .

[and] consider possession a behavior of "psychically dis-equilibrated persons with a mytho-maniacal constitution. . . ."

These wordy explanations ring most hollow when they are applied to certain irrefutable physical attributes of the possessed [immunity to fire, etc.] . . . [upon these] my logic wavered. . . .

In the absence of a scientific explanation, and in the face of our own certain ignorance, it seems foolish to disregard the opinions of those who know possession best.[42]

Such warnings are smugly disregarded by those who have built a "scientific" mythology founded upon the materialistic assertion that a spirit dimension is nonexistent. Upset at the emotional reactions aroused in audiences by *The Exorcist*, parapsychologist Loyd Auerbach writes:

To set the record a bit straighter, let me say that the only demons we, as scientists, deal with are one's own "demons" that may be conjured up by the subconscious and the imagination.[43]

With a healthy fear of evil spirits neatly debunked by psychologists, the barrier that has kept so many people from involvement with the powers of darkness is now gone. There is no longer anything to be afraid of, for nothing is there except fragments of one's own personality. So goes the refrain. All that is now needed is to accept a new *understanding*.

Unfortunately, that "understanding" begins with a denial of evidence and is concerned not with truth but with the dogmatic claim of the new religion of psychology that it alone is the true faith of humanity. We now stand in grave danger that psychology's glib pseudoscientific explanations of spiritual power are increasingly opening the West to the very phenomenon psychologists have sought so long to deny: demonic possession.

9

Ghosts in the Machine

Belief in the existence of *evil spirits* has been common to all cultures and races as far back as historians can trace—but has been largely rejected in the enlightened scientific West. Yet it would be presumptuous to assume that the human race represents the only intelligences in the entire universe or the only form that intelligent life could take. The scientific community takes very seriously the possibility that intelligent beings exist in other parts of the universe; nor is there any reason for denying the possible existence of nonhuman intelligences without physical bodies. Considering the pervasiveness of evil among mankind, clearly at least some of these entities may have evil intentions and, assuming that the brain is indeed a machine that a ghost can operate, could influence humans, even to the extent that has long been called "possession." Of course it is no longer in vogue to speak of *demons*. Even in his day, however, William James, Harvard University Professor of philosophy and psychology, decried this blind prejudice:

> The refusal of modern "enlightenment" to treat "possession" as a hypothesis . . . in spite of the massive human tradition based on concrete human experience in its favor, has always seemed to me a curious example of the power of fashion in things "scientific."
>
> That the demon-theory . . . will have its innings again is to my mind absolutely certain. One has to be "scientific" indeed to be blind and ignorant enough to suspect no such possibility.[1]

Professor James's pointed references to the prejudice that too often blinds men of science is well-taken, especially when modern science itself provides evidence that would seem to support the existence of nonphysical dimensions of reality that could be inhabited by "spirit entities." Some of the strange, ethereal particles of matter which physicists have been discovering in this century make the existence of a spirit world increasingly plausible. One component of the subatomic world, known as the "Z particle," is so elusive that only a few dozen have been captured. The United States has been in a race with scientists at CERN (the European Nuclear Research Center near Geneva, Switzerland) to build a giant "collider" capable of creating and capturing significant quantities of this exotic particle.

Subatomic Particles and "Ghosts"

In light of the many ghostly characteristics of our own physical universe now accepted by the scientific community, it seems at least reasonable that other worlds could exist which manifest in their entirety the qualities of elusive subatomic particles. Such worlds, by our standards, would have to be labeled "nonphysical" or "spiritual," because even physical objects therein would be undetectable by our most advanced instruments. "Spirits" might not seem ghostly at all in their own dimension; nor would they be any more mysterious than some of the qualities we now recognize in our familiar space-time-matter universe. Referring to the existence of a spiritual dimension, Sir Arthur Eddington wrote:

> The scheme of [the new] physics is now formulated in such a way as to make it almost self-evident that it is a partial aspect of something wider.[2]

That this "something wider" could be nonphysical is, as Eddington believed, suggested by the very qualities of the universe as we know it. The discovery of ghostly particles such as the neutrino makes the existence of discarnate spirits or other nonphysical intelligences much more plausible in a scientific context. With virtually no physical properties—no mass, no electrical charge, no magnetic field—the neutrino behaves very much like a "ghost." Neither gravitation nor electromagnetic force have any effect upon the neutrino, either to attract or to repel it. Consequently, a neutrino zooming in from intergalactic space at near the speed of light would almost instantaneously pass through the entire earth without hitting anything. This fact makes the suggestion that "ghosts" can pass through walls seem less fantastic. Astronomer V. A. Firsoff said:

> The universe as seen by a neutrino eye would wear a very unfamiliar look. Our earth and other planets simply would not be there. . . .
> A neutrino brain might suspect our existence from certain secondary effects, but would find it very difficult to prove, as we would elude the neutrino instruments at his disposal.[3]

It is clear that neutrino-bodied beings would be unable to see us with their neutrino eyes, just as we would be unable to "see" them. It would be folly, of course, for either of us to deny the existence of the other on that basis. There is no scientific reason to doubt that nonphysical beings undetectable by our most sophisticated instruments could exist. It is equally reasonable to assume that since our minds are nonphysical, some kind of "telepathic" communication could be established with "spirit beings" without visible or other tangible contact taking place. Arthur Koestler, "a reluctant convert" to a belief in psychic phenomena,[4] declared:

> The unthinkable phenomena of extrasensory perception appear somewhat less preposterous in the light of the unthinkable propositions of physics.[5]

The Key Role of Consciousness

Having said all of the above, we must not expect science to guide us into a verification and understanding of the "spirit world." It can take us only as far as the physical, mechanical phenomena it describes, but not into the world of spirit with its free will and ethics. We have already noted that even our awareness of physical phenomena is dependent upon consciousness, and, as the evidence seems to indicate, lies outside the realm of physical science. Consequently, that there should be a nonphysical dimension of existence is no mere chance development; it is demanded by the very nature of conscious awareness and the power to choose.

Consciousness gives us an *awareness* of matter; it is not a *property* of matter, since there is nothing physical about it. This understanding is reflected in that famous statement that Sir James Jeans so often repeated: "God is a mathematician, and the universe begins to look more like a great thought than a great machine." Elaborating further, Jeans wrote:

> Mind no longer appears as an accidental intruder into the realm of matter; we are beginning to suspect that we ought to hail it as the creator and governor of the realm of matter—not, of course, our individual minds. . . .
>
> It does not matter whether objects "exist in my mind or that of any other created spirit" or not; their objectivity arises from their subsisting [to paraphrase Berkeley] "in the mind of some Eternal Spirit." . . .
>
> Time and space, which form the setting for the thought [that created the universe], must have come into being as part of this [creative] act. Primitive cosmologies pictured a creator working in space and time, forging sun, moon, and stars out of already existent raw material. Modern scientific theory compels us to think of the creator working outside time and space—which are part of his creation—just as an artist is outside his canvas.[6]

With the observation that the Creator must be separate from his creation, Jeans has eliminated pantheism/naturalism as a viable theory. The capability of man to form conceptual ideas and to create exotic new technology would seem to indicate his creation in the image of the One who Jeans declares created everything out of nothing. Moreover, it seems evident that human minds, reflecting the image of their Creator, likewise exist outside the *physical* universe.

While our minds are conscious of an objective world which impresses itself upon our senses, consciousness itself is not dependent upon the physical world. We know this to be the case because thoughts themselves are not *physical*, nor do they depend upon any physical stimulation. This is evident from the fact that we can have thoughts about abstractions, such as purpose and meaning. In attempting to maintain the position that man is only a lump of matter responding to stimuli from the physical world about him, the materialist eliminates ethics, truth, esthetics, honor, and all the qualities that make life meaningful and distinguish humans from animals. As philosopher-historian Herbert Schlossberg has pointed out:

> What modern man cannot know through the senses, he feels safe in dismissing from further consideration.
> One of the first and most notable casualties of this reasoning is the idea of purpose. The senses are silent on such topics.[7]

The fallacy of materialism can futher be shown by the fact that mathematical processes can be carried on entirely in the mind. The numerical answer that results is simply a number with no relationship to any object in the physical dimension. Yet mathematical equations, for reasons which science can neither discover nor explain, perfectly describe every object and motion in the physical universe—and in limitless dimensions beyond even our wildest imagination. In fact, reflecting the conclusion of many other scientists, Jeans went so far as to say:

> The final [scientifically knowable] truth about a phenomenon resides in the mathematical description of it. . . . We go beyond the mathematical formula at our own risk. . . .
> The making of models or pictures to explain mathematical formulae and the phenomena they describe is not a step towards, but a step away from reality; it is like making graven images of a spirit.[8]

Jeans's rationale gives some insight into the biblical prohibition against idolatry—a practice universally accepted by other religions but abhorred by Moslems, Jews, and Christians. In fact, the Bible further explains this prohibition by declaring that idols provide demonic entities with identities through which they can influence mankind.[9] Again we see the clear distinction between naturalism/pantheism/polytheism and supernaturalism, and a major consequence thereof.

In agreement with the belief that the brain is operated by the nonphysical mind, it is quite clear that thoughts *precede* and *cause* neural activity in the brain. They do not *result* from anything happening in the physical brain, nor can thinking be explained on that basis. Thoughts about truth or justice, for example, could not originate through any physical stimulus (and thus could not result from any evolutionary process), because they are totally unrelated to any physical quality such as weight, texture, taste, or smell.

On the other hand, the fear of pain or illness, beginning in the non-physical mind as a purely mental event (aroused perhaps by suggestion or by some physical threat), can affect the physical body *psychosomatically*. It is erroneous, however, to imagine that human thought processes can create matter and thus to suggest that we have an *unlimited* potential for harming or healing ourselves or others with our minds. Nevertheless, within reasonable limits, even the courts recognize the reality of "mental cruelty" and award damages for such suffering. Anguish is not physical, yet it can cause physical problems in the body.

The Brain Doesn't Think at All

Because of the predominance of materialism, the human brain has generally been studied as though consciousness and thought could eventually be explained in terms of the electrical impulses and chemical reactions of neural activity. At least some researchers, however, are accepting the evidence that instead of *producing* thought, brain activity is a *result of* thought, and must therefore originate independently of the brain and apparently outside the physical dimension. The scientific materialist is naturally reluctant to accept such a conclusion, in spite of the evidence, because it undermines his entire worldview. Even someone like Harvard Medical School's Herbert Benson, who at times seems to give a nodding assent to the nonphysical nature of mind, persists in attributing the origin of *thoughts* to the physical substance of the brain. In his latest book, Benson writes:

> A healthy brain cell stores and transmits information which ultimately becomes what we know as *thoughts*. It's very difficult to describe exactly what happens in this process because the whole act of thinking is so complex, with enormous numbers of brain cells interacting in our mental processes.[10]

Yet a mere 20 pages further in the same book, Benson contradicts himself by referring to Sir John Eccles's experiments as though he agrees with his conclusions that the brain is a machine operated by a nonphysical entity, the mind. He also favorably quotes famed neurosurgeon and brain researcher Wilder Penfield: "The mind is independent of the brain. The brain is a computer, but it is programmed by something that is outside itself, the mind."[11] Not only the experiments of such researchers as Eccles and Penfield, but logic itself, compel us to conclude that the human brain, while of a much higher order than that of animals, doesn't *think* at all.

A computer does not think; the thinking is done by the operator and programmer, which in the case of the brain is the mind. The human brain simply provides the mechanism necessary for the nonphysical entity operating it to interface with the material world. Consequently, the current fad of trying to *develop* the "right brain" in order to counter Western culture's alleged bias toward "left-brained" thinking is indeed the "whole-brained half-wittedness" that some have labeled it.

Whether a person seems to be predominantly moral or immoral, aesthetic or vulgar, artistic or practical does not *originate* with and cannot be blamed upon a certain hemisphere of the brain, even though that part may be *used* by the brain's ghostly operator when expressing these characteristics. Yet this modern myth persists under the promotion of such highly regarded experts as Herbert Benson (who goes so far as to say, "We have become prisoners of the left sides of our brains")[12] and even in such bastions of advanced thinking as Stanford University, now recognized as the top academic institution in the country.

The following "exercise in creativity" taught in the highly touted "Creativity In Business" course at Stanford's Graduate School of Business may at least partially explain why Lee Iaccoca, the management genius who turned Chrysler Corporation around, has said that MBA's (Master of Business Administration graduates) being turned out by our universities "know everything and understand nothing." Most of the course involves far more overt Eastern mysticism than this particular exercise, which embodies one of the more "structured" techniques:

> If you don't know yet what your own key question is, ask your Essence [which the course defines as "the divine spark, the Self, the Divine Ego, the Great I Am, God, etc. within us all]. . . .
>
> [In a] more structured approach . . . you ask a question with your left brain and answer it with your right as a demonstration of your unused resources within. . . .
>
> Ask yourself a question by writing it down with your usual writing hand. Then empty your mind. Don't try to think out an answer. Remind yourself that the answer lives within you, and that all you have to do is record it with your *other* hand. . . . And have fun seeing what you have to say to yourself.
>
> Did you surprise yourself? . . . Of course this is just a demonstration of opposite-brain functions. Use any method that works for you. You don't need a pencil to get home to your Essence.[13]

The ability to form thoughts in the mind by an act of the will, as we have already noted, argues against the "All-is-One" maxim of naturalism/pantheism, and in favor of supernaturalism. Human thoughts, containing as they do much evil and error, could not originate with God. This fact alone would seem to demonstrate that human beings are not part of God, as the Stanford course implies. On the other hand, our thoughts involve concepts that cannot be explained as coming from the natural world. Though our thoughts can be affected by the physical world around us, our wills also enter into and can control the process. Certainly humans are not the stimulus-response mechanisms that B. F. Skinner's Behaviorism—and to some extent all of psychology—make them out to be. As C. S. Lewis put it:

> If minds are wholly dependent on brains and brains on biochemistry, and biochemistry (in the long run) on the meaningless flux of the atoms, I cannot understand how the thought of those minds should have any more significance than the sound of the wind in the trees.[14]

In view of the nonphysical nature of consciousness, it is intriguing that those who practice divination techniques for initiating contact with the "spirit" dimension all agree that the secret is in achieving the requisite state of *consciousness* through drugs, Yoga (and other forms of Eastern meditation), hypnosis, and mediumistic trance. It is not surprising, then, that this "altered state of consciousness" and the contact it brings with "spirit guides" has always been the traditional shamanistic method of achieving paranormal or psychic powers. It has also often opened the door to what has become known as "possession." This altered state is a condition which numerous courses, from the Silva Method to "Creativity In Business," are specifically designed to promote. While some would-be sorcerers seek "possession" voluntarily for the paranormal power and knowledge it brings, others have fallen into it unintentionally and with disastrous results.

In the Stanford Graduate School of Business "Creativity" course, *The I Ching Workbook* is recommended for "peer[ing] into your future . . . through divination . . . and discovering yourself." Meditation is the major technique used for achieving the "trance" state that is so critical to the "creativity" process taught in the course. A major purpose is to contact the "inner guide." Other methods are recommended as well, including dancing oneself into a trance, as practiced by followers of Sufism, Santeria, voodoo, and other occult religions. In their book based on the course, Professor Michael Ray and Rochelle Myers write:

> When we do trance dancing in our class, everyone puts on blindfolds to give each other complete privacy. . . .

> Get some music that has interesting and repetitive rhythms . . . something exotic from another culture . . . its mysterious quality allows you to move more easily into a trancelike movement. . . .
>
> Become one with the music. . . . Then, when the music stops, lie on your back on the floor. Collapse into the corpse pose. . . .
>
> Our students get everything from rushes of energy and tremendous confidence to out-of-body experiences. Some find it the only way they can really meditate and get into that blank but energizing state between sleep and wakefulness. They very often have spontaneous insights of what they consider to be a higher order.[15]

A large part of the materials and methods presented in the course are of this nature. It is Eastern *religion* dressed up in Western pop psychological terms and passed off as a pseudoscientific recipe for gaining the inspiration needed to guide corporate policy in the competitive world of twentieth-century computerized business. The techniques and the theories behind them come right out of shamanism, and the goal is the same: to meet one's "inner guide." There is therefore good reason to suspect that the "creativity" which this course and others like it produce comes from the same "spirit entities" that mankind has consulted for millennia through various occult techniques. That major universities such as Stanford are now presenting such religious practices as part of the new business technology is astonishing. And that these methods could well lead to "possession" must be at least strongly suspected.

Inspiration and Evil

University of California psychologist and pioneer consciousness-researcher Charles Tart admits reluctantly, "There's enough evidence that comes in to make me take the idea of disembodied intelligence seriously."[16] Stanislav Grof reports that some of the LSD subjects he has studied have had encounters with "astral bodies," and in some cases this has led to "the characteristics of spirit possession." Friedrich Nietzsche indicated that the inspiration for *Thus Spake Zarathustra* (his Bible of a new mankind "loyal to the earth") came as a form of possession. "It invaded me," he wrote. "One can hardly reject completely the idea that one is the mere incarnation, or mouthpiece, or medium of some almighty power." Famed architect Buckminster Fuller, after staying up half the night reading Marilyn Ferguson's "New Age Bible," *The Aquarian Conspiracy*, suggested that "the spirits of the dead" had helped her to write it. Ferguson laughed and said, "Well, I sometimes thought so, but I wasn't about to tell anybody."[17]

The New Age Vatican of Findhorn was founded upon the specific instructions of alleged "spirit guides." Eileen Caddy was apparently the first to receive this guidance through an "inner voice" that said: "Be still . . . and know that I am God. . . . Listen to Me, and all will be well. . . . I am closer than your breath, than your hands and feet. Trust in Me." All of the original adult members of this remarkable community (Sheena Govan, Dorothy Maclean, David Spangler, et al) were "channels" for a variety of entities that had brought them all together by similar "guidance," and some of which claimed to be their own "higher Selves." Harmony with nature was the common theme. Even the alleged spirits of "transformed" Russian prisoners that channeled through Anne Edwards preached the familiar gospel of naturalism/pantheism: that everything is "God" and that each person's "Higher Self," as a part of "God," can create its own reality.[18]

This message is being repeated through literally thousands of "channels" as the phenomenon of contact with "spirit guides" explodes around the world. Whoever these entities behind "channeling" are, the evangelization of the world with their "truth" seems to be the major purpose. However, they also seem to have a penchant for possessing human bodies; and when that occurs, events often take a frightening turn. Possession can occur because of the very nature of the relationship that one enters into in order to receive the power or knowledge that is offered, and in spite of the good intentions or the apparently innocent involvement of the unsuspecting.

Are "evil spirits" really involved? Consider these cases. A TM instructor sent to a South American country to inaugurate transcendental meditation there began to see "Satan" every time she looked at the picture of its founder, Maharishi Mahesh Yogi. Attempting suicide, she ended up in an insane asylum. After being initiated into Yoga by Swami Rama (one of the prize subjects of Elmer and Alyce Green in their biofeedback research at the Menninger Clinic), a Chicago housewife was tormented by psychic visitations from Swami and committed to a hospital psychiatric ward. Using the Silva Mind Control techniques she had been taught, a schoolteacher began to visualize her mentally handicapped pupils improving and seeming to achieve remarkable results. Then one night her brother received a frantic call at about 2 A.M. "My God, George! *Something's* in my apartment—something *evil*, and it's after me! Please come and help me!" A careful study of these and numerous other cases of this kind would suggest the very real possibility that alien and evil intelligences were involved.

The Exorcist and the Ouija Board

In the 1970's *The Exorcist*, William Blatty's runaway best-seller and movie, caught the attention of America and the world. To many people it was merely a horror story, frightening but entertaining. To others it was much more. Across America, admissions for emergency psychiatric care increased dramatically, some of the patients arriving in straitjackets directly from theaters where they had flipped out while viewing the film.

Blatty later acknowledged that *The Exorcist* was based upon a true story. In fact, the circumstances of the case were investigated by J. B. Rhine, founder and director of the parapsychological laboratory at Duke University, who called it "the most impressive" poltergeist phenomenon he had ever come across.[19] Blatty also revealed that the involvement with demon possession came through a Ouija board. It is therefore more than interesting that the Ouija board, which has been implicated by experts in numerous cases of apparent demon possession, overtook Monopoly to become America's most popular parlor game in 1967.[20]

Public libraries contain many volumes dictated by alleged non-physical entities which first made contact through a Ouija board with those who became their spokespersons. Jane Roberts is one of many examples. Like Carl Rogers and so many others, it was while skeptically experimenting with a Ouija board that Roberts began to receive messages from an extraordinary intelligence. Soon she was able to discard the board and thereafter speak in trance for "Seth," who from that time on seemed to "possess" her. Out of this encounter came literally thousands of pages of what became known as the famous "Seth material," some of it published in the series available in bookstores across America. The Seth writings are an ingenious interpretation, in psychological terminology, of naturalism's "perennial philosophy" and present an extremely complex explanation of alleged multidimensional psychic existence.

Of course Ouija board skeptics insist either that those on the board are making the planchette move or that the messages (as the Philip group claimed) are coming from their subconscious. Tests have been made, however, which eliminate both of those possibilities. Sir William F. Barrett conducted experiments in which the operators were thoroughly blindfolded and the alphabet around the board was scrambled without their knowledge, so that even their "subconscious minds" could not know the position of the letters. In addition, an opaque screen was held between the sitters and the Ouija to make doubly sure that those using the board could not see the letters. Under these rigorously controlled conditions the planchette moved faster than ever. In his report to the American Society for Psychical Research, Barrett said:

> For we have here, in addition to the blindfolding of the sitters, the amazing swiftness, precision and accuracy of the movements of the indicator spelling out long and intelligent messages . . . without halting or error . . . messages often contrary to and beyond the knowledge of the sitters. . . .
>
> Reviewing the results as a whole, I am convinced of their supernormal character, and that we have here an exhibition of some intelligent discarnate agency . . . guiding [the sitters'] muscular movements.[21]

It was through a Ouija board that Pearl Curran, a St. Louis housewife, first contacted a spirit entity which called herself Patience Worth. Patience claimed to have lived in Dorsetshire, England, in the seventeenth century, and during a 20-year period she gave eighth-grade-educated Pearl Curran "more than one-and-a-half million words in poems and historical novels." These highly acclaimed writings had religious themes and were mostly set in the time of Jesus. A composition of 350,000 words entitled *The Sorry Tale* was considered by a leading historical authority of the time "the greatest story penned of the life and times of Christ since the Gospels."[22] Another literary piece of 70,000 words by Curran was analyzed by Professor C. H. S. Schiller of London University, who found "the vocabulary contained not a single word to have originated after 1600." He stated:

> When we consider that the authorized version of the Bible has only 70% Anglo Saxon, and it is necessary to go back to Lyomen in 1205 to equal Patience's percentage (over 90%), we realize we are facing a philological miracle.[23]

This would indeed have been a miracle for Curran's mind to have produced, but not for another mind with such capabilities working through her, which is a possibility that must not be overlooked. Most psychologists, however, persist in the theory that Ouija board or other "spirit" communications merely represent an interplay between the left and right hemispheres of the brain and/or the therapeutic release of unconscious repressions. This was the thesis, for example, of psychiatrist Anita M. Muhl, former chief of the division of special education for the California State Department of Education. She considered the Ouija board and other forms of "automatic writing," though "dangerous for the amateur" if unsupervised, to be excellent tools for plumbing a patient's unconscious. And the danger which concerned her was not "possession" by evil spirits, but possible "fragmentation of the personality."[24]

Barbara Honegger, former White House policy analyst and past president of the Parapsychology Research Group, considers Muhl's *Automatic Writing: An Approach to the Unconscious* to be the authoritative psychological work on the subject. Yet Honegger, who also speaks of Ouija board communication as an interplay between brain hemispheres, nevertheless seems to acknowledge the existence of discarnate spirits. Some of these, she suggests, are still "earthbound" and need to "possess" living bodies long enough to "work their problems out, finish up their unfinished business." This would seem to be a dangerous assumption to make, particularly in view of the horrifying experiences, including insanity, murder, and suicide, that have resulted from "possession."

Clearly the fear that William James decried as "a curious example of the power of fashion in things 'scientific' "—the fear of admitting the possibility of *demonic* possession—still persists. The evidence that independent intelligences of great evil are indeed taking over the bodies of many who dabble in sorcery seems undeniable.

Evidences of Demonic Possession

In spite of the overwhelming skepticism among their colleagues, there are increasing numbers of psychologists and psychiatrists— former doubters concerning the existence of independent nonphysical intelligences—who now frankly affirm their belief in the reality of *evil spirits*. In his classic, *Channeling*, Jon Klimo refers to psychiatrist Ralph B. Allison, who says, "I have come to believe in the possibility of spirit possession . . . by demonic spirits from satanic realms, and that's an area I don't care to discuss or be part of—it's a theoretical possibility."[25] A host of psychologists and researchers could be quoted who have come to the same conclusion. In *The Unquiet Dead*, psychologist and author Edith Fiore tells how the failure of psychotherapy to treat and psychological theory to explain certain behaviors led her on a search that resulted in her belief in demonic possession. In Maya Deren's *Divine Horsemen: Voodoo Gods of Haiti*, the stark terror of possession is depicted, not only from the viewpoint of an observer but from one who has experienced it as well. Deren writes:

> I have left possession until the end, for it is the center toward which all the roads of Voudoun converge. . . . To know this area, one must, finally, enter. . . .
> Never have I seen the face of such anguish, ordeal and blind terror as at the moment when the loa [spirit] comes.[26]

Popular author and psychiatrist M. Scott Peck relates some of his experiences in graphic terms that reveal why the subject of possession arouses such fear, and why he went from skeptic to firm believer. Since Peck has had more than ordinary acquaintance with evil and has made it a special study, he did not come to his conclusions lightly. While he was Assistant Chief of Psychiatry under the Army Surgeon General, Peck also served as chairman of a special committee of three psychiatrists appointed by the Army Chief of Staff to study the "psychological causes of [the massacre at] My Lai, so as to help prevent such atrocities in the future." In his best-selling books, *The Road Less Travelled* and *People of the Lie*, Peck chronicles his odyssey from "vague identification with Buddhist and Islamic mysticism" to belief in both "God" and "Satan."

Peck refers to two specific cases that convinced him of the reality of demon possession. After participating in the "unscientific" procedure of exorcism, which he calls "psychotherapy by massive assault," Peck declared with awe that he had "personally met Satan face to face."[27] He went on to explain:

> When the demonic finally spoke clearly in one case, an expression appeared on the patient's face that could be described only as Satanic. It was an incredibly contemptuous grin of utter hostile malevolence. I have spent many hours before a mirror trying to imitate it without the slightest success.
>
> . . . when the demonic finally revealed itself in the exorcism of [another] patient, it was with a still more ghastly expression. The patient suddenly resembled a writhing snake of great strength, viciously attempting to bite the team members.
>
> More frightening than the writhing body, however, was the face. The eyes were hooded with lazy reptilian torpor—except when the reptile darted out in attack, at which moment the eyes would open wide with blazing hatred. Despite these frequent darting moments, what upset me the most was the extraordinary sense of a fifty-million-year-old heaviness I received from this serpentine being.

Almost all the team members at both exorcisms were convinced they were at these times in the presence of something absolutely alien and inhuman. The end of each exorcism proper was signaled by the departure of this Presence from the patient and the room.[28]

The conclusion Peck arrived at is not a matter of "scientific proof," but a conviction of human consciousness and conscience. Nor could it be otherwise when one confronts the spiritual realm. Eddington points out that if a physicist should try to apply scientific methods to the study of thought by examining the brain, "All that he discovers is a collection of atoms and electrons and fields of force arranged in space and time, apparently similar to those found in inorganic objects." From the physical evidence alone, "He might set down thought as an illusion—some perverse interpretation of the interplay of the physical entities that he has found."[29]

While human personality cannot be defined or demonstrated scientifically, but is nevertheless universally recognized, so it is with the manifestation of demonic power. Unfortunately, even though Peck acknowledges the reality and horror of demonic possession, his reliance upon psychology undermines his understanding of evil. Psychology pretends to provide a *scientific* explanation of human behavior, yet that is clearly impossible.

Peck laments the "lack of scientific knowledge" relative to evil, and hopes for the day when we will at last have developed, "through scientific research, a body of knowledge that constitutes a genuine psychology of evil."[30] If there is a *psychological* explanation for evil, however, then moral choice and personal responsibility are no longer involved. Moreover, if evil can be explained as psychologically programmed behavior, then what is the *Presence* that Peck says can be palpably "felt" by those present at an exorcism, and whose exit always signals the victory for the exorcist?

Ghosts in the Machine

While disagreeing on the details, the greatest philosophers prior to the twentieth century and the world's religions as far back as historians can trace have affirmed that the human soul (mind/consciousness) is not only as real as the flesh-and-blood body it inhabits but that it also survives physical death. Where and in what form is still debated. The experiments of Sir John Eccles, to which we referred briefly earlier, seem to require the existence of the soul as the necessary "ghost in the machine," without which the brain would be merely an incredible piece of hardware. To Carl Rogers, a nonphysical dimension of human existence opened enticing possibilities beyond anything known to physical science. He wrote:

> A whole new perception of human potential is threatening any complacency we still might feel . . . [leading] to the conclusion that mind is an entity far greater than brain . . . capable of incredible feats. . . .[31]

At the same time, Rogers seemed blind to the equally great potential for evil made possible through "spirit possession." Eccles's research uncovered insights that are not only fascinating but carry a note of warning as well. Much of his work focused upon the problem of how the "soul" (the Greeks called it the *psyche*) operates the body. Eccles devised a means of wiring the subjects of his experiments in such a way that his instruments could follow the neural activity in their brains as they performed, under his direction, simple tasks that required purposeful thought on their part. He noted that varying tasks utilized different parts of the brain, but that regardless of the task performed, the neural activity always *began* at a certain point in the brain and moved out from there. When those who had Parkinson's disease or had suffered a stroke and were incapable of performing the assigned task attempted to do it, that same point in the brain fired normally, but without any further neural activity. Eccles called this spot the Supplementary Motor Area. He believed this was where the "ghost" (or human spirit) in a living person made its connection with the brain and body.

Eccles's discovery pointing to the probable existence of a *ghost* in the machine confirmed intuition, religious tradition, and modern science in placing human consciousness outside the physical universe and thus beyond the reach of science and psychology. It also opened some frightening possibilities. Would it not be possible for spirits to exist without bodies? And could not such entities operate the human brain if given access, perhaps through an altered state of consciousness? If there must be one "ghost" in the machine, why could there not be more than one? It was this possibility that caused Jung to question his psychological theories and to refer to what he called "elemental demons who are supposed never to have been human souls or soul-parts."[32] As Klimo points out, what has long been known as demon possession has a logical explanation:

> If your own mind can affect your own brain, then the similar nonphysical nature of *another* mind might also be able to affect your brain, giving rise to your hearing a voice, seeing a vision, or having the other mind speak or write by controlling your body the same way you normally control your own body.[33]

10

In Search of Spirit Entities

It is not surprising that one of mankind's most compelling fascinations in every culture throughout history has been to communicate with the dead. Mediumship is one of the world's oldest professions and has always been an integral part of nature religion in its many forms. In stark contrast, the Old Testament, claimed as their Holy Scriptures by Jews, Moslems, and Christians, condemns those who "have a familiar spirit." Necromancy (or wizardry), the practice of consulting discarnate spirits (common among the nations around Israel), was forbidden to Israel by God.[1] Consequently, in the Western world, mediumship was generally practiced in secret until the predominant Judeo-Christian influence began to decline.

Since its modern revival in the early 1800's, spiritualism has attracted many prominent people. The fiery abolitionist orator William Lloyd Garrison, writers James Fenimore Cooper and William Cullen Bryant, and journalist-publisher Horace Greeley were among the early converts to spiritualism. Former Air Marshal Lord Hugh Dowding, hero of the Battle of Britain, and Mme. Adrienne Boland, the famous French aviatrix (who credited a spirit message with saving her life by guiding her over the Andes mountains), were leaders in the spiritualist movement. Thomas Edison spent years trying to devise an electronic means of communication with the spirits of the dead. Queen Victoria, whose reign of 63 years was the longest of any monarch in British history, routinely consulted mediums. Her favorite was her manservant, John Brown, through whom the Queen allegedly maintained contact with her husband,

Prince Albert, after his death in 1861.

Prince Charles is apparently continuing the tradition and has reportedly had some indication that his deceased uncle Lord Mountbatten may be guiding him from the spirit world. Sir Laurens van der Post, confidant of the Prince and his mentor in psychic research, believes he has had communication from his close friend Carl Jung since the latter's death. Even the Queen mother has reportedly attended seances in an effort to contact her dead husband, King George VI.

Communing with the "Other Side"

Seances in which contact was made with alleged discarnates were held in the White House while Abraham Lincoln was President. Both Lincoln and his wife believed in spirit survival and communication with the dead, and in fact made a number of attempts to contact their two dead sons. Powerful manifestations of poltergeist activity were witnessed by Lincoln and Cabinet members during these seances.

After Queen Victoria's death, in 1901, her spirit allegedly communicated regularly from the "other side" through a Mrs. Etta Wriedt of Detroit, whose mediumship was the subject of two books by Admiral Moore. Canadian Prime Minister MacKenzie King was introduced to Mrs. Wriedt by the Marchioness of Aberdeen, and it was through her seances that King became a convert to spiritualism. Whenever he was in London, England, King would consult several mediums there, among them Helen Hughes, who allegedly put King in touch with his dead mother. During his 22 years as prime minister, MacKenzie King kept his contact with mediums a closely guarded secret. The facts were revealed only after his death, in 1950.

Unlike King, two of England's prime ministers, the famous W. E. Gladstone and the first Earl of Balfour, were very open about their spiritualist beliefs and frequent attendance at seances. Balfour's sister was married to Professor Henry Sidgwick, the first President of the British Society for Psychical Research, of which Balfour himself later became president. More recently, in perhaps one of the most sensational and widely publicized developments in this ancient practice, James Pike, former Episcopalian Bishop of California, became involved in an attempt to contact his son's spirit after the latter had committed suicide. Repeated poltergeist activity of a very specific nature at the bishop's apartment in London (witnessed also by two friends) seemed to indicate that Jim, Jr., was still alive and wanted to communicate from the "other side." After much inner turmoil, intensified by the fear that he was becoming mentally unbalanced, Pike sought out the famous medium Enna Twigg.

At that first session in Mrs. Twigg's modest home in West London, Jim, Jr.'s, voice spoke to his father in the first person through the entranced medium. Always the skeptic, Pike listened carefully and with growing amazement, while the two friends who had accompanied him took careful notes. Although this familiar voice speaking through the medium mentioned details from the past that only son and father knew, Pike suspected that Twigg might be pulling these facts from his subconscious mind by some form of ESP and remained unconvinced. "I wanted to be very sure I wasn't being taken in," recalled the bishop.

Having been trained as a lawyer and having spent time during World War II in Naval Intelligence, Bishop Pike could hardly be classified as gullible or easily deceived. Yet he gradually became convinced, in spite of his initial skepticism, that his dead son was indeed communicating with him. In the process of speaking through the medium, the voice of Jim, Jr., mentioned a number of intimate personal details that could not have been pulled from the bishop's subconscious because he had no knowledge of them at the time. It was only later, after persistent investigation, that Pike was able to verify their accuracy. Moreover, everything that came through Twigg reflected Jim, Jr.'s, unique personality. Pike had the distinct feeling that he was indeed talking to his son. There were mannerisms, idiosyncrasies of expression, and personality quirks that were uniquely his. Yet Mrs. Twigg had never met Jim.

Having authenticated itself, the "spirit" speaking through the medium proceeded to explain that its purpose was to "prove" that there was no death. If Pike was at all aware that this declaration, according to the Bible, was one of the most basic lies, he apparently saw no significance in that fact. The alleged spirit of his son Jim revealed a thinly veiled contempt for Christianity, the faith which the Bishop had sworn to uphold, but which he had already abandoned in the process of his deepening involvement in occultism.

"Don't you ever believe that God can be personalized . . . he is the central Force," said the voice speaking through Twigg. It went on to explain that Jesus was merely a highly evolved man and *not* the Savior, only one of many enlightened beings who exist on a higher plane. This deliberate dilution of Christianity's exclusive claims with Hinduism's basic themes is the consistent aim of almost every "channeled" communication, regardless of how the entities identify themselves.

Modern Mediumship and Channeling

Accompanying the growing influence of Eastern mysticism in the West has been a renewed and sometimes surprising interest in mediumship. For example, it has been reported from various inside sources that the CIA has on occasion tried, through mediums, to contact the spirits of its dead agents. The purpose, of course, was to find out how and why they had died, who had betrayed them, and what secrets they may have learned or divulged under torture that had not been reported prior to their deaths.

Since Carl Jung restored respectability to spiritism by suggesting that mediums were contacting deeper levels of their own psyches or the collective unconscious, many psychologists and psychiatrists have been in the forefront of the modern revival of mediumship. In 1973, for example, Robert R. Leichtman, a psychiatrist who was also a psychic and medium, decided that his study of "the nature of genius" could be implemented by contacting the spirits of past geniuses. In fact, this idea had been suggested to him "by the spooks themselves," as he affectionately calls the discarnates.[2] Some of the dead geniuses whose spirits he "interviewed" through medium David Kendrick Johnson included William Shakespeare, Sigmund Freud, Thomas Jefferson, Sir Oliver Lodge, H. P. Blavatsky, Edgar Cayce, and of course Carl Jung.

In the mid-1980's an interest in mediumship once again exploded, but under the popular new term of "channeling." In the past, mediumship was largely confined to communicating with "Aunt May" or "Uncle George," who had been dead only a short while. Today's "channeling," however, purports to involve communications from "ascended masters" who have been dead for thousands of years and have reached the status of special gurus or even gods, or exotic entities from "higher dimensions of existence," or extraterrestrials from distant galaxies. As with past spiritist revivals, channeling is attracting a large following among the rich and the famous. Harvard University professor Harvey Cox suggests that the entities contacted in the new fad of "channeling" seem to be "yuppified versions of the demons and spirits of another time."[3]

Most mediums down through history have been frauds who played upon the sentimentality and superstitious fears of their clients, for whom they pretended (for a price) to make contact with the spirits of dead relatives. In the fifth century B.C. the Greek playwright Euripides declared, "I perceived how seer's craft is rotten and full of falsehood." Not much has changed since then, but most of the followers of today's popular channelers seem to be unaware of the massive amount of deliberate fraud that has traditionally been part of this scene. It has been particularly prevalent among the professional psychics of all kinds who hire themselves out to the public for a fee: the astrologers, palm readers, fortune-tellers, and mediums. The existence of organized, mediumistic fraud has been documented in *The Psychic Mafia*.

Ex-spiritualist M. Lamar Keene confessed that for 13 years he was part of a nationwide network of 2000 phony mediums who "traded information about clients, conspiring to cheat countless people out of millions of dollars." He claimed that massive card files on "believers" were kept at Camp Chesterfield, Indiana— described in brochures as "the hub of world Spiritualism"—for the use of mediums "on the inside." Though a staunch believer in alleged communications with the dead, psychic investigator Allan Spraggett wrote that his visit to Camp Chesterfield, which at the time attracted 50,000 or more eager pilgrims each summer, exposed him to seances where the fraud was "so crude that it was an insult to the intelligence."[4]

In *Out On A Broken Limb*, F. LaGard Smith tells how he tested Kevin Ryerson, one of Shirley MacLaine's favorite "channelers." In a personal session with Ryerson, Smith asked about his "dead" mother, who in fact was very much alive. "Tom McPherson," the entity allegedly speaking at the time through Ryerson (whom Smith judged not to be in a trance) proceeded to give "information" about Smith's mother as though she really were deceased.[5] Either the "entities" speaking through Ryerson were badly misinformed or Ryerson was putting on an act. Most of the communications being received through today's numerous "channelers" seem to be of the same questionable nature.

Nevertheless, there have been those few mediums who have produced convincing evidence of contact with intelligences not of this world. This evidence (contained in countless volumes of detailed reports accumulated over the past hundred years) has withstood all attempts at refutation. One preliminary indication that a medium may be genuine is his or her willingness to be tested scientifically. Among the greatest mediums of modern times was a fascinating woman named Eileen Garrett, who literally begged science to explain her incredible experiences and powers. To that end, Mrs. Garrett submitted herself to every test that psychic investigators could devise.

One of the Greatest Mediums

Before her death, in 1970, Eileen Garrett was called "the greatest living medium." The *New York Post* said of her, "In the aristocracy of the psychic world, Mrs. Garrett remains the most fascinating." The high regard in which she was held is indicated by the names of those whom she numbered among her close friends and associates: George Bernard Shaw, D. H. Lawrence, James Joyce, H. G. Wells, Carl Jung, Aldous Huxley, William Butler Yeats, and Sir Arthur Conan Doyle. Like most psychics, Garrett's paranormal powers were first exhibited in early childhood.

For more than 30 years a variety of entities spoke through Eileen, most claiming to be discarnate spirits of the dead. These "spirits" each exhibited individual voices and personalities that were obviously not Mrs. Garrett's. Their primary mission seemed to be to prove the survival of human consciousness beyond death. Manifesting knowledge and an independent awareness over which Mrs. Garrett herself had no control, these discarnate beings revealed information that was clearly unknown to her. Moreover, they evidenced clairvoyant perceptions and other psychic powers which she did not possess without these "spirits" in control.

Two principal entities, Uvani and Abdul Latif, known in spiritualism as "controls," consistently dominated Eileen Garrett's trance sessions. Uvani described himself as an Arab soldier who had died in battle hundreds of years before, while Latif claimed to have been born in Baghdad in 1162 and to have died there in 1231 after extensive travels and a time of service as a great Moslem physician in the court of Saladin, Sultan of Egypt.

"Latif" was well known in spiritualist circles, having communicated through a number of other mediums over a period of several centuries. While under his control, Eileen Garrett (like other mediums before her) was able to speak fluently and write in a scholarly and philosophical manner in Arabic, Hebrew, Hindi, Greek, Latin, Coptic, French, German, and Italian on a wide range of subjects. These disciplines included medicine, history, theology, physics, music, minerology, and anatomy. Sir Arthur Conan Doyle, creator of Sherlock Holmes (and a close friend and admirer of Mrs. Garrett), had his stenographers take down an entire book dictated by Abdul Latif through Garrett in trance. It was published as *Health: Its Recovery and Maintenance*.

Unlike most mediums, however, Mrs. Garrett was skeptical of her strange powers and unable to accept the identity of the entities that spoke through her. In an effort to discover the truth, she eagerly cooperated with investigators of psychic phenomena and even invested substantially with her own funds in psychic research. She was, in fact, the founder and major sponsor of the highly regarded Parapsychology Foundation.

When, as a young woman in London, Eileen Garrett had awakened from that first hypnotically induced trance to learn that a male voice identifying itself as "Uvani" had "spoken through her mouth," she had not only been dumbfounded but badly frightened.[6] Unable to accept what was happening to her, even when it was repeated again and again, Mrs. Garrett instead "agreed with her husband that she must be crazy."[7] That seemed preferable to admitting that she had been invaded against her will by the discarnate spirit of an Arab soldier who had been dead for centuries. The only way she could retain her sanity was to believe that Uvani and the other entities who followed him, once the door had been opened through hypnosis, were in fact mere psychological phenomena rather than the literal and real beings they claimed to be. In her autobiography Eileen Garrett recalled those early days of mediumship:

I found myself extremely unready to accept the suggestion that any personality outside of myself could use any part of my being. Suddenly I found a part of me lost . . . and this is the part that is so baffling and which I have taken to so many in the scientific world for study. . . .

For weeks . . . I never slept without a light burning in my room and wondered all the time if this Uvani saw and heard everything I did in my daily life.[8]

Compelling Physiological Evidence

Hindu Yogis are often able, while in deep trance, to exhibit astonishing alterations in their basic bodily functions and metabolism. This ability is similar to the transformation of features which M. Scott Peck says he witnessed in the two cases of demonic possession/exorcism in which he participated. Since mediumship is a form of "voluntary possession," it is not surprising that the same incredible physiological transformations are also exhibited by genuine spiritualist mediums. Eileen Garrett was no exception. Tests conducted on her while in mediumistic trance produced results that astonished the examining physicians and made it seem very unlikely that the entities speaking through her could be archetypal symbols from the collective unconscious or splits of her own psyche. For example, when Abdul Latif was in control, Mrs. Garrett became a diabetic, although that was not her normal condition, nor was it manifest when she was under the control of any other entity.

Take, for example, one series of rigorous medical tests that was conducted in New York by Dr. Cornelium H. Traeger, a specialist in arthritis and heart disease. When he began the tests, Dr. Traeger held firmly to the common opinion of psychologists that Uvani, Latif, et al had to be splits of Garrett's psyche and not distinct alien entities with their own minds. Eileen herself wanted desperately to believe this. While Garrett was possessed by different "control" spirits, Traeger tested her "blood count, bleeding time, clotting time, respiration, pulse, heart pressure and cardiac reaction by an electrical cardiograph, as well as by the injection of various drugs."[9] According to an associate, Dr. Elmer Lindsay:

The results were . . . so surprising that Dr. Traeger

hesitated to show them to his colleagues. No human heart could show records so diametrically opposed and divergent. . . .

The tests were carried out with the full cooperation of Mrs. Garrett's two chief guides, Uvani and Abdul Latif. . . . When the bleeding time . . . blood counts [etc.] were checked the results suggested an actual change in the physical composition of the medium's blood when she was entranced [and different for each control entity].[10]

Other elaborate tests, both in waking and trance states, were administered to Mrs. Garrett and her "controls" by Hereward Carrington, director of the American Psychical Institute. Again the results were startling. Bernreuter Personality Inventory tests and the Page's Behavior Analysis indicated that the various voices speaking through Garrett in trance were *not* splits of her psyche at all but *independent personalities*. When Carrington tested Mrs. Garrett and the various entities speaking through her with a lie detector, the polygraph confirmed that each entity differed fundamentally from the medium and from each other. Referring to cases of alleged "multiple personality" that are now recognized as very similar to the "possession" experienced by mediums, Willis Harman points out:

The current surge of interest in this topic has come about partly because of the discovery that in these cases of personality shift, physiological and bio-chemical changes may be observed as well. These can include brainwave patterns, chemical composition of bodily fluids, immune status, allergies, skin electrical responses, and others.

This development leaves little doubt that in some important sense the alternate personality "really exists" as surely as does the usual personality.[11]

Strange Mixture of Fraud, Nonsense, and the Paranormal

Though she was a medium herself, Mrs. Garrett granted no credibility to the seance sessions of her day. She found that most of the "communications" that came through alleged mediums from those on the "other side" were trivial and boring, and wondered why it should be so. T. H. Huxley refused to waste his time listening to the senseless prattle of "ghosts." Confusion, misinformation, trivia, and double-talk made up most of the "messages" that came out of the mouths of professional mediums in seances. The same is largely true of today's "channelers." Yet mixed in with the nonsense (or outright fraud) is much that is clearly beyond the normal powers of the mediums to produce and thus seems to come from some independent intelligent source. After years spent investigating numerous mediums, Cambridge philosophy Professor C. D. Broad summed up his findings in these words:

> There is no doubt that, amongst that flood of dreary irrelevance and high-falutin twaddle which is poured out by trance mediums, there is a kind of residuum of genuinely paranormal material . . . in some of the most striking cases the surviving person [discarnate spirit] seems . . . to speak in its own characteristic voice and manner through the medium's lips. [12]

There is a strange mixture of fact and fraud that has been noted by every investigator of the craft, going all the way back to William James. After much investigation, that eminent psychologist considered Lenore Piper to be the most impressive trance medium of his day. Yet she had a "control" that claimed to be the spirit of a dead French physician named Dr. Phinult who was unable to speak French. "Phinult" could not explain that curious fact.

In spite of occasional misinformation, the "spirits" communicated much paranormal data through Mrs. Piper in many "readings" that James and his colleagues found inexplicable. There were numerous phenomena that were unquestionably not coincidence; but if genuine, then genuine *what*? The question continues to plague the investigators. New York City clinician Armand DiMele declares:

> I have spoken to "spirit voices" who have . . . told me things about my childhood. Specifics, like things that

hung in the house. There's some undeniable evidence that something happens, something we don't understand and can't measure.

Yet I don't think that most of the people who claim to be channels are channels.[13]

A Most Impressive Seance

Harry Price, world-famous "ghost hunter" and exposer of fraudulent mediums, had carefully tested Mrs. Garrett on numerous occasions and was thoroughly convinced of her genuineness. One example of what Price called Garrett's "brilliant successes" occurred in his laboratory while Eileen was attempting to make "contact" with the discarnate spirit of Sir Arthur Conan Doyle three months after his death. Uvani was speaking through Eileen, giving some routine information about a friend of Price's who had died a year earlier. Suddenly Uvani's voice transmuted, and in extremely agitated speech another male voice broke in. Flight Lieutenant Irwin, commanding officer of a newly constructed British experimental airship, the R101, as the voice identified itself, had been killed two days before when the dirigible had crashed in France on its way to India. Eileen Garrett had already "seen" the crash in three separate visions which she had reported over the preceding months.

Irwin's voice proceeded to give a lengthy and highly technical analysis of design weaknesses and a detailed account of exactly how and why the airship had gone down. Price's stenographer recorded everything. Although news of the catastrophe had appeared in the papers, its causes were still unknown. Subsequent seances were attended by Major Oliver G. Villier, senior assistant intelligence officer in the Air Ministry, who had been intimately involved with the R101 and was able (through Garrett and Uvani) to ask Irwin pointed questions. The answers that came through in Irwin's unmistakable voice contained so many details of names and conversations of those involved in the construction and so many highly technical details (including more than 40 specific military secrets) that Eileen Garrett was nearly arrested as a spy.

Will Charlton had been chief supply officer of the R101 during its construction at the Royal Airship works at Bedford. After poring over the transcript of the seances, Charlton called it "an astounding document" because of its mass of both secret and highly technical detail understandable only to an expert with firsthand knowledge of this particular airship. This undeniable evidence, Charlton said, forced him to the conclusion that the spirit of Flight Lieutenant H. Carmichael Irwin, captain of the shattered craft, "did actually communicate with those present at the seance after his physical death."[14] After reading *The Airmen Who Would Not Die*, by John G. Fuller (later condensed in *Reader's Digest*), which documents this incident and fills in some astonishing further threads of the story, Charles H. Gibbs-Smith, formerly Lindbergh Professor of Aerospace History, National Air and Space Museum at the Smithsonian Institute, declared:

> This book had to be written; and I, for one, am profoundly grateful. . . . It will become a prime source for evidence of human survival after death.
>
> To deny the basic evidence of Fuller's excellent work would be as foolish as to deny the existence of the Battle of Waterloo.[15]

Psychoanalyzing the Entities

The impressive evidence of apparent communication with spirits of the dead, which Eileen Garrett repeatedly produced, has been the subject of numerous studies and books. Yet to the day of her death, in 1970, Garrett herself remained uncertain of the true identity of these mysterious entities. There could be no doubt that many different voices speaking through her had consistently revealed information which she could not possibly have acquired by any normal means. Eileen remained unwilling, however, to believe that she was actually possessed by minds other than her own—yet the fear never left her that this might in fact be the case. Searching anxiously for proof that the phenomena could be explained in terms of her own subconscious mind or a collective unconscious, Garrett gave herself tirelessly and unreservedly to scientific research. For this reason alone the case of Eileen Garrett holds such importance for researchers today. She submitted to tests by scientists in Paris and Rome, at Cambridge and Oxford, at Columbia University and Johns

Hopkins Medical School, and by J. B. Rhine at Duke University—desperately hoping all the while for proof that these entities were nothing more than splits of her own psyche.

Eventually Eileen persuaded the celebrated psychotherapist Ira Progoff to psychoanalyze the entities that spoke through her. Perhaps he could establish that they were not independent personalities which had invaded her consciousness, as they claimed to be. Progoff conversed at length with the entity Uvani, who had been the first to take possession of Garrett. He had done so without her permission while she was under hypnosis and had continued to speak through her against her will. In addition to psychoanalyzing Uvani and Abdul Latif, Progoff also carried on lengthy dialogue with two "god figures," Tahoteh and Ramah, who also possessed Garrett. Progoff wrote:

> It is clear . . . that the figure of Tahoteh wishes to present himself as a god . . . in no sense comparable to the Western understanding of what God is [but] . . . a member of a pantheon of gods, as would be the case in Greece or India. . . .
>
> Tahoteh [seems to be] presenting himself as a personification of a basic principle of life, and thus as a godlike figure but not as an ultimate God.[16]

As a result of in-depth discussions with Ramah, Progoff decided that he had reached "the God principle which is within us all." Progoff's conclusion presents once again the pantheism/polytheism/naturalism which these entities consistently preach. It is basic Hinduism dressed in the language of psychology. In terminology reminiscent of what "Philemon" taught Carl Jung, Progoff refers to "the principle of life energy in the cosmos embodied as a personality in the symbolic form of Ramah" residing in the depths of the "collective unconscious." Ramah spoke so convincingly that Progoff felt that the language and concepts could hardly be coming from Mrs. Garrett's subconscious. Nevertheless, he clung to that theory because, like Garrett herself, he found the idea of outside spirit entities invading a human personality scientifically unacceptable. So much for the objectivity of "science."

Possible Evidence of Identity

Much of the communication still being received through the entities today reflects the same psychologically interpreted pantheistic philosophy that the Garrett entities preached. A classic case in point is *The Starseed Transmissions*, channeled by "Raphael" through Ken Carey[17] and called by Jean Houston "perhaps the finest example of 'channeled knowledge' I ever encountered."[18] Houston, in fact, could have written their script, so closely does it resemble her own beliefs. "We are you, yourself," declare the entities, "in the distant past and distant future. We exist in a parallel universe of non-form, experiencing what you would have experienced had you not become associated with the materializing processes."

As in *A Course in Miracles*, the communicating entity at times claims to be Christ. Whether one believes the Bible or not, the following representative "transmission" is clearly a diabolically clever perversion of what the biblical Christ taught:

> I am Christ. I am coming this day through the atmosphere of your consciousness. I am asking you to open the door of your reason, to allow me into your heart. . . .
>
> I came to you first through a man named Jesus . . . [and now] the bridegroom returns. Whoever will come after me will have to die to all definitions of self, take up my spirit, and follow along the lines of my vibrational field.[19]

Many Christians would consider today's proliferation of such communications to be a fulfillment of the biblical warning: "God's Spirit specifically tells us that in later days there will be men who abandon the true faith and allow themselves to be spiritually seduced by teachings of demons. . . ."[20] Those who reject that possibility must explain why the philosophy which the entities preach is so consistently antibiblical. Certainly the content of their message strongly suggests that they could well be the "teaching demons" referred to in the biblical warning. If this is not who they are, then what is their identity? We cannot simply dismiss the question of the source of the message by saying that it is not important.

If the entities are lying to us about their identity, that would cast a shadow over everything else they say, even though much of it may be "true" in a general sense. And if in fact (as some suggest) the "truth" is coming from the subconscious (or the collective unconscious), then why does the unconscious mind find it necessary to concoct fictitious entities in order to communicate with itself? There is something basically wrong about presenting "higher truth" by means of misinformation and symbols that are deceptive.

Could it be that the "entities" hope to make their fantastic claims of being "Christ" and "God" or beings from a "higher vibrational plane" more palatable by insisting at the same time, as they so often do, that their identity isn't important? Psychiatrist Ralph B. Allison, who has come to believe that the evidence supports the existence of disembodied minds, nevertheless told Jon Klimo in an interview:

> When I talk to the alleged spirits, they say, "Don't worry about where we come from or what's our address, or where we've lived before.". . .
>
> Who am I to argue? I don't know who they are. So I'm just telling you what they tell me. They don't come with ID cards. . . .
>
> I'm in the business of helping people, and I could care less where the information comes from.[21]

Evidence of a Nonhuman Source

Some psychologists have attempted to explain channeling or mediumship by resorting to a super-ESP theory, which suggests that the medium is somehow tapping into all of the knowledge in the universe contained in Jung's collective unconscious. Once again it seems to be a case of straining at a gnat and swallowing a camel. The proposal of such an incredible theory would not be necessary if the existence of nonhuman intelligences, to which the evidence seems most obviously to point, were accepted. Recognizing the extreme irony, paranormal debunker Marcello Truzzi points out that this "super-ESP" theory "isn't any less extraordinary than the thing it's trying to explain away—channeling."[22]

In a recent bulletin from the Institute of Noetic Sciences (founded by ex-astronaut Edgar Mitchell), Institute president Willis Harman refers to some very remarkable data. While it does not help to *identify* the entities involved, *it does eliminate the possibility that the communication is coming from any human agency either through the unconscious or ESP of any kind*. This particular evidence points conclusively to the existence of distinct entities as the real explanation of mediumship and channeling.

Harman likens the reluctance of today's scientific community to accept the existence of spirit entities to the attitude toward meteorites on the part of the French Academy of Science in the eighteenth century. They insisted that those who claimed to have seen "flaming stones" falling out of the sky had to be hallucinating, because "there are no stones in the sky to fall." Pointing out that theories of the medium's ESP abilities or subconscious mind or a collective unconscious have no possible connection to communications coming out of nonhuman electronic devices, Harman writes:

> Very briefly, the "electronic voice phenomenon" which Mr. [George] Meek [of Franklin, North Carolina] has explored is the following. Under certain conditions a tape on an audiotape recorder, set on "record" but with no signal input of the usual sort, has been found when replayed to contain an intelligible voice recording that purports to be a communication from a person sometime deceased.
>
> The phenomenon has been repeated many times, with many assortments of witnesses. . . .
>
> Only this year a group of researchers in Luxemburg was carrying out similar experimentation when they received "instructions" to have a TV camera set up on a tripod and focus on the picture tube of an old TV set. In a manner similar to the "electronic voice phenomenon," the videotape recorded a number of still pictures, each lasting a fraction of a second.
>
> Some of these appeared to be photographs of identifiable persons, now dead, typically the way they looked as

young adults. Other pictures appeared to be landscapes, which a "spirit guide" explained as "test signals."[23]

To present further evidence here would serve no purpose. What is now needed is to establish the origin and identity of these mysterious "minds from beyond."

11

Minds from Beyond

No one finds the existence of "spirit entities" and the suggestion that they might be influencing human beliefs and behavior more repugnant than the Committee for the Scientific Investigation of Claims of the Paranormal (CSICOP). It is headed by State University of New York philosophy professor and tireless antisupernatural crusader Paul Kurtz. Even though its membership includes such luminaries as Carl Sagan, Isaac Asimov, and B. F. Skinner, CSICOP seems to be losing its stubborn battle to educate the public against what it considers to be a modern revival of superstition. Organized in 1976, CSICOP held its fourth world conference in April 1986 in Boulder, Colorado (which, ironically enough, although a university city, is overwhelmingly New Age). CSICOP's members are frustrated "that the most technologically advanced society in history still favors tabloid headlines about ESP, UFOs, and poltergeists to the studied opinions of scientific journals."[1]

Credit must be given, nevertheless, to Kurtz's organization, and in particular to Randall Zwinge (better known as the "Amazing Randi") and his colleagues, for exposing deceptive techniques used by some television evangelists. It was Randi who first disclosed that flamboyant "faith healer" Peter Popoff's "revelations" of names, addresses, and ailments of the ill were actually being transmitted from his wife backstage into a tiny radio receiver hidden in his ear. In spite of such exposés, however, there is growing concern that CSICOP is fostering an antisupernatural hysteria, which University of Oregon psychologist Ray Hyman, though himself a critic of psychic research, describes as "a 'witch-hunting' mentality that has nothing to do with science." In fact sociologist Marcello Truzzi, a cofounder of CSICOP, "left the organization when he grew concerned that it was becoming an 'inquisitional body.' "[2]

Prejudice Posing as Science

Kurtz insists that "psychics are either deluding themselves or the public, or both."[3] While that may be true in many cases, the professional skeptics who speak for CSICOP seem to come to this blanket conclusion more from a bias against the supernatural than from a thorough examination of all of the evidence. Ironically, Kurtz and his fellow antisupernatural dogmatists may unwittingly be contributing to the very delusion they seek to expose and dispel. Those who deny the existence of a disease because the virus causing it has never been identified only help to spread the plague. C. S. Lewis's "senior devil" Screwtape, at least, seemed to have this up his sleeve as an optional strategy.

Those who worship at the altars of scientific materialism are exceedingly jealous of any rival religion that seems to challenge their revered dogmas. The popular image of the impartial scientist on a quest for truth is not always valid. It was not only the church that hounded Galileo, but his fellow scientists as well. The classic case of Ignaz Semmelweis is only representative of similar travesties perpetrated down through history by scientists defending their prejudices. In 1847, as a young physician in charge of an obstetrical ward in Vienna's famous Allegemeine Krankenhaus, Semmelweis began to require doctors to wash their hands after dissecting corpses and before examining the living, and also between examinations of individual patients. The mortality rate dropped dramatically from one in six women to one in fifty.

Instead of being acclaimed, Semmelweis was scorned, belittled, and hounded from the hospital by his colleagues. Needless to say, the mortality rate shot back up as soon as he left. Unable to find employment in Vienna, he was forced to go as far as Budapest to obtain a position in another hospital. There he accomplished the same dramatic reduction in mortality in his wing; yet again he was ridiculed and shunned for his hygienic regime, in spite of the lives he saved. Haunted by the cries of dying mothers and the contempt with which his lifesaving methods were viewed by his fellow doctors, Semmelweis died in a mental institution, a broken man.

Is it possible that disbelief in invisible germs in the 1850's is analogous to the disbelief in invisible entities and psychic powers (or psi) today? It is easy to see why the idea of *extrasensory* perception is so distasteful to the materialist. For all of his protestations of *objectivity* in examining the possibility of psi, the dyed-in-the-wool skeptic has predetermined the only conclusion he can reach by denying the existence of the very thing he claims to be scientifically testing. It is obviously wrong to demand a *physical* explanation for *spiritual* experiences. That is like denying the reality of *smell* because it can't be *felt* or insisting that because *honesty* and *justice* have no *taste* they should therefore be disallowed. As Leslie Shepard points out in *The Encyclopedia of Occultism and Parapsychology*:

> It is difficult to combine an attitude of impartial inquiry with a stance of scientific authority when there is an implicit initial assumption that all claims of the paranormal are erroneous and fraudulent.

Defending its dogmas seems to have become more important to CSICOP than respecting truth. Keith Harary dismisses CSICOP as "a cult of believers in the absence of psychic functioning," and points out that CSICOP audaciously claims to represent the scientific community, when in fact it doesn't. Another critic of CSICOP says, "We know it [psi] works and if they want to sit back there with the Flat Earth Society and say, 'It can't exist because it threatens my world view,' that's fine."[4] Referring to the traditional "scientific skepticism toward various 'supernatural' and 'paranormal' phenomena," Robert Anton Wilson declares in *The New Inquisition*:

> To deny dogmatically is to say that something is impossible. In a century in which every decade has brought new and astonishing scientific shocks, that is a huge, brave and audacious faith indeed.[5]

The Birth of Parapsychology

It was out of a desire to understand psychic phenomena on a rational level that a new branch of psychology known as parapsychology was formed.[6] Parapsychology has been defined as "the attempt to apply scientific method and/or critical investigation to phenomena which are 'paranormal' . . . [i.e.] outside the normal paradigms of science and critical reasoning."[7] It is therefore not surprising that parapsychologists have experienced much difficulty in attempting to establish scientific verification for psychic phenomena, and much skepticism from the scientific community as well. Nevertheless, among the early investigators into psychic phenomena were some of the most renowned scientists and psychologists in history.[8]

Harvard professor William James was one of the pioneers in this new field of investigation. Turning away from his earlier belief that human personality and behavior could be explained in materialistic/ deterministic terms, James became a supporter of religious and mystical experiences and embraced the belief that "higher powers exist and are at work to save the world. . . ." After much investigation, James also became, like Freud and Jung, a firm believer in psychic phenomena. His writings growing out of his monumental work in this field were edited and published in 1960 under the title *William James and Psychical Research*.

Another distinguished Harvard University professor of psychology, William McDougall, who became chairman of the psychology department at Duke University, was also one of the pioneers in psychical research. It was at Duke under McDougall's direction that J. B. Rhine established his world-famous Parapsychology Laboratory, where psychokinesis (mind over matter, or PK) was first scientifically demonstrated. After Rhine's death, in 1980, his work was carried on by his wife, Louisa, who was also a respected parapsychologist.

The Question of Survival

In every culture down through history, paranormal powers have always been associated with *spirit* entities variously believed to be gods, ascended masters, or spirits of the dead. The idea that human "mind power" could be responsible is a new invention that was required when the former belief in spirits became unacceptable. While the scientific study of ESP, PK, and other psychic powers may seem unrelated to mediumship, parapsychology actually began as an attempt to examine the question of the soul's survival beyond the body's death. The first subjects of early experiments were "spirit mediums" (also known as "trance mediums"), some of whom have, during the last hundred years, produced convincing evidence of paranormal powers, which they generally credited to spirits of the dead.

The British Society for Psychical Research (SPR) was formed in 1882 with distinguished Cambridge professor Henry Sidgwick as its first president. The SPR was determined to take a "scientific" approach in examining whether the soul and/or spirit could survive bodily death. Frederic W. H. Myers, one of the SPR's early leaders, declared: "We must experiment unweariedly; we must continue to demolish fiction as well as to accumulate truth; we must make no terms with any hollow mysticism, any half-conscious deceit."[9] After his death, an entity claiming to be the spirit of Myers produced, as Myers had promised he would, one of the most convincing pieces of evidence for mediumship on record. In the so-called "cross-correspondences," fragmentary communications, meaningless in themselves, were received by mediums widely separated around the world, which, when put together, fit like pieces of a puzzle to provide a coherent series of messages.

To a large extent the SPR grew out of the Cambridge University Ghost Club. In its early days the SPR attracted a number of young intellectuals who, having turned "to psychic research as a substitute for their lost Evangelical faith,"[10] were to become famous as leaders in the Fabian Society. In 1885 the American Society for Psychical Research was formed in New York, with William James as one of its early members. Researchers in both societies devised elaborate experiments and spent decades working with trance mediums in an attempt to verify whether discarnate spirits of the dead were in fact speaking through them as they claimed. There are exhaustive published reports of this research.

In the final analysis the evidence did not establish the proof for "survival" that had been sought. It did seem clear that intelligences other than the mediums' own minds were involved, but whether these entities correctly identified themselves when speaking through the mediums in trance remained a puzzling dilemma. Researchers to this day have not been able to answer that question on "scientific" grounds. The experiments added further support, however, to the belief that man has a soul and/or spirit that probably survives death. Moreover, the nonphysical nature of the mind seemed to open the possibility to the exercise of psychic powers.

Growing Scientific Acceptance

Former president of the Association for Humanistic Psychology and considered by many to be the successor to Margaret Mead, Jean Houston declares that "we are about to acquire the powers of Genesis. . . . We are living in mythic times and we are getting mythic powers."[11] By "mythic powers" Houston means something beyond the physical products of technology and reaching out into the *spiritual* dimension. Research into psychokinesis (PK) by Duke University professor J. B. Rhine, the father of American parapsychology, uncovered persuasive evidence for the existence of *mind* as a nonphysical entity capable of influencing the material world. Commenting upon his discovery, Rhine declared:

> It staggers my imagination to conceive all the implications that follow now that it has been shown that . . . energies operate in PK [that involve] a mental force that is as yet entirely unrecognized in any of the physical sciences. . . .
>
> The evidence of PK along with that of ESP establishes the case for the reality of mind. . . . Now for the first time mind is what the man in the street thought it was all along. . . .
>
> The man in the pulpit too was right in preaching that the human spirit is something more than the material of his body and brain. For the first time, science offered a little support to his view . . . of man's nature . . . the result of principles hitherto overlooked by the sciences.[12]

The research of Rhine and others who followed in his footsteps was disregarded or derided by the scientific establishment for many years. Parapsychology was the unwanted stepchild which none of the sciences was willing to take in and nourish. More recently, however, on the basis of increasing evidence, many leading scientists are converting from skepticism to firm belief in the paranormal. One example is Brian Josephson, recipient of the Nobel prize in physics in 1973 and a professor at Cambridge University (which, like the University of California at Berkeley, awarded its first doctorate in parapsychology in the late 1970's). He "describes himself as '99 percent convinced' of the reality of paranormal events . . . [and] that the case for psychokinesis is particularly strong."[13]

Willis W. Harman is another person whose impressive credentials would seem to mark him as an unlikely candidate for the mysticism he now espouses. A Stanford University professor of engineering-economic systems, Harman is also a senior scientist at SRI and one of the early organizers and an executive board member of the Association for Humanistic Psychology. As long ago as 1975, in his special address to the Annual Parapsychological Association Convention, Professor Harman stated:

> The paramount fact that has emerged [from psychic research] is the duality of his [man's] experience. He is found to be both physical and spiritual, both aspects being 'real' and neither fully describable in terms of the other. "Scientific" and "religious" metaphors are complementary; neither contradicts the other.[14]

Such a concession from a scientist as influential as Harman understandably raises the anxiety level of the materialists who had hoped that science would by now have laid "religious myths" to rest. Some of the reasons why science could never replace religion have already been addressed. In his keynote speech at the August 1979 annual convention of the Institute for Transpersonal Psychology, Harman pointed out:

> A couple of generations ago most educated people were quite certain that materialistic science had clearly won the "warfare between science and religion," and that such improbable ideas as "mind over matter" were banished once and for all.
>
> It now appears that . . . mind can remotely [i.e. at a distance] exert influence in the physical world.[15]

Practical Applications of Psychic Powers

Perhaps one of the most incredible things about psychic power is that it still has its believers in spite of the abysmal failure of its popular seers to predict accurately. As skeptic Al Seckel pointed out early in 1988, one-third of Jeane Dixon's predictions for 1987 were hardly psychic ("the IRS and the public will be confused by the new tax laws," etc.), the second third "were so vague that it is impossible to say if they came true or not," and the remainder were laughable. "In the one-third of her predictions that most clearly call for 'psychic' powers, the only correct one was that Elizabeth Taylor would not remarry again in 1987." Not only did the sensational predictions of numerous popular psychics (marriage for Senator Edward Kennedy, spoon-bending TV appearances by Prince Charles, an assassination attempt upon Soviet leader Gorbachev, etc.) not happen, but, as Seckel pointed out under the facetious heading "Tabloid Psychics Failed to Predict '87 Would Be a Bad Year for Them":

> . . . not one of the tabloid psychics predicted any of the genuinely surprising news stories of 1987: the Dow Jones Industrial Average falling more than 500 points in a single day . . . the downing of a jetliner by a revengeful ex-employee believed to have shot the flight crew . . . the unexpected withdrawal of Gary Hart from the presidential race over a sex scandal and his equally unexpected reentry into the race . . . [etc.][16]

In spite of the many failures, however, the fact that psychic powers have often been put to practical use is now a matter of indisputable record. In numerous criminal cases psychics have provided key information which they unquestionably derived by some unknown means beyond normal human capabilities. In one well-known case, Los Altos, California, psychic M. Kathlyn Rhea was called in by police who had been unable to locate two missing persons. Rhea not only pinpointed with astonishing accuracy the locations (in rough terrain) of the victims' two widely separated bodies, but correctly gave the cause and manner of death in each case (one had died of natural causes and the other had been murdered by heavy blows to the head). Without the psychic information supplied by Rhea, police doubted that one of the bodies would ever have been found.[17]

Similar cases are numerous and well-documented. More recently Etta Louise Smith of Pacoima, California, was "jailed for four days after saying that a 'psychic vision' enabled her to lead Los Angeles police to the body of a slain nurse." After questioning Smith for ten hours, the police arrested her, unable to believe that she could have known the location of the body by the incredible means she claimed. Four days later, however, when the murderer confessed and implicated two other people, none of whom had any connection to Smith, she was released. On March 30, 1987, a Van Nuys Superior Court Jury awarded Smith $26,184 for false arrest and imprisonment. As the *Los Angeles Times* reported:

> Jury foreman Janet Fowler of Burbank said that most jurors believed Smith's story that she had a psychic vision and they felt that an award equivalent to a year's salary for Smith was fair.[18]

No one has put psychic power to more practical use than experimental psychologist Keith Harary, SRI physicist Russell Targ, and businessman Anthony White, who have teamed together to form Delphi Associates. Located in San Mateo, California, the unusual partnership offers clients "psi-derived prognostications for business decisions. And they are turning a nice profit."[19] The projects which Delphi has done for clients have included such widely varied services as predicting silver futures and psychically surveying oil company land by "remote viewing" in order to choose between geologically established drilling sites, "assess underground conditions and give a rough estimate of what the well's output will be." With an understandable air of satisfaction, Russell Targ declares:

> And if there is anything Delphi Associates has already shown, it is that "psychic functioning is alive and well."
>
> People are making money with psi, and Delphi is supporting itself.[20]

A Psychic War?

Periodic reports from the scientific community are still being issued denying the existence of psychic powers. The latest came with the announcement in December 1987 that a two-year, 425,000-dollar study by the National Academy of Sciences had concluded that "130 years of research has produced 'no scientfic justification' to support widespread belief in the existence of extrasensory perception, mental telepathy or similar phenomena."[21] In fact, only about 65,000 dollars was allocated for the study of what was described as "the so-called 'incredible technologies,' including parapsychology [psychic research]," so the outcome was not surprising.

Nevertheless, inside informants continue to insist that the United States government is taking psychic power seriously enough to spend millions on secret research, and that the Soviets are doing likewise. Neither side can afford to let the other get too far ahead in this area. It is no longer science fiction to imagine a future confrontation between the world's superpowers involving not only reading the minds of enemy leaders and predicting strategic events, but mentally jamming computers and erasing magnetic tape at a distance, and even creating confusion or causing key personnel to act against their own interests. Representative Charles Rose (D-NC), a member of the House Select Committee on Intelligence, "calls the possibility of 'psychic war' all too real." Charles Wallach, one of the most visible experts in this area, has proposed the establishment of a "non-speculative, scientific, investigatory *Journal of Psychic Warfare*."[22]

It has been estimated that "the Soviet Union has about thirty government-run parapsychological laboratories," while officially the U.S. has none.[23] Rose favors increased expenditures for "research on the national security implications of PSI,"[24] arguing logically that "if the Russians have it and we don't, we are in serious trouble." Having done psychic research for the U.S. government and having also spent time in discussion with Soviet parapsychologists in the USSR,[25] Keith Harary (who has profited by taking his own advice) declares impatiently:

It's time to stop arguing about whether psychic functioning exists and to start *using* it.[26]

The dangerous possibilities can no longer be dismissed by smug skepticism. Brooklyn's Maimonides Medical Center parapsychologist Charles Honorton says, "The likelihood of negative application [of psi] frightens me greatly."[27] Harary and Targ are convinced that Soviet parapsychologists are involved in experiments for "behavior manipulation from a distance."[28]

Due to its top-secret status, it is difficult to obtain accurate information about military or other government experiments involving psychic power. However, bits of information are periodically leaked to the press, such as the following news brief early in 1987 in *U.S. News & World Report*: "Foreign Relations Chairman Claiborne Pell last week reserved a vault in the attic of the Capitol—a room often used to examine top-secret documents. Purpose: to assemble government officials to hear Israeli psychic Uri Geller reveal what he has divined of Soviet strategic intentions. Geller, who claims to be able to bend spoons with mind power, once briefed former President Jimmy Carter."[29]

Minds from Beyond?

Geller has borne the brunt of much of the ridicule coming from the critics of psychic research. Along with a number of other professional magicians, the "Amazing Randi" has boasted that he can reproduce most of Uri Geller's feats with a combination of sleight of hand, misdirected attention, and patented paraphernalia.[30] Theatrical magicians complain that the scientists who test psychics are not competent to detect fraud because they know nothing of stage magic. In fact a cloud of skepticism hangs over Geller and he "has not been accepted by most parapsychological investigators."[31]

Yet one of those who tested Geller was W. E. Cox, formerly on J. B. Rhine's staff at Duke University and himself a magician who has served as chairman of the Society of American Magicians National Occult Committee. Uri passed the three tests which Cox imposed, the most impressive involving a watch into which Cox had previously inserted a strip of tinfoil to jam the balance wheel. Yet Uri started the watch by concentrating upon it. When Cox later opened it he found that the tinfoil had been broken and moved out of the way in a manner that could not be explained naturally. This is only one of many similar feats produced by Geller and other psychics that could not possibly be dismissed as some kind of magician's sleight of hand. Said Cox:

> Insofar as the question of deception by Geller is concerned, I believe . . . that it has been ruled out as the explanation of these three effects.[32]

While Stanford Research Institute (now called SRI) was preparing to put him through tests of his psychic powers for a documentary film, Uri Geller complained that most parapsychologists misunderstood the true source of this mysterious force. "They keep talking about *my mind*," he said. Uri then explained that in his opinion psychic power didn't emanate from his mind at all but from *other minds*—entities from another planet who were telepathically channeling the power through him for their own purposes, and that he *had* to obey.

"I have no choice," Uri told ex-astronaut Edgar Mitchell and several SRI scientists, "because *they* direct me. I can't go against [*them*]."

None of the SRI scientists brushed Uri's astonishing statement aside as paranoia. Russell Targ replied: "The things you are telling us agree very well with things that Hal [SRI colleague Harold Puthoff] and I believe, but we can't prove." Added Mitchell: "Uri, you're not saying anything to us we don't in some way already sense or understand."[33]

The Burning Issue

Uri's comments, rather than reflecting something new, solely compatible with modern science, and related to the space age and extraterrestrial intelligences, are in fact right in line with ancient occult tradition. At the heart of all occultism are rituals embodying secret words, symbols, potions, movements, etc. which are carried out with the hope of securing from invisible entities either special knowledge or supernatural power. Whether the entities are called "ETI's" by Uri Geller or "Masters of the Great School" by Napoleon Hill or "inner guides" by Stanford University's Graduate School of Business seems to be immaterial. This is classical sorcery (or shamanism), in which the reliance upon nonphysical entities has always been the cornerstone. Anthropologist Michael Harner reminds us:

> To perform his work, the shaman depends on special, personal power, which is usually supplied by his guardian and helping spirits.
>
> Each shaman generally has at least one guardian spirit in his service . . . [and] without a guardian spirit it is virtually impossible to be a shaman. . . .[34]

After all of the research, we are left with two possibilites for explaining the psychic powers and paranormal knowledge displayed at times by such persons as a Uri Geller or an Eileen Garrett: 1) human minds, or 2) nonhuman minds. Clearly no *individual* human mind has either the power or the knowledge to produce the verified paranormal phenomena. The weight of evidence points to the involvement of nonhuman minds.

It is at this point, however, just as it would seem that we could identify these entities, that we notice something peculiar. The message which they most consistently preach denies their individual existence as separate from mankind. In spite of the various identities they assume, from dead relatives to space brothers to ascended masters, there is the claim of being the varied expressions of a universal consciousness, of which all things are a part. If this is true, it would mean that human minds, being themselves part of the one Universal Mind, would have unlimited potential—even the ability to create their own reality. That possibility must be explored.

12

Creating One's Own Reality

It is important to remind ourselves of what we have established to this point. Whether one is involved in psychotherapy, witchcraft, channeling, or self-improvement techniques, the underlying philosophy is the same. The entire New Age movement embodies ancient occult ideas repackaged in pseudoscientific language for modern consumption. It is naturalism/pantheism/polytheism in opposition to supernaturalism/monotheism. In this scheme of things, man is a creature of the impersonal and uncreated cosmos rather than of a personal Creator, and contains within himself (by virtue of his oneness with the cosmos) all wisdom, knowledge, and power. This is not ordinarily apparent because we have "forgotten" our true identity; and these limitless resources, which are now known only to the alleged "higher self," lie buried in Jung's "collective unconscious." In order to tap this inner potential, New Age methodologies have borrowed from Eastern religions the dubious concept of gaining insight ("enlightenment") and effecting changes in behavior and well-being through "altering" consciousness.

In altered states of consciousness a new "reality" is experienced, often accompanied by the conviction that the entire universe is simply a projection of one's mind. From this it follows that to change our *awareness* (the basic element of consciousness) is to change our universe. In his new book, *Global Mind Change*, Willis Harman explains that "by deliberately changing their internal image of reality, people are changing the world." Of course this is not a new belief, but has been the basic element of Eastern mysticism for thousands of years. The fact that the countries which have been practicing this philosophy the longest, notably India and Tibet, are among the most deprived areas of the world should be evidence enough that something is wrong. In spite of that fact, however, Westerners are looking to the Eastern gurus for "enlightenment."

If Wishes Were Horses

And now we have an explosion of messages from alleged "higher beings" promoting this perennial philosophy. The "channeled entities," no matter how they represent themselves, consistently teach that we create our own reality with our minds. "Seth," for example, declares, "You are given the gift of the gods; you create your reality according to your beliefs. . . ."[1] Jon Klimo calls this teaching "Seth's chief contribution."[2] Ramtha, who tells us, "Love yourself, you are God," also declares that "we create our own realities within which to express ourselves, against which to react, from which to learn, and in which to evolve." Again Klimo reminds us that this view "is virtually identical with . . . many other channeled materials."[3]

For many years Rosicrucian ads in magazines and newspapers have been offering initiation into the "psychic faculties of man [which] know no barriers of space or time," yet we see no one displaying the powers alluded to. In spite of that obvious failure, any number of popular self-improvement seminar leaders and mind-dynamics courses are now promoting this same delusion that was once the exclusive stock in trade of small esoteric organizations and witch covens. The Silva Method teaches that whatever the individual can visualize in his or her mind can be brought into existence in the physical world by that same mental power. "Get What You Want Through Self-Directed Mind Power" declares a competing technique's brochure, sounding an appeal that is very hard to resist for those who want to impose their will upon the universe. Marilyn Zdenek, highly acclaimed by university professors, business lead-and celebrities, teaches a seminar titled "Inventing the Future: Advances in Imagery That Can Change Your Life." Foretelling the future is no longer good enough; now we are going to make it all turn out our way.

Here is the stuff of fairy tales, of the dreams of Camelot, of the philosophy to which the simple response remains: "If wishes were horses, everyone would ride." No matter how sincere both teachers and pupils may be, they have left the real world of verifiable data and common sense to create their own fantasyland. Yet New Age writers claim that not only the "channeled" spirit entities but also the new physics confirms the Hindu belief that there is no objective universe; it is all *maya*, an illusion that we have created with our minds. Supposedly we can be "liberated" from this collective delusion through changing our awareness. In a classic flimflam, we are being persuaded to believe that the normal objective reality experienced in ordinary consciousness is unreal and that the illusion experienced on drugs, in Yoga, or in other altered states of consciousness is the true reality.

That thesis, however, rather than being supported by science as claimed, is in fact denied by it according to the scientists who gave us the new physics. It is true that Sir James Jeans, Sir Arthur Eddington, Erwin Schroedinger, and others among the greatest scientists of this century spoke of the stuff of the universe as "mind stuff." By that statement they did *not* mean, however (as today's popularizers of Eastern mysticism would have us believe), that we create reality with our minds and that there is therefore no real world out there for us to perceive. They simply meant that we cannot have a direct experience of the objective world around us, but that all we can know of it is a mental sensation or image.

The reader, for example, has no direct experience of the book presently being read. Light photons bouncing off the page cause a visual image in the eyes, which is carried to and interpreted by the brain. Nerves in the fingers connect to a neural network, which carries a sensation of touch (texture, weight, etc.) to the brain—and that mental impression is all the reader can know of the physical substance of the object being held and read.

In no case do we have a direct experience of the thing itself, but only what is mediated by the five senses and interpreted by the brain. In fact the new physics, rather than supporting mysticism, tells us that we cannot know anything of the physical universe around us except through this mental image, and as represented by mathematical symbols. Yet mysticism claims to give an unmediated experience of the cosmos itself. Thus the mystical experience, contrary to popular claims, is not supported by science and involves delusion rather than enlightenment.

Certain writers assure us that the new physics somehow demonstrates that the very act of observing an event in the physical world mysteriously interferes with it—and that this proves that we do create reality with our minds. By "faith" the average person accepts this assertion as "scientific fact," even though it quite clearly contradicts the daily experiences of a lifetime. What is generally not explained is that this "interference" occurs only in a very special situation and for obvious reasons.

Radar beams (radio waves) must be continuously bounced off a plane flying across the sky in order to calculate its speed, direction, and position at any time. Of course radar or light bouncing off a plane has only an infinitesimal effect upon it. When observing a tiny subatomic particle, however, it is necessary to bounce off of it a particle of its same size. Obviously that "interferes" with the particle being observed. The resulting interference should be no more surprising or mysterious than the fact that bouncing an airplane off of an airplane would also "interfere" with its flight. In neither case, however, does such interference come from the *mind* of the observer, and therefore it cannot be used to support the belief that we influence, much less create, the world about us by our thoughts.

Hinduism and Modern Science

Encouraged by New Age apostles such as Fritjof Capra (*The Tao of Physics* and *The Turning Point*) and Gary Zukav (*The Dancing Wu Li Masters*), the belief is growing that modern physics and ancient mystical traditions have striking parallels that lead to similar views of reality and thus justify a merger between the two. The facts are quite the opposite. Rather than supporting Eastern mysticism because it is so similar, modern physics actually has little in common with it.

In addition to his claim that he has a direct experience of the essence of the universe (which science denies is possible, as we have just seen), the mystic also claims to "experience" the unity of all things, including his own "oneness" with the cosmos, as though the universe were his own body and the expression of his mind. In contrast again, the physicist declares that the universe is a separate reality and therefore this experience of "oneness" with the All is a deception. Mysticism denies any reality external to the mind, while the physicist declares that the external world is in fact real and that we have no way of comparing our mental impressions of the universe with its true character and essence. For these reasons Ken Wilber declares: "What an absolute, radical, irredeemable difference [separates science] from mysticism!"[4]

Most physicists disagree with the thesis of Capra and Zukav, which would not be the case if it followed from the evidence. In fact, Capra admits that his theory (which is so popular among New Agers) did not result from insight gained through scientific observation, but actually came about through a powerful mystical experience he had in 1969 "on a beach in Santa Cruz [California]."[5] In *The Tao of Physics* he writes:

> Five years ago, I had a beautiful experience which set me on a road that has led to the writing of this book. I was sitting by the ocean one late summer afternoon . . . when I suddenly became aware of my whole environment as being engaged in a gigantic cosmic dance. . . .
>
> I "saw" the atoms of the elements and those of my body participating in this cosmic dance of energy, I felt its rhythm and "heard" its sound, and at that moment I *knew* that this was the Dance of Shiva, the Lord of Dancers worshipped by the Hindus.[6]

Presumably this religious experience of "cosmic consciousness," or the "oneness of all," that is attained in an altered state provides an insight into the actual reality underlying the universe—a reality that we do not ordinarily recognize because our perception is flawed. Before accepting such a thesis, however, one cannot help wondering how and why, if all is perfect, our perception could be imperfect. From what source did this imperfection arise to mar the perfection of the All? If all is indeed one, then how could we even have the illusion of separation from the universal consciousness and unified whole, of which we are allegedly an intimate part? And why is there so much conflict within the individual human heart and so much jealousy, hatred, greed, and antagonism exhibited toward fellow members of the race?

Whether the altered state of consciousness that brought "enlightenment" came about through drugs or Eastern meditation, the fact remains that Capra's present obsession is not the result of scientific investigation or evidence but of a classic Hindu mystical experience. In *The Tao of Physics* and *The Turning Point*, Capra argues for an integration of Eastern and Western thought in order to bring about what he perceives as a necessary "revolution in all the sciences and a transformation of our world view and values." It would not seem advisable, however, to base such a "revolution" in scientific thinking upon a religious insight such as Capra experienced in an altered state of consciousness.

In the Mind of Some Eternal Spirit

Sir James Jeans demolished the view of Capra, Zukav, et al long before it became popular. Jeans demonstrated that there is in fact an objective world and that this would not be the case if reality were the creation of individual minds. He did this very simply by presenting three criteria which are essential for objective reality: *surprise, continuity,* and *change.* What he meant is easily illustrated.

Twenty million people are suddenly awakened from a sound sleep by an earthquake in Mexico City, an earthquake which kills many of them by collapsing the homes and apartments they occupy. The fact that so many people were *surprised* by this event, indeed awakened by the shaking and roaring of an earthquake that they certainly were not even dreaming of, is evidence enough that an objective reality imposed itself upon its victims. It would be madness to suggest that a hurricane or a fire that guts a hotel was created in the minds of those who experienced it. Yet new-consciousness gurus continue to promote and sell various techniques for creating one's own reality, and the customers are still eagerly paying for seminars that will supposedly teach them to develop this amazing human potential.

Such ideas are being taken seriously even by our top government officials. Consider, for example, the statements of ex-astronaut Edgar D. Mitchell in an address to members of Congress and Congressional staff on behalf of the Congressional Clearinghouse on the Future:

Within ten years, psychokinetic functioning will be

reasonably well accepted. It knocks down the previous model of the human; there is something more fundamental than the material we are made of.

We can control, external to our bodies, the matter that is around us, and control internally the functioning of our bodies, by the way we think.[7]

There are only two years left of Mitchell's projected ten years for this new paradigm to be in operation, and we are no closer than we were 3000 years ago when the same ideas were being taught by Yogis in India. Consider Jeans's second reason why this dream must forever remain a delusion: the *continuity* of objective reality. After a 20-year absence you return to your high school for a reunion. The same rooms in which you once attended class are there, complete with desks, blackboards, and cracks in the ceiling—everything that you had never given a thought to during the 20-year interval. Everything has remained in place without your mind supporting its existence.

Such *continuity* proves the objectivity of the world independent of human minds, a *continuity* without which life would be impossible. Imagine the chaos if reality were in fact the product of billions of individual minds of independent and forgetful (or even insane) nature. Whose "reality" would be dominant, and how often would one person's self-created "reality" suddenly be overturned by another's imposing itself?

There have also been many *changes* at your high school during your absence. The old gymnasium has been torn down and a new and much larger one stands in its place. *Change* such as this, coming without our knowledge in places we have forgotten, clearly has occurred without our minds creating it. This too demonstrates the objectivity of the physical universe about us. So Jeans argues that these three elements—*surprise, continuity*, and *change*—prove that the world about us is not created by our minds but has in fact an objective reality of its own independent of anything we may think or do.

Nevertheless, the universe seems more like a great thought than a great machine. Consequently, Jeans concluded that it must subsist "in the mind of some Eternal Spirit," who is in fact its Creator. Far from mentally creating reality, mankind has been struggling to discover the incredible secrets of a universe which is at once so awesome in size and yet so intricate in minutest detail that it reflects the genius of a Designer whose mind is infinitely beyond human capabilities. The theory that we can create our own reality would seem to represent the envy and rebellion of little minds with delusions of grandeur who have an insatiable desire to play God.

Nevertheless, the belief that we have already conspired to create the delusion we now call reality, and from which our imaginings can deliver us, grows ever more popular. In *Shifting Worlds, Changing Minds: Where the Sciences and Buddhism Meet*, Jeremy W. Hayward argues that everything we see and experience in the world about us is mere illusion: "Our belief that we are like that creates each other." The mere fact that the universe obviously existed before homo sapiens came along to "create" reality with his imagination ought to be sufficient to end such theories, yet they persist. In a March, 1988 *Los Angeles Times* review of *Shifting Worlds*, Jonathan Kirsch writes:

> In other words, Hayward insists, my wife's beauty and grace and kindness, her engagement in our family and her commitment . . . are essentially an illusion, a fabrication of my consciousness, which is itself an illusion.
>
> "To think that there is a real, objective and external Universe, independent of mind and observation," writes Hayward, "is no longer an acceptable attitude with which to approach . . . reality.". . .
>
> I persist in believing that . . . the fact that the stuff of a chaotic universe can take the form of a human being— with all of our marvelous gifts of passion and intellect, our fascination for the world around us, our commitment to life and love—is nothing less than miraculous, and perhaps the best argument that we are, after all, the handiwork of the Almighty.

The Most Wonderful Truth—or the Cruelest Hoax

In spite of its obvious folly and impossibility, the delusionary dream of playing God is so appealing that few people can resist the temptation when this carrot is dangled in front of them. In each issue one major New Age magazine boldly offers to its large circulation of readers: "Tools & Teachings To Create Your Own Reality."[8] Seminars offering techniques for developing one's alleged infinite "potential" are, as we have already mentioned, proliferating. Typical of the courses being presented to a public only too eager to believe any "positive" message is the following from a full-page ad in the January-February 1988 *New Realities*:

> Contact your Higher-Self. Discover the Inner Power to create your Ideal Reality.
>
> As you listen [to the special tapes] . . . instantly the powerful learning, cognitive, and creative potentials of [your] brain open wide. The mind's full power comes alive at last. . . .
>
> [On] side 2 . . . you consciously hear [the] soothing voice which leads you through a pleasant guided state of relaxation to the receptive "Alpha State."

As we have already indicated, highly educated Westerners are embracing, as *science*, a Hindu gospel that must take much of the responsibility for making India one of the poorest, most superstition-bound countries in the world. This gospel offers to Calcutta's one million beggars who have been born and live and will die in its streets the good news that their running sores, gnawing hunger, and poverty do not really exist, but have been created by their own "negative" thinking. There is no suffering, disease, or death; one merely misperceives what is actually there. All one needs to do to change one's experience of life is to change the way one perceives it. In that same address to Congressional leaders, Edgar Mitchell declared:

> Our physical and emotional well-being is totally under our control and we can train ourselves to control ourselves. It puts responsibility for health and well-being on the individual.
>
> I am not a victim. I choose on some level, whatever happens to me. Within ten years, the AMA will endorse this viewpoint.[9]

As Norman Vincent Peale, Denis Waitley, and many other motivational speakers would persuade us if they could, anyone can change his entire world by changing his thoughts. Now this is either the most wonderful truth or else it is the cruelest hoax imaginable. Who could reasonably doubt that it is the latter? Yet this delusion, surprisingly, continues to grow in popularity in spite of the obvious fact that no one (not even a patient in a mental hospital) lives in his own mentally-created reality separate from the rest of the world.

Who walks in sunshine while others all around him are in the rain? Or who continues to fly safely through the air on a plane that the other passengers and crew, because of their negative thinking, "imagine" has sustained a powerful explosion and is falling from the sky? Or who can (by positive thinking) cause a stock that he or she owns to maintain its value, when to everyone else's perception and according to the figures coming out of the New York Stock Exchange that particular stock has drastically fallen in value? Nevertheless, millions are persuaded by gurus of the new consciousness that they have such "potential," and are purchasing and practicing various techniques for cultivating altered states in pursuit of this pot of gold at the end of the New Age rainbow.

Mystical fantasies in altered states aside, the daily experience of all mankind has always demonstrated that there is a common reality shared by all human beings upon planet Earth regardless of whether they are positive or negative thinkers. Ecological disaster or nuclear war, for example, do not threaten only those negative people who are pessimistic enough to believe in such horrors. The possibility of World War III is just as much a threat to those who display "Visualize Peace" stickers on their car bumpers, practice transcendental meditation faithfully, and think nothing but positive thoughts day and night as it is to anyone else.

Nor can it be argued that the majority belief is imposed upon the minority. This idea forms the basis for the attempt to mobilize hundreds of millions of people to meditate for peace in the hope that a "critical mass" of peaceful thinking will be reached and will thus tip the scales in the Universal Mind itself and bring about peace upon earth. If it requires millions or even billions of persons thinking the same thought together to effect such changes, then obviously one person could not possibly create his or her own individual reality in competition with billions or even thousands of other minds.

The story is told of two overweight men whose holistic physician prescribed 18 holes of golf each week, but without balls or clubs. The game was to be played by visualization. Swinging imaginary clubs at imaginary balls the first time seemed a bit odd, but right off the first tee each player managed a 280-yard visualized "drive" straight down the fairway. As one might imagine, it was a very close match. In fact, by the time they reached the 18th hole, a 450-yard, par-4 dogleg, the game was tied.

"I've never parred this hole before," said one of the men, "but I've got a feeling that today is my day!" Whereupon he "drove" his imaginary ball the 300 yards to where the fairway angled off to the green. The second man did likewise.

With his imaginary six-iron the first man took aim and "swung" for the pin, following the invisible ball in his mind. "It's bouncing onto the green!" he exclaimed excitedly. "It's heading for the pin! It's in the cup! An eagle! Beat that!"

"I don't have to beat it," said the second man. "I win, you lose! You hit my ball!"

A Cruel and Evil Philosophy

Beyond the problem of whose reality would prevail lies another contradiction. Most of those who teach that we can each create our own reality also theorize a Universal Mind as the source of infinite power and knowledge—a Mind which, oddly enough, has no mind of its own, but depends upon what *we* think. Moreover, to make visualized fantasies in our minds the key to war or peace, famine or plenty, and the state of individual lives is to delude and inhibit the choices and effort required for genuine solutions. Yet this is fundamental New Age teaching. Ernest Holmes, one of the early New Age gurus and founder of the Church of Religious Science, wrote:

> Science of Mind teaches that the originating, supreme, creative Power of the Universe . . . is a cosmic Reality Principle which is present throughout the Universe and in every one of us.

> Science of Mind teaches that . . . we are all creating
> our own day-to-day experiences . . . by the form and
> procession of our thoughts.
> Man, by thinking, can bring into his experience what-
> soever he desires. . . .[10]

What the popular and growing delusion that we each create our own reality actually creates is disappointment and depression when it proves not to be true. Moreover, it promotes the unrealistic attitude that, rather than face a problem in the real world, the solution is to fantasize a different illusion, which becomes one's new "reality." Instead of correcting this madness, many psychologists encourage it. In fact, a growing number of today's psychotherapies are based upon this very theory. Such therapies incorporate visualization and the acting out of fantasies, a process which encourages the idea of escaping from problems rather than confronting them and working out a real solution.

The perennial philosophy (common to all nature religions) teaches that the Universal Mind has divided itself into fragments in order to have experiences on "different levels." The channeled entities with one voice proclaim that "we are the way God has individuated itself to experience itself and explore its creative possibilities. All life is an exploration of the infinite possibilities within and of the one 'house of many mansions.' "[11] It is astonishing that anyone could be blind to the basic evil in such a philosophy.

The desire of the New Age "God" to "have experiences on 'different levels' " in order to "explore its creative possibilities" is hardly an acceptable excuse for rape, murder, famine, and war. The litany of evil and sorrow that is so real to the multitudes suffering in the world today is almost endless, and none of it is *wrong* by the new consciousness standards. The sense of outrage that this pantheistic theory arouses in anyone with a normal conscience was expressed in a recent article in, of all places, *New Age Journal*. In criticism of guru Shirley MacLaine, it declared:

> I found the implications of her philosophy basically
> cruel and callous. . . . MacLaine's basic truth is that we
> create our own reality. . . .

Are you poor? You chose poverty because you need to learn certain lessons. . . . Do you have cancer? . . . Did you lose a loved one? . . . You participated in creating that reality . . . nobody is a victim . . . evil is just a matter of your point of view.

It sounds like the perfect yuppie religion, a modern prime-time rerun of nineteenth-century Social Darwinism. Both blame the victim. Only now, the poor are not poor because they are "unfit" . . . [but because] they want to be poor. . . .

If I were a dictator, I could think of nothing better than to have a nation dedicated to following MacLaine's agenda.[12]

The "Universal Mind" is a very convenient "God" who won't hold its devotees accountable to any moral standards, but will help those who know the "laws" to create their own reality and do their own thing. William A. Tiller, Stanford University physicist and a leader in the New Age movement, declares: "Our *intentions* influence the level of mind of the universe and bring forth manifestations in our environment."[13] In fact this concept seems to provide a cover for man's desire to play God. This has been the goal of sorcery for thousands of years and is the aim of modern sorcerers, who often call their belief system "Religious Science." Again Ernest Holmes laid it out clearly:

Mind as Law is helpless without direction [from man]. We are co-partners with the Infinite in the management of our own affairs . . . we are surrounded by a Universal Creative Mind which receives the impress of our thought and acts upon it.

But because of Its very nature, this Mind [God] cannot act without an image of thought [supplied by man].[14]

A Delusion Fueled by the Blindest of Pride

As a matter of fact, natural events proceed on their course quite independently of the thoughts or absence of thoughts being supplied by mankind. To think otherwise is such folly that its persistence can only be the product of a delusion fueled by the blindest of pride. Try to imagine the incredible processes involved within trillions upon trillions of atoms, molecules, and cells within our own bodies and environment or in distant suns and galaxies—all of the activity in the microcosm or macrocosm hidden from the eyes and completely unknown to the thoughts of man. Then stand in equal awe at the perversion that could suggest that it is *our universe* created by *our minds*, and that the Mind who conceived and created it all before we existed is subject to our command and can do nothing without the compelling "impress of our thoughts"!

Consider the spontaneous ease with which lightning blacks out a city, a snowstorm closes roads and airports, a tornado tears off rooftops—all of this not only without any help from human minds, but in spite of both curses and positive affirmations. Then contrast this with the hours of seminars and self-hypnosis/subliminal-suggestion tapes, the meditation and Yoga, the positive declarations repeated endlessly—all of this intense effort aimed at "creating a new reality," yet with so little visible effect. When a power failure blacked out one of her seminars in Dallas in mid-1987, Shirley MacLaine led her audience of about 1000 in visualizing the problem being cleared up. The attempt failed to produce a demonstration of what Shirley teaches, and the crowd of eager learners had to go home.[15]

How do those who receive payment for teaching other people techniques for releasing from within an alleged "infinite potential" explain the puniness not only of their disciples' "mind powers" but of their own in relation to the incredible forces surrounding us? The answer to that question and the recovery of these allegedly "forgotten" natural powers through Eastern mystical practices has been the promise of most of the cults formed during the past 20 years in the Western world.

Scientology is typical and presents a clear picture of the general New Age thesis. Blending psychotherapy, Eastern mysticism, and science fiction, Scientology proposes that all humans are eternal, omnipotent, omniscient beings called Thetans. After creating the universe, we Thetans incarnated the creatures we had made. As lower forms of life *evolved* ever higher, we *reincarnated* repeatedly.

By the time we had *evolved* into humans, so the theory goes, we had "forgotten" who we were.

Scientology offers a psychotherapeutic process for breaking through the "engrams" picked up from traumas in prior lives, so we can "realize" once again our true identity as an "operating Thetan" (or God) beyond the limitations of space, time, and matter. Oddly enough, those who achieve this fantastic breakthrough continue to bumble their way through life like the rest of us, mysteriously unable to display their "god-powers." The key elements involved (which reveal the close link between Eastern mysticism, cults such as Scientology or transcendental meditation, and the more respected and much larger cult of psychotherapy) are the twin theories of *evolution* and *reincarnation*.

In fact, evolution has always been recognized as the vehicle that makes reincarnation seem credible. There is no point in being reincarnated back to earth countless times unless one is evolving higher. Of course one could, as the result of "bad karma" (so the theory goes), drop lower on the scale as well. As evolution gained official status as the only religious view sponsored by the government in public schools, it was only natural that its religious twin, reincarnation, would enjoy a renaissance in the West, and so it has.

Amoral, Senseless, and Hopeless

Since reincarnation is a belief basic to witchcraft, it is not surprising that it is *amoral*. Instead of solving the problem of evil, it perpetuates it. If a husband beats his wife, the cause-and-effect law of karma decrees that he must be reincarnated as a wife who is beaten by her husband. That husband (who will have been prepared by his karma to be a wife-beater) will in turn have to come back as a wife beaten by her husband, and so forth endlessly. The perpetrator of each crime must become the victim of the same crime, which necessitates another perpetrator, who in turn must become a subsequent victim at the hands of another, ad infinitum, ad absurdum. Rather than solving the problem of evil, karma and reincarnation perpetuate it. Think of the evil that must yet be perpetrated upon future reincarnations of Hitler in order to "pay" for his crimes!

With few alleged exceptions, the average person has no recollection of the many past lives that he or she has supposedly lived.

Without any memory of previous mistakes and lessons learned, what is the point of living again and again, only to bear the burden of bad karma and the dire consequences of deeds one cannot remember? It is argued that *subconsciously* we have such memories (which can be induced and dealt with through hypnotherapy) and are thus benefiting at an unconscious level. If that were true, we should see evidence that humans, individually and collectively, are living better, more divine lives. That is patently not the case. Reincarnation is thus a *senseless* philosophy.

That reincarnation is also *hopeless* follows logically. The karma built up in the present life must be worked off in a future reincarnation. But in the process of working it off, more karma is accumulated, which must in turn be worked off in the next life, and so forth endlessly. This is why the Hindu speaks of the *wheel* of reincarnation, and why Gandhi called reincarnation "a burden too great to bear." There is no release; it goes on forever. Yoga was developed as a means of escape from this endless wheel of death and rebirth, but whether it actually is or not must be taken by faith. And faith in the efficacy of amoral and senseless laws whose existence is not supported by the facts would appear to be misplaced.

What happens in this life is presumably decreed by the karma of the last life, which in turn was determined by the karma built up in the life previous to that one, and so on endlessly. When we trace the path of karma back to the beginning, we arrive at a stage when, according to Hindu tradition, the three *gunas* (or qualities) of the godhead were in perfect balance in the void, the nothingness from which all comes and to which all returns. Something happened to cause an imbalance in the godhead, and the *prakriti* (manifestation) began, bringing about the illusion which we experience as the universe today. Consequently, *bad karma actually began with an imbalance in the godhead itself and is built into the very fabric of the universe*. There is indeed no escape, Yoga or no Yoga. It is thus *hopeless*.

In most Buddhism there is no reincarnation of individual souls, but a survival of consciousness. Upon death the individual consciousness, like a drop of water joining the ocean and becoming an unidentifiable and undivided part of the whole, once again enters and merges into the pool of universal consciousness or world soul, from whence it somehow at some unknown time separated. (The *Star Wars* film series promotes George Lucas's belief that this "pool of consciousness" constitutes the "Force" that can be tapped into by initiates for mystical powers.) In Hinduism the individual identity that was taken on for a time is the source of all pain and must be retained through countless reincarnations ("transmigrations of soul"). Escape (*moksha*) from "time, sense, and the elements"—or Self-realization—comes when the individual soul (*atman*) recognizes that the appearance of separation is an illusion and "realizes," through the state of consciousness reached in Yoga, that it is in fact identical with the universal soul, or *Brahman*.

Amoral, senseless, hopeless—reincarnation is nevertheless winning adherents by the millions in the West. And although consciousness is clearly outside the realm of physical science, there has been an ongoing effort to connect what is undeniably a mystical religious belief with what has been generally accepted as scientific. This is happening in many areas, but as we have already noted, much of the leadership in this movement to the East and the undeserved aura of respectability are clearly coming from psychology.

Psychiatrists utilizing hypnotherapy are "regressing" their patients back to memories of childhood or even of the womb, in spite of the fact that the myelin sheathing in the brain of the prenatal, natal, and early postnatal infant is not sufficiently developed to carry memories. They are regressing their patients to prior lives as well. And, offering the ultimate escape from present moral responsibility, some therapists are even "regressing" patients into "earlier stages of evolution" in order to help them find the cause of present problems buried within the "deeper memories" of their experiences as apes, salamanders, or polliwogs.

Such therapies, which are no more scientific than reading tea leaves, blend two of the greatest hoaxes that have ever been foisted upon mankind: psychotherapy and evolution. We have given considerable attention to the former, and we must now take at least a brief look at the latter in our search for the identity of the entities which down through the centuries have fostered both beliefs.

13

From Slime to Divine

Although Freud ridiculed all religion, much of his thinking was nevertheless closely related to ancient mystical and occult beliefs and practices. His twin theories of the unconscious and psychic determinism followed his discovery that under hypnosis patients could apparently "remember" early childhood incidents of which they had no conscious memory. He concluded that these hidden traumas, particularly those occurring prior to the age of six, were the driving force in determining one's present personality and reaction to circumstances. The relationship between the Freudian belief that the present is determined by the *prior years of one's life* and the teaching of reincarnation that the present is determined by one's *prior lives* is no coincidence, as subsequent developments in psychotherapy have demonstrated.

It was Carl Jung's theory of the collective unconscious that supplied the connection. Inspired by his spirit guide, Philemon, Jung set the stage for applying reincarnation directly to psychotherapy by the proposal that his "depth analysis" could peel off layer upon layer of consciousness in order to uncover primeval archetypes where one literally reached the level of the "consciousness" of simpler life forms, such as the amoeba. This necessitated the proposal that "memory" resides not only in the brain but in the genes themselves, and that the entire cosmos, including each electron, is thus "conscious." Building upon that foundation, many psychotherapies have attempted to put the twin theories of evolution and reincarnation to practical use for changing lives.

"Remember When You Were a Fish"

Jean Houston, who has a doctorate in psychology and religion, travels about 250,000 miles a year on the new consciousness/self-improvement circuit. In some of her workshops she leads participants to awaken ancient prehuman "memories" as a means of gaining insight into their personalities and working through "emotional blocks." The following excerpt is from a reporter's account of one such session:

> "Remember when you were a fish," Houston suggested in Sacramento. Nearly a thousand people . . . dropped to the floor and began moving their "fins" as if to propel themselves through water.
> "Notice your perception as you roll like a fish. How does your world look, feel, sound, smell, taste?"
> "Then you came up on land," Houston recalled, taking us through the amphibian stage. . . .
> Then Houston suggested, "Allow yourself to fully remember being a reptile. . . . Then some of you flew. Others climbed trees." . . .
> We became a zoo of sounds and movements made by early mammals, monkeys, and apes.
> Houston then called us to remember being "the early human" who loses his/her protective furry covering" and . . . evolves into modern human.[1]

Where are Randi the Magician and CSICOP when we need them? We appreciate the whistle being blown on phony television healers—but they are not the only charlatans. Falsely claiming to heal someone's physical ailments with God's power is admittedly religious fraud, but why is pretending to heal emotional problems by conjuring up nonexistent memories of a past life as a fish or a lizard accepted as valid science?

This "exercise in evolutionary memory," as Houston calls it, is patently nonsense. The fact is that no one has such "memories," but participants fantasize in order to play along with the regressive therapy game and not appear to be out of step. One suspects that this exercise in futility would be universally recognized as folly if it did not offer the carrot of escape from moral accountability—an escape which is so desirable that a great deal is willingly overlooked in reaching for it.

Houston is supported in her "evolutionary memory therapy" by such theorists as Paul MacLean, who heads up the Laboratory of Brain Evolution and Behavior at the National Institutes of Mental Health (NIMH). The basic theory is that our brains are comprised of three distinct parts—reptilian, mammalian, and neomammalian—with each part still containing the neurological and chemical patterns of our animal ancestors. Such fanciful ideas, though lacking any scientific evidence, have had a great deal of influence in this country and abroad. Involved for years in governmental conferences, Houston chaired and organized "a symposium for leading U.S. government policymakers entitled 'The Possible Society: An Exploration of Practical Policy Alternatives for the Decade Ahead.' " She tells of guiding "about 150 extremely high-ranking government officials for about three days . . . we had these officials on the floor, guiding them into internal journeys, looking for the possible society."

If it seems odd that "higher consciousness" takes us back to life as an amoeba, Houston assures us that this altered state also opens us to "memories" of the future as well. Once again it is naturalism/pantheism. The deified collective unconscious is a substitute for the supernatural God of the Bible. And our identification with this alleged universal Source of wisdom and power effectively makes gods out of us as well. The observation of the participating reporter at the Sacramento conference continues:

> The climax of the already intense exercise that had taken us more than an hour followed: "Now I want you to extend yourselves even further—into . . . the next stage of your own evolution."
>
> We became a room of leaping, joyous, sometimes alone, often together human beings who eventually joined hands and voices. The impact was electric. . . .
>
> We had become a wriggling sea of bodies—nearly a thousand housewives, therapists, artists, social workers, clergy, educators, health professionals . . . [who] had

crawled over and under each other, enjoying ourselves and re-learning what was deep within our [past and future] memories.

Mysticism or "Science," Mathematics Doesn't Lie

Perhaps no other idea within the last few centuries has had more impact upon twentieth-century mankind than the theory of evolution. It has directly or indirectly influenced nearly every aspect of our modern culture. Evolution was an established religious belief at the heart of occultism and mysticism thousands of years before the Greeks gave it "scientific" status. As Theodore Roszak has pointed out, mysticism is "the parent stock from which the theory of biological evolution springs."[2] It is the core belief of Hinduism and witchcraft, and is at least as old as the theories of reincarnation and karma, in which it is a key element. Michael Harner reminds us that "millennia before Charles Darwin, people in shamanic cultures were convinced that humans and animals were related."[3] This belief is reflected in the idea of "werewolves" and "vampires" as well as "power animals" with human characteristics who serve as "spirit guides." Occult literature, ancient and modern, contains repeated references to evolution, as do communications through past mediums and present-day channelers.

Even as a "scientific" theory, evolution predates Darwin by many centuries. In *Evolution: A Theory in Crisis*, medical doctor and molecular scientist Michael Denton points out that materialist philosopher Empedocles proposed a theory similar to Darwin's in about 450 B.C. One hundred years earlier Anaximander and Empedocles was said to have postulated that sea slime was the environment from which life forms had their beginnings. Out of this primeval soup, he theorized, emerged sea life, which then evolved into more complex forms suitable for terrestrial living.

After 2500 years, this ancient naturalistic speculation remains the foundation for most modern evolutionary theory, in spite of the fact that with today's mathematics we know (what Anaximander and Empedocles may be excused for not knowing) that this imaginative idea is patently absurd. Eminent British astronomer Sir Fred Hoyle reminds us of the well-known fact that "even if the whole universe consisted of organic soup" the chance of producing the basic enzymes of life by random processes without intelligent direction would be approximately one in 10 with 40,000 zeros after it.

It is impossible even to comprehend such a number, but a comparison can be made. The likelihood of reaching out and by chance plucking a particular *atom* out of the *universe* would be about 1 in 10 with 80 zeros after it. And if every atom became another universe, the chance of reaching out at random and plucking a particular atom out of all of those universes would then be 1 in 10 with 160 zeros after it. Hoyle concludes that "Darwinian evolution is most unlikely to get even one polypeptide [sequence] right, let alone the thousands on which living cells depend for survival." Why then is this completely impossible theory still honored? Hoyle accuses the evolutionists of self-interest, unfair pressure, and dishonesty:

> This situation [mathematical impossibility] is well known to geneticists and yet nobody seems to blow the whistle decisively on the theory. If Darwinism were not considered socially desirable . . . it would of course be otherwise.
>
> Most scientists still cling to Darwinism because of its grip on the educational system. . . . You either have to believe the concepts, or you will be branded a heretic.[4]

Darwinism: The Unbelievable Religion That Persists

"Heretic" is an appropriate term, because evolution, like psychotherapy, is actually a religion—a religion to which Hoyle himself remains strangely committed. While he has defected from the Darwinian camp, Hoyle has simply switched his membership to another "denomination" of evolutionists with an even more bizarre belief: that life came in from outer space. Of course this theory only raises a further question: Where and how did *that* life originate? We are obviously back where we started. Hoyle does admit that perhaps "God" is the One who sent life in from space, but that belief puts all evolutionists completely out of business and is therefore not likely to gain many adherents.

In *Chance and Necessity*, Nobelist molecular biologist Jacques Monod gives a dozen or more reasons why evolution could not possibly occur. He explains, for example, that the essential characteristic of DNA is its perfect replication of itself; that evolution could only happen if something went awry in that mechanism; and that it is absurd to imagine developing even a single cell, much less the human brain, from a series of random and harmful mistakes in the DNA mechanism. Yet after giving reason after reason why life could not possibly be the product of chance, Monod concludes that it *must*, nevertheless, have happened that way.

Does Monod have any scientific reason for this conclusion? No. He simply refuses to accept the only other alternative—creation by God—and declares with a shrug, "Our number came up in the Monte Carlo game." By contrast, professed agnostic Robert Jastrow shocked many of his fellow scientists when he implied at the 144th national conference of the Association for the Advancement of Science that the evidence seems to demand an intelligent Creator for the universe. Most of his colleagues were not happy with this inference. Jastrow has written:

> Astronomers are curiously upset by . . . proof that the universe had a beginning. Their reactions provide an interesting demonstration of the response of the scientific mind—supposedly a very objective mind—when evidence uncovered by science itself leads to a conflict with the articles of faith in their profession . . . there is a kind of religion in science. . . .[5]

British Museum of Natural History senior paleontologist Colin Patterson has pointed out: "Evolutionists—like the creationists they periodically do battle with—are nothing more than believers themselves. I had been working on this stuff [evolution] for more than twenty years, and there was not one [factual] thing I knew about it. It's quite a shock to learn that one can be so misled for so long."[6] Speaking before a group of his fellow biologists, D. M. S. Watson, popularizer of evolution on British television (as Carl Sagan has been on American TV), reminded them of the common *religious faith* they all shared:

> Evolution itself is accepted by zoologists not because it has been observed to occur or . . . can be proved by

logically coherent evidence to be true, but because the only alternative, special creation, is clearly incredible.[7]

Apparently unaware of the religious roots of their theory in occultism and mysticism, the early "scientific" evolutionists of the nineteenth century were materialists who attempted to use evolution to disprove Christianity. They recognized that if life evolved by chance, then belief in the God of the Bible would have been proven unnecessary. Roszak suggests that "so many scientists rallied to Darwin's banner" because he drove "every last trace of an incredible God from biology." He goes on to admit, however, that Darwinism "replaces the old God with an even more incredible deity— omnipotent chance."[8]

Certainly the embarrassing absurdity ought to be clear to today's engineer whose belief in evolution forces him to accept that his most sophisticated *design* will prove to be drastically primitive in comparison with the simplest organism supposedly produced by *chance*. Michael Denton writes:

> It is the sheer universality of perfection, the fact that everywhere we look, to whatever depth we look, we find an elegance and ingenuity of an absolutely transcending quality, which so mitigates against the idea of chance.
>
> Is it really credible that random processes could have constructed a reality, the smallest element of which—a functional protein or gene—is complex beyond our own creative capacities, a reality which is the very antithesis of chance, which excels in every sense anything produced by the intelligence of man?
>
> Alongside the level of ingenuity and complexity exhibited by the molecular machinery of life, even our most advanced artifacts appear clumsy. We feel humbled, as neolithic man would in the presence of twentieth-century technology.[9]

The irrefutable verdict of ironclad mathematics makes it absolutely clear that evolution, as Popper says in his autobiography, is not science but "a metaphysical research programme." Had this plain fact been heeded, the famous Leakey family and other seekers after missing links would have been saved entire lifetimes devoted to the search for nonexistent evidence. Fanatical religious faith, however, seldom yields to facts or reason. Even Popper still clings to vestiges of evolution in spite of mathematics and logic.

The Facts of Nature

If evolution is the true process of life, we should expect to find a great deal of supporting evidence in nature. Among the literally millions of fossilized life forms unearthed by paleontologists we ought to have an extraordinary amount of evidence showing the intermediary stages between species. But, in fact, *not one example* has ever been found in the fossil record for any of the literally billions of "links" demanded by evolutionary theory. As the Associated Press reported:

> Darwin's missing links are still missing after 120 years. Fossil hunters have not found the fossils needed to explain the glaring differences between major species. . . .
> So some respected paleontologists are now backing the hypothesis that new species come about . . . in sudden bursts of evolution. The big bang in biology which again smacks suspiciously of creation and gives comfort to the theologians. . . .
> Science, the religion of the intelligentsia, is faced with clamorous apostasy.[10]

Colin Patterson, editor of the prestigious magazine of London's Museum of Natural History, has written that he didn't know of "any real evidence of evolutionary transitions either among living or fossilized organisms."[11] Robert Barnes writes in *Paleobiology*: "Intermediate forms are non-existent, undiscovered, or not recognized." After interviewing American paleontologist Niles Eldredge, whose work critically addresses the lack of transitional forms in the fossil record, a British newspaper reported:

> If life had evolved into its wondrous profusion of creatures little by little, Dr. Eldredge argues, then one

would expect to find fossils of transitional creatures which were a bit like what went before them and a bit like what came after. But no one has yet found any evidence of such transitional creatures.

This oddity has been attributed to gaps in the fossil record which gradualists expected to fill when rock strata of the proper age had been found. In the last decade, however, geologists have found rock layers of all divisions of the last 500 million years and no transitional forms were contained in them."[12]

If the Darwinian view were true, there should be such an abundance of transitional life forms in the fossil record that distinguishing one class of organism from another would be nearly impossible. There should be so many part-reptile/part-bird forms, for example, that any attempts at classification would be an exercise in frustration. Yet, as Denton points out, you don't have to be a biologist to recognize a bird, whether it's a canary or an ostrich. For more than a century the cry from the evolutionary camp has been, "To reject Darwinism is to reject *science* in favor of dogma." Yet scientists now find themselves forced to admit that Darwin's theory doesn't fit the facts. In Denton's words again:

If anyone was chasing a phantom or retreating from empiricism it was surely Darwin, who himself freely admitted that he had absolutely no hard empirical evidence that any of the major evolutionary transformations he proposed had ever actually occurred.[13]

The followers of Darwin were so confident that they would find the evidence that they treated a speculative theory as though it were fact. In their unscientific and dishonest behavior they deceived not only themselves but generations who relied upon their word. Textbooks at all levels of education around the world perpetuate this fraud, and today's students are still being denied the facts in the interests of maintaining the reputations and careers of a few.

While there have always been dissenters to the Darwinian view, the impression has been given that a biblical Christian bias motivated its detractors. However, many of the greatest men of science opposed Darwinism right from the start. These included Faraday, Maxwell, and Lord Kelvin, along with leading biologists and anatomists of the time (including Louis Agassiz and Richard Owen). All of them rejected the theory of evolution simply because the facts of nature did not support it.

Even Alfred Wallace, the codiscoverer with Charles Darwin of the principle of natural selection, had his problems with the theory. His concern went beyond the physical considerations to the obvious spiritual shortcomings. There was clearly no way to account for *consciousness* in the Darwinian theory. Wallace recognized this and repeatedly insisted that a purely materialistic explanation of biological evolution failed to account for the spiritual nature of man. "And for this origin," he declared, "we can only find a cause in the unseen universe of spirit."[14] By that, however, he did not mean the God of the Bible, who had been thrown out of his universe, but "intelligences [that] very probably exist in a graduated series above us."[15] In fact, Wallace was heavily involved in the spiritualist movement of his day.

Evolution is not science but a religion, which its supporters have clung to in spite of the evidence. They are simply unwilling to accept the only other alternative, which is moral accountability to a Creator. Having been the core belief of occultism for thousands of years, evolution has lately been dressed in the language of science and deliberately passed off on a gullible public as fact. The perpetrators of this massive deception have taken millions of dollars in grants from foundations to pursue a phantom that mathematics conclusively says does not exist. They need to admit that they are working on a mathematically impossible theory and desist from pretending that it is supported by scientific evidence.

There was only one way to avoid returning to the God that the Enlightenment had declared dead. Materialists were forced to attribute Godlike qualities to nature and thus fell into the trap of naturalism/pantheism. Instead of accepting the overwhelming evidence of intelligent design as proof that a great Mind had planned and created the universe, it was taken to mean that the cosmos itself was a great Mind with a universal consciousness of which we all partake at some deep level beyond ordinary awareness. The goal of evolution, as portrayed for thousands of years before Darwin, has always been to journey through endless reincarnations until we have once again achieved union with the Universal Mind, or All.

Evolution of Consciousness—Slime to Divine

The next stage in evolution is believed not to involve further physical development but a quantum leap to a higher state of consciousness. Barbara Brown, associated with UCLA Medical Center and called by Milton Greenblatt, president of the American Board of Psychiatry and Neurology, "the most commanding person in the [biofeedback] field," declares that we are "evolving to a higher level of mind . . . [called] 'supermind'."[16] At Esalen, Michael Murphy and George Leonard have offered a seminar on "The Evolution of Consciousness," in which it is suggested that "a transformation of human consciousness as momentous as the emergence of civilization is underway." Marilyn Ferguson agrees: "The human mind may have reached a new state in its evolution, an unlocking of potential comparable to the emergence of language."[17] The attainment of this fabled "higher" state of consciousness, which has been the common doorway to magic powers for sorcerers, is today the means of salvation offered by the ecumenical union of the two religions of evolution and psychotherapy. As Theodore Roszak put it:

> An evolutionary leap in consciousness: the idea . . .
> that the world shall be redeemed by a contagious psychic
> mutation hatched in the grey matter of a chosen few.[18]

Darwin himself seemed to recognize the spiritual implications of his theory. In *The Descent of Man* he wrote: "Man may be excused for feeling some pride at having risen, though not through his own exertions, to the very summit of the organic scale; and the fact of his having thus risen, instead of having been aboriginally placed there, may give him hopes for a still higher destiny in the distant future." Whether Darwin fully realized it or not, the mystical goal of the theory of evolution he now championed had always been to become "God." In *The Atman Project* Ken Wilber lays it out clearly: "If men and women have ultimately come up from amoebas, then they are ultimately on their way towards God." In *Up From Eden* Wilber identifies this belief in man's ascension to Godhood as the heart of what has been "known as the 'perennial philosophy' . . . the eso- teric core of Hinduism, Buddhism, Taoism, Sufism. . . ." As Klimo summarizes it, the "truth of truths" of the channeled material is "that we are God," and only need to "realize" it. As one brochure offering "A Weekend Exploration and Reclaiming of your own Divine, Innocent, and Infinite Power" explains, "The God Powers Experience" is for those who are "Willing To Be God Again."

Certainly the fact that one must take leave of one's normal senses and reason, and journey into inner space in an altered state of consciousness in order to "experience" this great truth, ought to be cause for considerable caution. Nevertheless John White trium- phantly proclaims that "science confirms" the Hindu axiom: "I am the universe; I am Universal Mind!" Even if that were in some metaphysical sense true, it would hardly be worth getting excited about. Imagine a positive-thinking atom proclaiming itself to be the universe, or a single cell in the intestines proclaiming itself to be man, and we have some idea of what it means for one of us to claim to be the universe or "God." Such a claim chanted repeatedly in the most "positive" frame of mind changes none of the obvious facts of life: pain and sorrow, death and taxes, and the necessity to work for and eat and digest one's daily bread.

Scientism's demythologized fulfillment is no better. Carl Sagan would have us thrill to the thought that there are hydrogen atoms in our bodies that were once part of a distant star system—and may even resume that honored place in the future. It all has a hollow ring.

All of the objective evidence denies this "scientific pantheism." Yet in her seminars to packed audiences, Shirley MacLaine blithely tells her eager followers: "Just remember that you are God, and act accordingly." Common sense protests. Isn't it the height of folly to urge mere humans to "act" like "God"? If we really are God, as Shirley wants us to believe, then why aren't we already acting the part? And why must we attend a MacLaine weekend seminar and pay her 300 dollars to tell us what we already ought to know if that's who we really are? The magnitude of the delusion is matched only by the pride that feeds it.

A Seductive Promise

It can hardly be a coincidence that so many voices on the American scene are preaching this same gospel today. Werner Erhard, founder of the Forum (formerly est), declares, "You're god in your universe." Benjamin Creme's Lord Maitreya ("The Christ" who "is now here" according to full-page ads around the world) states, "Man is an emerging God. . . . My plan and my duty is to reveal to you a new way . . . which will permit the divine in man to shine forth." Sun Myung Moon has written, "God and man are one. Man is incarnate God." Maharishi Mahesh Yogi, founder of TM, perverts the biblical God's statement, "Be still and know that I AM God," by telling his followers that the purpose of TM is to "Be still and know that you are God. . . ." Haiti's followers of voodoo, who know the "altered state" well, have a saying: "The Catholic goes to church to speak about God, the vodounist dances in the hounfour [temple] to become God." In full agreement, Ernest Holmes declared, "All men are spiritually evolving until . . . each will fully express his divinity. . . ." To the Christian, Moslem, or Jew, this is the ultimate blasphemy. Alan Watts, Episcopal priest turned Zen Buddhist Master, fully demonstrated his renunciation of his former faith when he declared:

> The appeal of Zen, as of other Eastern philosophy, is that it unveils . . . a vast region . . . where at last the self is indistinguishable from God.[19]

If we claim that we are God, we have demeaned the very concept of God. We haven't lifted ourselves up to God's level, but have dragged God down to our level. If everything is God, as Hinduism teaches, then nothing is God because the very word "God" has lost its meaning. And if the New Age leaders who are bringing this enlightenment are demonstrating what it means to "act like God," then they have clearly demeaned the long-accepted concept of the Supreme Being.

The spirit guides have been pushing this "Ye are gods" idea for thousands of years and it has not improved human life one iota. According to the Bible, this seductive promise originated with Satan and is in fact the cause of all human problems. There are many astute observers of the current scene who, whether they agree with the Bible or not, consider this deification-of-man philosophy to be the major cause of society's growing ethical and spiritual decadence. In his famous Harvard commencement address on June 9, 1978, Aleksandr Solzhenitsyn identified the root cause of moral decline in the Western world as "self-deification of man as supreme . . . a rationalistic humanism . . . [that makes man] the center of everything." Historian Herbert Schlossberg, in warning of the consequences of this growing belief, adds this ominous note:

> Exalting mankind to the status of deity dates from the furthest reaches of antiquity, but its development into an ideology embracing the masses is a characteristic trait of modernity. [20]

It is odd that psychiatrist M. Scott Peck claims to have embraced Christianity while still promoting its very antithesis, the perennial philosophy—which he admits contradicts the evidence. He writes: "Everywhere there is war, corruption and pollution. How could one reasonably suggest that the human race is spiritually progressing? Yet that is exactly what I suggest. . . . To explain the miracles of grace and evolution we hypothesize the existence of a God who . . . wants us to become Himself (or Herself or Itself). We are growing toward godhood." He is clearly not referring to the God of the Bible. In fact he tells us that, like Jung, he means the collective unconscious:

> But we still have not explained how it is that the unconscious possesses all this knowledge which we have not yet consciously learned . . . we can only hypothesize . . . [that] our unconscious is God. . . .
> I am indebted for this analogy to Jung, who describ[ed] himself as "a splinter of the infinite deity. . . ."
> Since the unconscious is God all along, we may further define the goal of spiritual growth to be the attainment of godhood by the conscious self. It is for the individual to become totally, wholly God . . . then God will have assumed . . . through our conscious ego a new and potent life form. [21]

While all of the above may sound exciting to the New Age neopantheist, to the supernaturalist it is both preposterous and evil. In fact, the Old Testament accepted by Jew, Christian, and Moslem identifies the promise that man could become God as the identical lie with which the serpent deceived the human race at the very beginning. In *Up From Eden* Ken Wilber traces the serpent through many religions and cultures. He points out that, in contrast to the biblical characterization of the serpent as evil personified, it has in other religions around the world been the symbol of wisdom and eternal life and has always been identified with the "perennial philosophy."

David Spangler, cofounder of Findhorn, declares: "The being that helps man to reach this point [of becoming a god] is Lucifer . . . the angel of man's evolution. . . ."[22] Again the Bible identifies Lucifer, the serpent, as Satan, the master of evil. And the channeled spirit entities in turn would seem to betray their own identity by their unanimous and consistent proclamation of the promise of godhood. Knowing full well the remarkable correlation, Wilber commends to others precisely what the Bible identifies as the serpent's promise, "Ye shall be as God." Magnanimously he declares that he has "no quarrel" with the biblical view, but that "it simply forms no part of the perennial philosophy whatsoever, and thus is not a view I am here advancing."[23] A contradiction of such cosmic proportions, however, can hardly be dismissed in such a cavalier manner.

There is no escaping the choice that must be made. We are in fact confronted with the great conflict of the ages. Timothy Leary knew whereof he spoke when in his address at the 22nd Annual Conference of the Association for Humanistic Psychology he declared:

> You could argue that human history is the exciting and invigorating tension between the humanists—those who believe in inner potential and the divine spark within— and those who don't.[24]

Of course, by the word "divine" atheistic humanists such as Leary and those who cheered this statement at the AHP conference are not referring to any Supreme Being. It is pantheism/naturalism again, the deification of the entire universe—including man. As New Haven, Connecticut, surgeon and Yale University professor Bernie Siegel expresses it: "Within each of us is a spark. Call it a divine spark if you will, but it is there. . . ."[25]

This inner "spark" is the cosmic force alleged to be innate in all things, but which in mankind, we are assured, has evolved to the point of self-consciousness. On that basis it is able to reach for new heights—to be attained through the fabled quantum leap.

If, as the Bible declares, the promise of godhood is a satanic ploy, then one would expect to find it at the heart of Satanist religion. In fact that is the case, and it provides an underlying relationship between the growing Satanist movement and basic New Age philosophy—a connection that most New Agers find surprising.

14

Satanism, Rock, and Rebellion

Michael Aquino is both a self-proclaimed Satanist and a Lieutenant Colonel in the United States Army. "The Army has known about my religion for the entire span of my Army career, which began in 1968," says Aquino, "[and] has paid very little attention to it, as it would . . . any other slightly unusual religion today."[1]

That statement was part of Aquino's defense of his "slightly unusual" religion when he and his wife, Lilith (the name, in occult mythology, of Adam's demon-wife before Eve), appeared February 17, 1988, on America's most popular television daytime talk program, the "Oprah Winfrey Show." Winfrey was clearly surprised by the Aquinos' description of Satanists as "very decent, very law-abiding people [with] . . . a very high set of personal ethics . . . [who have] nothing to do with evil."

"It's just difficult for me to understand that the devil is a good thing . . . that Satan isn't evil, which is the opposite of what everybody in this world has been taught," responded Oprah Winfrey, obviously perplexed. "In every state of the nation authorities are investigating some form of what they call satanic activity. . . . Children are telling the same stories about infants being murdered before their eyes in strange devil rituals. The list of bizarre stories goes on and on."

Openness As the Only Virtue

Oprah's surprise reflected a basic inconsistency in popular

233

thinking. If, as today's culture generally accepts, there are no moral absolutes, then calling Satanism just as moral as any other belief system is not surprising at all. In vain one searches the New Age "states-of-consciousness" clichés and hype about "spiritual values" for any basis of evaluation. In fact the mere suggestion that there ought to be some definite standard of *right* and *wrong* is rejected out of hand as narrow-minded. As Jean Houston persuades those whom she has led into altered states specifically designed for receptivity to suggestion: "And no one has any right . . . to impose guilt . . . you are bound only by your own ethics and authentic responsibilities."[2]

Surely, then, Satanism could not be *wrong*, because nothing is wrong. The Satanist's "own ethics and authentic responsibilities" are just as valid as those of anyone else. Those who no longer believe in the personal God of the Bible haven't come to believe in *nothing*, but must in fact accept *everything*, because they no longer have any legitimate basis for rejecting anything. As Allan Bloom reminds us in *The Closing of the American Mind*, in today's relativistic society, "There is no enemy other than the man who is not open to everything."[3]

New Agers are especially vulnerable to the popular belief that has dominated American universities for decades: that the one virtue is openness to everything and the refusal to be against anything. It is this very openness which makes the New Age so appealing. Among consumers of the wide variety of products offered in the burgeoning mystical supermart, there is a naive and dangerous tendency to embrace anything so long as some spiritual shibboleth is pronounced. "New Agers . . . never tackle issues; they hug them," Richard Blow points out in *The New Republic*. "The New Age way is not to deny differences between people, but to deny that they matter." This unwillingness to distinguish between right and wrong was carried to its logical extreme in an editorial in the transpersonal psychology journal *The Common Boundary*:

> It isn't too difficult to differentiate between the devils and the angels, but it requires a fairly sophisticated discrimination to see that an angel is just the flip-side of a devil, and that true harmony demands a "holy marriage" between the two: a union which results in the birth of an

entirely new principle that transcends the whole devil/angel duality.[4]

By this "sophisticated new principle" of openness to *everything*, which is generally taught in most universities today, "God," if you choose to believe in some "higher power," is whatever you want to call it (or him or her), from Mother Earth to Krishna to the All or some evolutionary Force—or Satan. No difference is allowed among these deities, because to do so would be discrimination. Moreover, it really makes no difference what labels are attached, because in the final analysis "God" is everyone's "Higher Self." It would be inconsistent with New Age philosophy to criticize Satanism, even if it included molestation of children, suicide, murder, and human sacrifices—which it does (but all of which both Aquinos vehemently denied).

There was really no need for them to deny anything. On what basis can any behavior, no matter how horrifying, be "discriminated" against? The murderer is only fulfilling karma. As Edgar Mitchell, Shirley MacLaine, et al tell us, there are "never any victims." If this is true, then Hitler, Himmler, and company were only assisting in the "reality" which their six million Jewish victims had created for themselves.

Why should such an assertion cause those who deny moral absolutes to cringe? Aquino, at least, is consistent. If we have no better reason than public opinion for prohibiting human sacrifices, child molestation, pornography, or homosexuality, then the Nuremberg trials of "war criminals" were a farce. Hitler's systematic extermination of Jews was not a question of *right* or *wrong* but of whether the majority of Germans were in favor of it at the time. Today, however, we have gone even beyond that point: Behavior is no longer acceptable because of its approval by the majority (much less on the basis of moral considerations), but now *minority rights* are the all-important factor, even when the majority of people are opposed. And Satanists, seeing themselves as an "oppressed minority," are now ready to press for their "rights" on that basis. And on what basis could they be refused?

If one's child is sacrificed on a Satanist altar there is the great consolation of knowing that karma is being fulfilled, and that the child has actually chosen this fate in order to learn some essential lesson in its cosmic advance toward godhood. As Shirley MacLaine said on an earlier Oprah Winfrey Show, in response to a mother's question concerning the recent death of her 20-month-old baby, "When someone dies, respect their need to do it. . . ."[5] Oprah had agreed with Shirley's New Age ideas. She knew she *shouldn't* agree with Aquino's. Yet it was the clear connection between the two that she found disturbing.

The New Age Connection

The "perverted" idea of Satan as *evil* was a gross misconception which Lieutenant Colonel Aquino indignantly said he would "lay at the doorstep of the Christian value system. . . ." His former mentor, however, Anton LaVey, founder of San Francisco's First Church of Satan, has not been so reluctant to reveal what Satanists actually believe. On its 20/20 News Special, ABC had already shown LaVey on camera stating, while not the whole truth, at least more than Aquino was willing to admit:

> We perform human sacrifices, by proxy you might say—the destruction of human beings who would, let's say, create an antagonistic situation towards us—in the form of curses and hexes, not in actual blood rituals because certainly the destruction of a human being physically is illegal.[6]

Aquino explained that Satanism involves the recognition and development of an "inner quality of soul" which gives mankind the right and power to oppose all laws of nature and to conquer or use to one's own ends all natural forces. This anarchy against nature goes far beyond the legitimate defense mounted by science and technology against the often harmful and destructive forces of nature. Aquino elaborated further upon Satanism in terms hardly distinguishable from Huxley's explanation of the perennial philosophy and (as Winfrey must have recognized) uncomfortably similar to the basic beliefs of the New Age movement, with which she has expressed strong sympathy and agreement.

"We are not servants of some God," declared Aquino; "we are our own gods!" This is the very heart of New Age teaching, yet Aquino stated it as Satanist doctrine.

Winfrey seemed surprised. "Well, the way you explain this," she said, "is very much the way a lot of people who are into metaphysics now and the New Age movement and New Age thinking, they say the very same thing. Are you saying that it's the same?"

There was no hesitation in Aquino's response. "Yes, except that I would say we [Satanists] have a more precise grasp of . . . this quality of the human psyche or the human soul. . . . We would say that we understand what's actually happening a little better than many New Agers."

"How do you explain across this country," she persisted, apparently trying to clear the confusion, "children who are listening to heavy rock metal music and supposedly talking to the devil? Recently in New Jersey a 14-year-old boy who'd been getting straight A's did a paper on Satanism . . . and in two weeks had turned his entire life around, ended up stabbing his mother 12 times, and killed himself—all in the name of Satan!"

Aquino dismissed such happenings as the activity of "misguided kooks or young children with a very disturbed family background" who were giving Satan an undeservedly bad name. He complained that Satanists were being accused of crimes "on virtually no evidence at all." Ridiculing the charges of ritual murder, Lilith said, "You can't find any bodies . . . the constant answer is, 'We haven't found any bodies, but we know this is going on.' " Michael Aquino vowed that Satanists were going to fight discrimination and persecution. "We have seen quite enough of this kind of thing going on in the United States with regard to our religion, and we are not about to sit silent and watch it proceed further."

Later in the program, the second member of the audience to gain the microphone turned out to be a law-enforcement officer. After identifying himself, he said: "To say that there are no bodies and that these [Satanists] are not committing crimes is the farthest from the truth . . . in every case that I've investigated, now extending over 200, I have found this particular book. . . ." He held up a well-worn copy of Anton LaVey's *Satanic Bible*, which Aquino had insisted contained only good doctrines.

In the new consciousness, of course, "good" depends upon individual taste, so a Satanist's definition is as "good" as anyone's. And when it comes to actual practice, Satanists such as the Aquinos are more consistent in their beliefs than New Agers. The latter talk of surrender to nature, Mother Earth, or the cosmos; yet at the same time they attempt to develop powers of the mind for creating their own reality, their own nature, or their own cosmos. As MacLaine had said to Winfrey, "You have ultimate . . . freedom. So you're creating your own reality just like you want to do it." At least Aquino admitted that Satanists see themselves as alien to the universe, outside the established reality and overthrowing it with magical power—and he correctly identified this as the same power which the New Agers seek to tap into and use to their own ends.

On the other hand, it is hardly consistent for Aquino to pretend to childish innocence and virtue, and to describe Satanists as "decent, very law-abiding people," when at the same time he states that the essence of Satanism is an arrogant and hostile rebellion against universal law. It is equally deceitful to claim that the generally accepted view of Satan as evil is false, and preposterous to lay this "misconception" at the door of Christianity. In fact, the biblical depiction of Satan as the archenemy of God and man is very consistent with the view that Aquino himself expressed.

The Hebrew prophets declared that Satan was the most beautiful, wise, and powerful being that God had created; but, deluded by pride, he had aspired to become a "God" himself. It was the ultimate rebellion, in which a multitude of angels-turned-demons apparently followed him. Mankind also chose to join in this high treason against the Lord of the universe. Satan's all-consuming pursuit of this ambition has made him the personification of evil and perversion. That the biblical Satan and the god of Satanists are one and the same, even as to their influence upon mankind, is clear from what Aquino told the television audience:

> We believe that this quality [to go against God's natural order] in the human soul that makes it different from all other life forms . . . was deliberately inculcated in humanity in its distant evolutionary past by an active agency that is operating in defiance of the universal norm [God's laws].

And that agency has been caricatured and that agency has been mythologized as Prometheus, as Lucifer, as Satan, and in the greatest antiquity by the ancient Egyptians as Set.

Satanism, Rock Music, and "Inspiration"

In addition to the similarities between the New Age and Aquino's philosophy, Oprah Winfrey also pointed to a connection between Satanism and rock music. Such a relationship should be obvious. Yet the extent to which some popular music has become the vehicle for deliberately and successfully influencing millions of America's youth with Satanism seems to have aroused little public concern.

Many of the big-time rock stars have been heavily involved not only in the occult but also in overt Satanism. Even since his death, in 1971 at the age of 27, Jim Morrison (leader of one of the most popular American rock bands of the 1960's, The Doors) continues to have a powerful influence. In terms strikingly similar to Aquino's description of the force behind Satanism, the eulogy on the back cover of Morrison's biography describes him as the "obsessed disciple of darkness who rejected authority in any form, the explorer who probed 'the bounds of reality to see what would happen'. . . ."[7]

John Lennon told of mystical experiences as a young teenager: "I used to literally trance out into alpha . . . seeing these hallucinatory images of my face changing, becoming cosmic and complete."[8] He called Yoko Ono his "don Juan," referring to the Yaqui Indian sorcerer who initiated Carlos Castaneda into the sorcerer's world.[9] Trying to describe his own "inspiration" process, Lennon said: "It's like being possessed: like a psychic or a medium."[10] According to Keith Richards of the Rolling Stones: "The Stones' songs came spontaneously like an inspiration at a seance. The tunes arrived 'en masse' as if the Stones as songwriters were only a willing and open medium."[11] Of the Beatles, Yoko Ono has said, "They were like mediums. They weren't conscious of all they were saying, but it was coming through them."[12] Many others tell of similar inspiration. Marc Storace, vocalist with the heavy-metal band Krokus, told *Circus* magazine:

You can't describe it except to say it's like a mysterious
energy that comes from the metaphysical plane and into
my body. It's almost like being a medium. . . .[13]

"Little Richard" had similar experiences and identified Satan as
the source of his inspiration: "I was directed and commanded by
another power. The power of darkness . . . that a lot of people
don't believe exists. The power of the Devil. Satan."[14] Jim Morrison called the spirits that at times possessed him "The Lords,"
and wrote a book of poetry about them.[15] Folk rock artist Joni
Mitchell's creativity came from her spirit guide "Art." So dependent was she upon "Art" that nothing could detain her when he
"called."[16] The prevalence of such "spirits" among many top rock
stars seems to go beyond the realm of coincidence. Superstar Jimi
Hendrix, called "rock's greatest guitarist" and known as the *Voodoo Chile of The Aquarian Age*, "believed he was possessed by
some spirit," according to Alan Douglas. Hendrix's former girl-
friend, Fayne Pridgon, has said:

He used to always talk about some devil or something
was in him, you know, and he didn't have any control
over it, he didn't know what made him act the way he
acted and what made him say the things he said, and
songs . . . just came out of him. . . .
He was so tormented and just torn apart . . . and I
used to talk about my grandmother and all her weird
stuff, you know, and he used to talk about us going down
there and having some root lady or somebody see if she
could drive this demon out of him.[17]

Revolution for a New World

The power of music to mold the thinking of generations has been
fully demonstrated. It was Elvis Presley, admired and highly honored
by millions in spite of his thorough involvement in drugs and
occultism, who started it all. His swinging hips were a mild expression of the rebellion against all authority to which Aquino referred—
a rebellion that reached new heights as its influence accelerated

through groups such as the Beatles and Rolling Stones. That revolt of youth has now blossomed into a flagrant glorification of the ugly and perverted, and a brutal assault against what has long been considered decent and moral.

Aquino's "active agency [Satan] that is operating in defiance of the universal norm" appears to be largely in control. The motivation seems so admirable: deliverance from narrow-minded judgmentalism and an openness to new truth—and all for the good cause of building the youthful idealists' "new world." Jimi Hendrix, talented but tormented "voodoo child," was one of the crusaders of this seemingly worthy cause. Why then did he plead for deliverance from demons that possessed and destroyed him? The openness—the "exploration and imagination" he espoused—still seduces his admirers today. As part of his legacy he said:

> Things like witchcraft, which is a form of exploration, and imagination, have been banned by the establishment and called evil.
>
> It's because people are frightened to find out the full power of the mind.[18]

It is not only Satanists who flaunt their rebellion and in effect thumb their noses at the Creator. Calling the Jehovah of the Old Testament "a mean, nasty, paranoid, mafio, coppo, condominium owner," Timothy Leary says, "I submit that Eve's a good place to start if you're looking for a humanist psychologist hero. How about a round of applause for Eve!" There were cheers and laughter from the psychologists' convention audience. In *The Courage To Create*, Rollo May, who has an undergraduate degree from Union Theological Seminary, praises Eve for her independent spirit in rebelling against God's command not to eat the forbidden fruit. What the Bible calls sin May calls the "felix culpa" or "fortunate fall." Though himself one of the founders of the Association for Humanistic Psychology, Stanford's Willis Harman has said:

> It is not an accident that this value confusion of modern society follows so closely after the period, a half century or so ago, of the "great debunking" of religion

by positivistic reductionist science—the period Roger
Sperry [has] referred to as dominated by the "materialist
and behaviorist doctrine."

The weakening of Judeo-Christian values in Western
society was a direct consequence of the "scientific"
erosion of belief in the transcendental nature of the human
spirit.[19]

It is interesting that Harman identifies "value confusion" (i.e.,
rejection of moral standards) with antagonism toward Judeo-Christian beliefs. The Bible, which presents these now-largely-rejected
values, prophesies that in the "last days" the "spirit of disobedience" that has been at work in mankind since it joined the
serpent's rebellion will be embodied in the Antichrist, ruler of a
world united against God. He is called "the man of lawlessness"
who, in his rejection of God's authority, declares that he himself is
God.[20] The ultimate rebellion, of course, is the New Ager's claim to
be God. The cloak of immunity which such a claim provides renders
one free from accountability to any authority higher than self.

Written nearly 2000 years ago, the biblical prophecy that this
rebellion would gather momentum until it engulfed virtually the
whole world is an amazingly accurate description of current developments. Much of the credit for two generations of youth in an
international rebellion against all authority and moral values must
be given to entertainers such as the Beatles and the Rolling Stones,
whose "openness to everything" is characterized by bitter hostility
toward a Judeo-Christian value system. Derek Taylor, the Beatles'
press agent, said:

They're completely anti-Christ. I mean, I am anti-Christ as well, but they're so anti-Christ they shock me,
which isn't an easy thing.[21]

The Seductive Call of "Freedom"

It was apparently too late when Jimi Hendrix discovered that he
was controlled by minds other than his own. Much of today's rock
music, like Aquino's Satanism, represents an angry and arrogantly

self-centered revolution aimed at overthrowing all morals and the very order underlying the universe, and filling the vacuum by a deified self. The promised freedom, however, has proven to be destructive not only of values but of the individual as well. That same freedom from the restrictions of conscience is a by-product of a belief in the ability to create one's own reality. It surfaces once again in a context seemingly far removed from Satanism or the rock music scene: Stanford University's Graduate School of Business.

In their "Creativity In Business Course," Michael Ray and Rochelle Myers have adapted from the Siddha Yoga of Ray's guru, Swami Muktananda, exercises for developing mind powers. One of the techniques involves the destruction of generally accepted moral values and what is called the voice of judgment (VOJ), which of course includes conscience:

> **Do the forbidden** [in your imagination]. Sass a parent, disobey a boss, throw your hand at a bridge partner— anything you've always wanted to do. Luxuriate in the emotional aftermath, then pick up the pieces.[22]

New Age educators such as Ray and Myers might object to having their goals likened to the anarchy that characterizes Satanism and rock music. After all, MBA's are hardly your average hard-rock enthusiasts. A fundamental rebelliousness, however, is the common denominator in all attempts at mentally creating one's own reality, whether or not those who espouse this belief see themselves as doing it for love and good or for hate and evil. If "All is One," then such distinctions are meaningless, and each individual is his own ultimate authority. William C. Miller, one of Ray's colleagues at Stanford's Graduate School of Business and an 1800-dollar-per-day consultant to many Fortune 500 companies, dedicates his book *The Creative Edge* to "the divine spirit we all share." He advocates the same Eastern meditation in order to contact "your innermost intuitive self . . . [part of] the spiritual core of all humanity" as the ultimate source of wisdom for business decisions. There is no higher authority.[23] Ray's calculated destruction of conscience results in this same deification of self as the supreme authority:

> The answers to all your questions . . . are within you.
> Your biggest job in life is to learn to trust your Essence to
> provide all the answers you can ever use.
>
> [Quoting, as an example, a businessman]: "The moral
> code is imposed from outside when one is too young to
> discern oneself. . . . Like training wheels on a bicycle,
> they support us when we are young and clumsy . . . but
> then get in the way. . . .[24]

That may seem attractive, but it leaves us without any moral
direction. Five billion little make-believe "gods" each following his
own dictates doesn't make for peace upon earth. Expressing this
appealing but deceptive pseudofreedom, graduates of Harvard's
School of Public Health (Class of '87) defiantly "tossed into the air
hundreds of condoms encased in envelopes that bore the Latin
message AD VENEREM SECURIOREM ('for safe sex')." In contrast, ABC *Nightline* Moderator Ted Koppel delivered this sober
statement in his commencement address to 1987 graduates of Duke
University:

> We have actually convinced ourselves that slogans will
> save us. Shoot up if you must, but use a clean needle.
> Enjoy sex whenever and with whomever you wish, but
> wear a condom. No! The answer is no. Not because it
> isn't cool or smart or because you might end up in jail or
> dying in an AIDS ward, but no because it's wrong,
> because we have spent 5,000 years as a race of rational
> human beings, trying to drag ourselves out of the prime-
> val slime by searching for truth and moral absolutes.
>
> In its purest form, truth is not a polite tap on the
> shoulder. It is a howling reproach. What Moses brought
> down from Mount Sinai were not the Ten Suggestions.[25]

Koppel's call for the recognition of a higher authority than selfish
desires is not a popular one. Anton LaVey speaks not only for
Satanists, but for today's relativistic society as well when he declares: "The highest of all holidays in Satanism is the date of one's
own birth, for we worship the individual and celebrate self-love."

One observer of today's scene writes: "A current ad for Calvin Klein's Obsession For Men perfume shows a young, attractive man—hair slicked back, suit pressed, and in love in the way only an '80s man can be: he's staring straight into a mirror."[26] This is actually an ancient Hindu method of worshiping the "God within." It was looking into a mirror that gave Lennon the vision of his cosmic Self, a practice that John Denver picked up from Muktananda (who was also his guru), who advocated bowing down and worshiping oneself in front of a mirror.

The "Electric Shamans"

The same spirit that is inspiring much of the rock music scene seems to be exerting its influence in every area of society. While rock music makes its appeal to the latent rebelliousness of youth, the various psychotherapies, meditation, and other new consciousness techniques appeal to the yuppies and more established citizenry. All, however, are simply different pieces cut out of the same cloth. When asked to describe a Van Halen concert, David Lee Roth (at that time the group's lead vocalist) replied: "It's like therapy." Carl Jung would have agreed; so many of these stars have their "Philemons." In the world of rock, however, the entities no longer seem to feel it necessary to wear a mask to hide their identity.

The satanic connection is now something about which to boast. No longer is anyone shocked by albums and lyrics honoring Satan. AC-DC's "Highway to Hell," the Rolling Stones' "Their Satanic Majesty's Request" (put together by the suicidal Brian Jones), and David Lee Roth's "Running With the Devil" are typical of this genre of rock. The source of such artistic expression is clear: Marc Storace of Krokus talks about "meditat[ing] with the dark powers" and "allow[ing] them entrance" to the soul.[27] Roth, who called himself "toastmaster for the *immoral majority*," was very aware that the ultimate goal was to conjure up *evil* spirits and surrender to them. He told an interviewer:

> I'm gonna abandon my spirit to them, which is actually what I attempt to do. You work yourself into that state and you fall in supplication of the demon gods. . . .[28]

Strangely enough, no matter how much the various means may seem to be at odds, the underlying perennial philosophy is invariably the same. Though led down the same path, each stratum of society is convinced that it is involved in building a new world that meets its own ideals. As it is with the New Age, there is nothing *new* about this dream. It is, in fact, a regression to earlier cultures that were dominated by witch doctors, voodoo priests, and other shamans. Lauding the connection between rock music and voodoo ("drum beat by drum beat, movement by movement—a force which compels a man forward . . . against that final terror . . . the dark sense of death"),[29] Ray Manzarek, keyboard player for The Doors, relates:

> You see, when the Siberian shaman gets ready to go into his trance, all the villagers get together and shake rattles and blow whistles and play whatever instruments they have to send him off [into trance and possession]. There is a constant pounding, pounding, pounding. And those sessions last for hours and hours.
>
> It was the same way with *The Doors* when we played in concert. The sets [concerts] didn't last that long, but I think that our drug experiences let us get into it that much quicker. We knew the symptoms of the [altered] state, so that we could try to approximate it.
>
> It was like Jim [Morrison] was an electric shaman and we were the electric shaman's band, pounding away behind him. Sometimes he wouldn't feel like getting into the state, but the band would keep on pounding and pounding, and little by little it would take him over.
>
> God, I could send an electric shock through him with the organ. John could do it with his drumbeats. You could see every once in a while—twitch!—I could hit a chord and make him twitch. And he'd be off again.
>
> Sometimes he was just incredible. Just amazing. And the audience felt it, too![30]

From Wall Street to Haiti and Back

One is reminded of Wade Davis's description of the vodoun

ceremony leading to possession: "The drum pounded relentlessly, deep solid blows that seemed to strike directly to the woman's spine. She cringed with each beat. . . . And upon this wave of sound, the spirit arrived . . . slowly she lifted her face to the sky. She had been mounted by the divine horseman; she had become the spirit. . . . Apparently the spirits could be greedy, for soon two other *hounsis* were possessed. . . . The drums beat ceaselessly. Then, as suddenly as the spirits arrived, they left. . . ."[31] Such practices have played an important part in many cultures around the world in the past and are being revived in various forms throughout a wide range of American society today.

The connection between voodoo and rock representations of shamanism and the "trance dancing" exercise in the "Creativity In Business" course is clearly more than coincidental. The similarity is not only in the music ("repetitive rhythms . . . exotic . . . mysterious") but in the trance ("collapse into the corpse pose"), the "rushes of energy," and the "out-of-body-experiences" which Michael Ray describes and recommends. Moreover, the altered state is specifically entered not merely to "loosen up analytic types" (as Ray would say) but in order for the shamans-in-training of the business world to make contact with a "spirit guide . . . to whom you can turn for guidance."[32]

Like so many other popular promoters of contact with "spirit guides" in an academic or psychotherapeutic setting, however, Ray again suggests that such entities are creatures of our imagination. Yet they have some very real powers and personalities of their own. We can hardly ignore the fact that those who present today's most popular form of this ancient practice, rock's "electric shamans," generally agree, like their ancient predecessors, that the spirits involved are demons in the service of Satan. Moreover, the fanatically rebellious conduct on and off stage, and the tragic and premature deaths of so many rock stars, seem to confirm this identification. Haiti provides a current example of what America's future society of sorcerers could be if we continue in the present direction. Davis writes:

> Vodoun is not an isolated cult; it is a complex mystical worldview, a system of beliefs concerning the relationship between man, nature, and the supernatural forces of the universe. . . .

In Haiti, as in Africa, there is no separation between
the sacred and the secular . . . vodoun not only embodies
a set of spiritual concepts, it prescribes a way of life. . . .
Each believer not only has direct contact with the spirits,
he actually receives them into his body. . . .

"Haiti will teach you that good and evil are one. . . .
For the vodounist there seem to be no absolutes.[33]

Building the Sorcerer's World

So the destruction of absolutes in which American public education has played such a large role since the days of John Dewey, and
which today's university students imagine is a modern concept, has
been at the heart of sorcery from time immemorial. As we have
already seen, the power to create one's own reality must include the
power to create one's own values as well. While most Americans
have not yet become convinced that the former is possible, it is now
the general consensus that the latter is everyone's right.

Witness, for example, the hue and cry that went up in certain
quarters when it was suggested that in conjunction with all of the
information being made available to teenagers about sex and birth
control and access to clinics dispensing contraceptives, sexual
abstinence might be recommended as well. Civil libertarians presumably feared that, while condoms, IUD's, and birth control pills
are merely neutral, value-free *techniques*, abstinence might reflect
a moral (or, even worse, a religious) *value judgment*. When several
states passed laws requiring parental consent before undergoing
abortion, it was virtually a foregone conclusion that a number of
courts would rule them unconstitutional. Somewhere in the Constitution a phrase was found from which could be wrenched the
opinion that children—who need parental consent in order to have
their ears pierced—could not be required to have parental consent
for abortions.

Parental *values* must not be allowed to influence children's *rights*
to set their own standards. It is the very "freedom" from any
authority higher than self which Satanists imagine is their peculiar
trademark, but which the government itself champions. This ram-
pant relativism, which is now taken for granted by the general
public, is one more evidence of the overwhelming influence of

Eastern mysticism upon the West. In Hinduism there are no absolutes and no sin; each person's *dharma* is unique. The "All is One . . . you are the universe" message of cosmic consciousness has provided relativism and its twin, rebellion, with a justification previously unknown in the Western world. Wisdom, knowledge, truth, and moral standards are no longer to be sought in parental counsel, great literature, or sacred writings. They are to be found by looking deep within one's own soul. Each generation imagines itself to be the author of this belief, and is seduced once again by the delusion of a freedom that ultimately fails to deliver on its promises.

The exaltation of self always espouses at first an openness to all truth and equality among all. Inevitably, however, as in Orwell's *Animal Farm*, "we are all equal" becomes "some of us are more equal than others." Mankind cannot do without its heroes. The youth who seem to defy all authority are at the same time obedient to those who have persuaded them to disobey. Even those who are trying desperately to believe that they are autonomous gods and "One with the All" stand at the same time in awe of the various gurus who have brought them this liberating "truth." Oddly enough, "liberation" from belief in the God of the Bible and its moral code seems to produce a fanatical allegiance to another god, whether a rock star, a guru, or a Hitler.

Some Disturbing Similarities

The sense of *déjà vu* is so strong as to be almost nauseating. Throughout the Western world we are seeing a repetition of the conditions in Germany that contributed to the founding of the Nazi regime. Some of the more perceptive New Agers have noticed the similarities between their movement and the Germany of the 1920's and '30's, and it troubles them greatly. One writer in *New Age Journal* tells of reading "a little book published in 1923—*The Revolt of Youth*, by Stanley High." He says, "It is a disturbing book . . . an eyewitness account, glowingly recorded, of the youth culture that followed the horrors of World War I . . . [that] could well have been entitled *The Greening of Germany*. Reading it, one is unsure whether this is Germany of the twenties or America of the sixties that High is describing." The article continues:

> Back to nature go the hippies of the day, the *Wander-vogel* . . . led by a battered assortment of guitars . . . the "hope for the future of Germany."
>
> Natural camaraderie prevails, with freedom of sexual companionship. . . . "Nothing is so roundly hated as the superimposition of conventional authority, and nothing so loved as nature." . . .
>
> The political interests are tending to disappear, the great spiritual forces are on the ascendency . . . there is an inexplicable reaction against conventional Christianity. . . .
>
> I had been privileged to walk with the youth of another world . . . the apostles of a wholly new life for young and old alike . . . with their spirit the old heaven and the old earth—suspicion and selfishness and hate—will pass away."

This is not Charles Reich praising hippiedom, this is Germany of 1923!

There are other similarities, even more disturbing and ominous. There was the revival of Eastern mysticism, yoga, Zen, Taoism, meditation, astrology, vegetarianism, the awakening belief in reincarnation and karma—and of course the emphasis upon "enlightenment" through tapping into the infinite "source of wisdom" within the psyche. The realization that "All is One" and that each person is "God" was, of course, the underlying belief. Hitler himself was deeply involved in mysticism and pursued the dream of occultic power with a passion, sending expeditions to India and Tibet in search of Hindu and Buddhist secrets. Herman Rauschning, Governor of Danzig, who knew the Fuehrer intimately, claimed that Hitler confided in him: "I will tell you a secret. I am founding an Order. . . . the Man-God, that splendid Being, will be an object of worship. . . ."

There is no normal explanation for the staggering mystery that was Hitler: a small-time ex-corporal with obsessive delusions who rose out of obscurity to make the entire world tremble. Bewildered historians have asked how a man so narrow in view, so enslaved by stultifying dogmas, could have achieved such incredible success. Yet this comic figure with the bobbing mustache and frantic gestures outmaneuvered the world's leaders time and again with his insane boldness, conquered Europe with terrifying swiftness, and held the destiny of nations in his mad grip. There is no ordinary answer to the enigma that was Hitler. Reflecting upon his experiences with the Nazi dictator, Rauschning declared with awe:

> One cannot help thinking of him as a medium . . . the medium is possessed . . . beyond any doubt, Hitler was possessed by forces outside himself . . . of which the individual named Hitler was only the temporary vehicle.[34]

No less obsessed with the occult was Heinrich Himmler, head of the infamous SS, which was not only a military organization but a secret order of black magicians. Himmler reportedly spent more money on occult investigations and genealogical research, tracing the mystical origins of Aryan supermen back to India and Tibet, than the Americans spent upon the initial development of the atomic bomb. The ultimate mission of the SS was to usher in a New Age, a New World inhabited by a New Man. In the dedicated fulfillment of this task, given to Hitler by the "invisibles" that inspired him, the SS murdered 14 million men, women, and children. World War II itself claimed the lives of almost 50 million people. Yet the Nazi leaders saw themselves much as Aquino described Satanists on the Winfrey Show—decent, sensitive, and affectionate family men who appreciated good music and didn't even like to see animals suffer.

Defectors from the Temple of Set tell of the visit of Aquino, at that time a Major in the U.S. Army, to the SS castle at Wewelsburg, Germany. Nicholas Goodrick-Clarke gives a description and brief history of Wewelsburg in *The Occult Roots of Nazism*. Here at the height of Nazi power Himmler presided over magical rituals very much like those engaged in not only by Satanists today but by many New Agers. On the Winfrey Show, Aquino denied any sympathy for Hitler's politics and claimed he was only interested in the "occult practices of the Third Reich." Upon visiting Wewelsburg, Aquino reportedly obtained access to the inner sanctum, where he went into deep meditation, made contact with "the force that empowered Hitler," and loosed it upon the world once again.

Whether this "contact" was something real or imaginary, it is highly disturbing that similar meditation is being promoted and practiced across America as we unwittingly create a society of sorcerer's apprentices.

15

Shamanism on the Rise

The VIII International Conference of the International Transpersonal Association, held in Davos, Switzerland, brought together participants from numerous countries concerned for the future of planet Earth. Speakers were mostly medical doctors and psychologists of international reputation. The workshops were all hard-core occultism and mysticism dressed in a flimsy disguise of science or psychology. The following description, from the conference brochure, of a typical workshop presents some idea of what these influential leaders from around the world considered essential for working out a better future for this planet:

The Shamanic Journey, Power and Healing

The Shamanic Journey is one of mankind's most ancient visionary methods of entering non-ordinary reality and exploring the hidden universe usually glimpsed only through myth and dream.

Participants will undergo an experiential initiation into the journey, aided by traditional drumming and dancing techniques designed to achieve the Shamanic State of Consciousness.

Participants will learn how to use the shaman's journey to heal and maintain health, acquire knowledge, and solve daily problems.[1]

Health is a universal concern. When suffering from serious illness, especially if diagnosed as terminal, the ill are likely to reach out in desperation and grasp at any straw. The field of holistic medicine, of which famed mystic Edgar Cayce has been called the American founder, offers a new hope to those whom medical science has failed. The major distinctive of holistic (or wholistic) medicine is that it deals with the whole person: "mind, body, and spirit," as the ads generally declare. One immediately wonders what qualifies medical doctors, dentists, chiropractors, psychiatrists, and other holistic practitioners to "treat" a *spirit*. Of course, that has always been the province of religion, and particularly of witch doctors and other shamans.

It is certain that the average physician never took a single course in medical school that even defined *spirit*, much less taught how to diagnose and cure in that realm. While great care is taken with training, testing, and licensing those who treat the body, there are no criteria for those who claim to treat the spirit. This is because *spirit* has always been recognized as a *religious* term, and the government's regulatory agencies are supposed to allow complete freedom in that area. It is amazing that most people flocking to holistic health practitioners seem to overlook the critical question that ought to concern everyone: *What religion* is being passed off as medical science under the label of holistic health?

Shamanism and Holistic Medicine

The answer to that question is obvious, yet its significance seems to elude us: Once again it is naturalism/pantheism/polytheism's ancient metaphysical or occult beliefs (generally with a heavy Hindu or Buddhist flavor) being presented in new packages for the West. Anthropologist Michael Harner, who is one of the world's leading experts on shamanism, has pointed out that holistic medicine is simply shamanism being practiced in our culture under new labels. Harner writes:

> The burgeoning field of holistic medicine shows a tremendous amount of experimentation [with] . . .techniques long practiced in shamanism, such as visualization, altered states of consciousness, aspects of psychoanalysis, hypnotherapy, meditation, positive attitude, stress-reduction, and mental and emotional expression of will

for health and healing.

In a sense, shamanism is being reinvented in the West precisely because it is needed.[2]

The fact that there are no regulations, standards, or governmental agencies to assure that certain *spiritual* criteria are met and safeguards observed presents both practitioners and their patients with dangers that few people even consider. A recent editorial in *Shaman's Drum* warns that Westerners who are now jumping into the practice of shamanism because of its growing popularity "tend to downplay or deny shamanism's inherent dangerous aspects. . . ." As we have already mentioned, shamanism involves the development of alleged mind powers, which are always connected with a "spirit guide" contacted through an altered state of consciousness. Harner goes on to explain:

> A shaman is a man or a woman who enters an altered state of consciousness—at will—to contact and utilize an ordinarily hidden reality in order to acquire knowledge, power, and to help other persons.
>
> The [shaman's] guardian spirit is often a *power animal*, a spiritual being that not only protects and serves the shaman, but becomes another identity or alter ego for him.
>
> The shaman frequently sees and consults with his guardian spirit, travels with it on the shamanic journey, has it help him and uses it to help others to recover from illness and injury. . . .
>
> The shaman moves between realities, a magical athlete of states of consciousness . . . a "power-broker" in the sense of manipulating spiritual power to help people, to put them into a healthy equilibrium.[3]

As in psychotherapy, so also in the medical profession: The practice of shamanism is literally exploding. In *Visualization: The Uses of Imagery in the Health Professions*, Errol R. Korn and Karen Johnson (medical director and administrative director, respectively, of a pain rehabilitation center near San Diego, California) take shamanic techniques long used by medicine men and present them as the latest medical science. They conclude that "the use of altered states of consciousness alone on a regular basis . . . is sufficient to lead to wellness and actualization."

Los Angeles physcian Art Ulene, a popular television medical consultant and a TM graduate, suggests that the altered states reached through Eastern meditation involve "more than the physiological changes that Dr. [Herbert] Benson called 'the relaxation response.' " Says Ulene, "You'll know when it happens to you . . . some people say it's like smoking marijuana. . . . Your mind reverberates with emptiness."[4] In agreement, Yale University medical professor Bernie Siegel writes in his *New York Times* best-seller, *Love, Medicine & Miracles*:

> The goal is to reach a light trance state, sometimes called the alpha state . . . [which] is the first step in hypnosis, biofeedback, yogic meditation, and most related forms of mind exploration.
>
> With guidance and practice, meditation can lead to breath-taking experiences of cosmic at-oneness and enlightenment. . . .
>
> Among many psychological techniques applied to physical illness, the most widely used and successful has been the one called imaging or visualization.[5]

The Heart of Shamanism: The "Inner Guide"

It should be understood that these ideas are not coming out of careful medical research, but have been adopted by the doctors presenting them because this "new truth" has been received as a transforming revelation in an altered state of consciousness. And in nearly every case there has also been an experience of the most powerful use of shamanic visualization: contact with and usage of the "inner guide," which is often a "power animal." Bernie Siegel, for example, writes: "Just as healers in primitive tribes tell people to utilize power animals, I suggest that patients use similar animated symbols."[6] Explaining that a "safe place" must first of all be visualized in the imagination in order to meet this guide, Korn and Johnson write:

> With you in this safe place is a living being that is very
> much concerned with your welfare. . . . When you be-
> come aware and notice this guide, establish contact . . .
> and this you can do by actually talking with the crea-
> ture . . . and then telling the animal or person just exactly
> what you wish to get out of this encounter. . . .
>
> It is important that the clinician realize that the guide
> can be used to give advice to the client . . . [to] provide
> support and protection . . . messages that will solve the
> problems that the client is having . . . and to provide
> total symptom removal for brief periods. . . .[7]

We have already referred to Ulene's inner guide, contacted while
in an altered state, a rabbit that calls itself "Corky." "Don't ask me
where that name came from," says Ulene. "He also said he was a
boy." While hardly a "power animal," Ulene's bunny serves the
same shamanic function. "I was first introduced to guided imagery," Ulene tells us, "while making a film of relaxation techniques
with Dr. David Bresler, a psychologist at UCLA." To help readers of
his book, *Feeling Fine*, experience a similar life-changing transformation, Ulene explains the same technique we are hearing now
from hundreds of sources:

> Slowly look around your relaxing scene until you
> spot a living creature. Don't be surprised by what you
> find. . . . Move in closer on the creature. Ask it to move
> a little closer to you. (Bear with me; I haven't lost my
> senses.) . . .
>
> Now that the creature is up close, it's time for the two
> of you to get acquainted. . . . Talk to your creature. Tell
> it your name. Ask *its* name. Believe it or not, you'll get an
> answer. . . .
>
> When you and your creature have said all there is to
> say, it's time to return to *this* world again. Say goodbye
> and promise you'll return again. Then slowly open your
> eyes. . . .
>
> In the days to come we'll show you how to use this
> technique for pain relief and problem solving. We all

> have this inner diagnostician, a creature advisor who
> can come to us in time of need. Our creatures may not
> have the proper degrees, but their brand of medicine
> works. . . .[8]

Lest we fear that contact is being made with actual spirit entities, Ulene provides us with the familiar psychological assurance: "The animal, of course, is nothing more than a symbol for your inner self, and talking to the animal amounts to talking to yourself, but on a brain wavelength you don't often use." Like Ulene and many others who share this faith in the infinite wisdom and power of the "Higher Self," cancer researcher O. Carl Simonton declares that the "inner guide" is simply "a symbolic representation of aspects of the personality not normally available during conscious awareness."[9] Richard L. Watring argues, however, that such an explanation, in the face of the wealth of convincing evidence to the contrary, betrays a materialistic bias that "denies the existence of a supernatural realm."[10]

Korn and Johnson also insist that the "guide" represents the power and wisdom of one's own unconscious. Yet it is claimed that the "spirit guide" can provide the answer to every question, which is clearly beyond the capability of individual consciousness. And to explain these entities as representing a collective unconscious fails for reasons already discussed. Moreover, we have also demonstrated that the "All is One" philosophy which they preach is false.

Confronted by Inescapable Conclusions

It is affirmed by almost everyone who has experienced contact with them that these entities *seem* to have a real existence of their own. Certainly the followers of voodoo or Santeria, who have experienced possession, testify that some separate entity has taken control. Moreover, not all psychologists see these spirit guides as simply games played by the unconscious. Clinical psychologist and channeler Jose Stevens of Berkeley, California, is convinced that the entities that speak through him have an independent existence of their own.[11] Wade Davis believes in their power, having experienced it not only through witnessing the phenomenon of possession but by personal contact with his own inner guide.

Michael Harner suggests that the shamanic technique of visualizing a spirit guide actually opens the door for an independent entity to reveal itself. One must not "dismiss such visions as hallucinations," Harner writes. "It is a mental formation visualized and externalized, which may even exist for a time independent of its creator."[12] Medical scientist Andrija Puharich, holder of more than 50 patents, concluded after extensive research that increasing numbers of persons today are getting in touch "with some source outside of themselves." Puharich considers these entities to have powers far beyond human capabilities. He writes:

> I am personally convinced that superior beings from other spaces and other times have initiated a renewed dialogue with humanity. . . .
> While I do not doubt [their existence] . . . I do not know what they look like, how they live or even what their goals are with respect to humankind.[13]

For thousands of years shamans and mediums have been convinced of the real existence of the entities communicating with them. On what basis do the psychologists, physicians, self-improvement entrepreneurs, and business leaders who have adopted and promoted the long-established shamanic techniques for contacting these same entities deny their separate reality? There is no reason other than what William James called "the power of fashion in things 'scientific'." It is no longer in vogue to admit the existence of personal demons or angels or Satan or even a personal God. However, as we have already seen, it is the height of both naivete and vanity to pretend that humans are the only intelligent life in the universe, or that it would be impossible for intelligences to exist without physical bodies—or that none of these beings could possibly be *evil*.

Regardless of differing spiritual orientations, we seem to be confronted by certain inescapable conclusions: 1) The entities communicating with mankind are independent nonhuman intelligences with not only an existence of their own, but a particular agenda; 2) they lie repeatedly both about their own identity and about human potential, trying to attribute their activity to some power resident within the human psyche or within an alleged but nonexistent universal mind or collective unconscious. There is more than enough evidence to demonstrate that these beings are deliberately seducing those with whom they make contact. Moreover, their ploy, as we have seen, is simply a continual reenactment down through history of the original seduction of Eve by Satan.

Everyone is free to scoff at the story of Eve and the serpent presented in the Bible. No honest person, however, can deny that the identical offer of equality with God is the very heart of New Age philosophy and the gospel which the entities preach. Clearly each of us faces today the same decisive choice of whether to accept this offer (which is the ultimate rebellion) or to reject it.

On the one hand, for any human to imagine that he or she is or could become God would seem to betray itself as a lie by the very monstrosity of such an imposture. Yet the seduction is very difficult to resist. This is particularly true of those who have actually made contact. The experience of meeting these entities is so real, and what they offer in many cases seems so in line with the good of humanity, that, once initiated, a person is convinced that he is part of a superior consciousness and feels compelled to convince others to open themselves to the same life-changing transformation.

Initiation: Opening the Door

Wade Davis tells us how, as a young man in Canada on a North American Indian shamanic "vision quest," he had acquired a power animal that gained for him the respect of "a malevolent sorcerer," one of Haiti's most powerful and feared *bokors*:

> I explained to Marcel that I had my [power] animal, and that was the reason I was not afraid of him. That was why I feared no man.
>
> Once this came clear to Marcel, he became visibly excited. . . . Later that day Rachel overheard him explaining to several of his people that this *blanc* was unlike the others because he had been initiated.[14]

The experiences even of those who claim that such entities are merely splits of their own psyches nevertheless sound very real, and contain Sir James Jeans's three criteria for reality which we have already discussed. Moreover, there is a consistent pattern in the way that nearly all initiates are brought into this pantheistic worldview, which then becomes the basis for their new holistic approach to medicine, psychotherapy, business, science, and life in general. Bernie Siegel learned how to make contact from oncologist O. Carl Simonton and psychologist Stephanie Matthews, who achieved reknown through their use of visualization in research with cancer patients. Siegel tells how the Simontons (who learned the technique from Jose Silva, who in turn learned it from his spirit guide) led him "in a directed meditation to find and meet an inner guide":

> I approached this exercise with all the skepticism one expects from a mechanistic doctor. Still, I sat down, closed my eyes, and followed directions.
>
> I didn't believe it would work, but if it did I expected to see Jesus or Moses. Who else would dare appear inside a surgeon's head?
>
> Instead I met George, a bearded, long-haired young man wearing an immaculate flowing white gown and a skullcap. It was an incredible awakening for me, because I hadn't expected anything to happen. . . .
>
> George was spontaneous, aware of my feelings, and an excellent advisor.[15]

Professor Michael Ray tells of his initiation into the mystical realm that became the framework for the beliefs he presents in the "Creativity in Business" course. Like Fritjof Capra, who embraced a new view of physics through a Hindu mystical experience, Ray came to a new view of business in a similar manner. After being introduced by his psychotherapist to the Siddha Yoga of Swami Muktananda (guru to many other business leaders and stars of the entertainment industry), Ray had a mind-blowing experience. He tells what happened when an assistant to Muktananda ran a peacock feather across the "third eye" in the center of his forehead:

> I saw a bolt of lightning, like a pyramid of light. I began literally bouncing off the floor and trembling. I

cried. I felt tremendous energy, love, and joy.

What I had experienced, I later learned, had been *shaktipat*, or spiritual awakening of kundalini energy inside me [the *serpent* force coiled at the base of the spine awaiting release through an altered state].[16]

One could easily equate Ray's experience with what Castaneda and Huxley describe as occurring through drugs. Herbert Benson says that his Relaxation Response "acts, in a rather extraordinary fashion, as kind of a door to a renewed mind and changed.life."[17] We have already pointed out that this altered state removes all basis for objective evaluation, renders the participant vulnerable to suggestion, and is not the condition in which to adopt new world views. Yet such mystical experiences are the glue that holds the New Age movement together.

It is on the basis of such rites of initiation that the Seigels, Capras, Bensons, Korns, and Simontons have become evangelists dedicated to transforming America into a high-tech shamanic society. Best-selling author Gerald Jampolsky has become famous for his use of *A Course In Miracles* in his psychiatric practice and in his books and lectures around the world. He tells how he was prepared for the message of the *Course* through his own initiation when guru Muktananda administered the *shaktipat*:

. . . it seemed as though I had stepped out of my body and was looking down upon it. I saw colors whose depth and brilliance were beyond anything I had ever imagined.

I began to talk in tongues. A beautiful beam of light came into the room and I decided at that moment to stop evaluating what was happening and simply be one with the experience, to join it completely . . . I was filled with an awareness of love unlike anything I had known before.

And when I started reading the *Course*, I heard a voice within say, "Physician, heal thyself; this is your way home," and there was a complete feeling of oneness with God and the Universe.[18]

The New Evangelists

There can be no doubt that increasing numbers of leaders in every area of society are having powerful religious experiences and that as a result they have acquired a pantheistic worldview. Their lives have undoubtedly undergone a remarkable transformation. Such individuals are certainly entitled to have whatever experiences they desire; and they are also entitled, in their enthusiasm, to share with others what has happened to them, and even to do all they can to persuade others to undergo the same shamanic rite of initiation into the world of sorcery. We would not question the sincerity of these evangelists. They should not, however, deceptively present the perennial occultic religion of the spirit guides as medicine, psychology, self-improvement methods, science, or something other than what it actually is. Much less should they use highly suggestible altered states of consciousness for persuading others to join their faith.

Door-to-door salesmen could make a sale in every house on the block if the potential customers would consent to being led into an altered state of consciousness, a form of hypnosis where they are highly vulnerable to suggestion. It is through the induction into such mental states, however, that America is being subtly converted to the religion of shamanism—and by the very people who enjoy the highest degree of public confidence: its physicians, scientists, educators, psychotherapists, and clergymen. Increasing numbers of these highly regarded professionals are violating the public trust by deliberately evangelizing with Eastern mysticism those who look to them for help and guidance. Moreover, in the process, these evangelists of a basically Hindu gospel deny that they are presenting religious beliefs and assure their converts that they can embrace this new faith without in any way changing their present belief system. Here is how Bernie Siegel's spirit guide, "George," convinced him to become such a missionary:

> I was still toying with the idea of a career change. When I told him ["George"], he explained that . . . I could do more by remaining a surgeon but changing my *self* to help my patients mobilize their mental powers against disease.

I could combine the support and guidance of a minister or psychiatrist with the resources and expertise of a physician. I could practice "clergery," a term my wife coined. . . .

George said, "You can go anywhere in the hospital. A clergyman or therapist can't. You are free to supplement medical treatment with love or death-and-dying counseling, in a way that nonphysicians are not." . . .

["George"] has been an invaluable companion ever since his first appearance.[19]

The editorial in the Winter 1987-88 issue of *Shaman's Drum* declared: "There are signs that core shamanism may now be taking root in modern society . . . [including] modern medical settings . . . [and even] in the Soviet Union's scientific circles." It mentioned in particular "percussive instruments like the rattle and drum," which are used in trance dancing (as we have already discussed) and "the employment of animal allies discovered through journeying in alternate realms of consciousness." Why this growing acceptance of an ancient religious practice in secular Western society? The editorial explained that shamanism "is not considered a religion . . . but a *method*, empirical in nature rather than 'mystical,' and therefore more appealing to a secular-oriented audience."

This editorial can hardly be dismissed as shamans blowing their own horn. At a recent conference Marilyn Ferguson told of how the New Age "seems to be everywhere—kids are talking about their past lives . . . publishers are hiring channelers to aid them in their businesses." At the same conference ufologist Kenneth Ring gave a number of reasons why he believes we are witnessing the beginnings of "the shamanizing of humanity."[20] Many other astute observers of the contemporary scene are coming to similar conclusions. In the latest Institute of Noetic Sciences bulletin, Willis Harman declares:

We are living through one of the most fundamental shifts in history—a change in the actual belief structure of Western industrial society . . . allowing us to recapture the insights of thousands of years of exploration of human consciousness [i.e. shamanism]. . . .

Guidance from a Source "Too High to Question"

The sincere New Age evangelists are presenting theories that can't be substantiated medically or scientifically. Instead, we are assured that by entering an altered state of high suggestibility, cut off from all objective criteria for evaluation, we will *experience* this new truth for ourselves. Moreover, our trusted leaders who preach this gospel learned it from "spirit guides" whose identity and allegedly pure motives they have accepted by *faith*. As Klimo points out, all of the channeled entities insist that the inner guidance they provide is coming from a source too high for us to check out, and therefore we must simply accept what is said, believe that it is for our own good, and obey it.

It is amazing how many persons who were raised in the Moslem, Jewish, Catholic, or Protestant faith and rebelled against authoritative or dogmatic pronouncements of their religion nevertheless accept unquestioningly a message from the "collective unconscious" through some exotic entity with incredible claims (or even from the alleged spirit of a relative recently deceased who was less than infallible upon earth). Brilliant man that he is, Puharich seems (like Siegel, Jampolsky, Benson, Capra, et al) to have bought the farm. He writes:

> Considering that I have had two years of intermittent experience [of contact with them], I am remarkably ignorant about these beings.
>
> On the other hand I have complete faith in their wisdom and benevolent intentions toward man and living things on earth. My lack of hard knowledge about them is the kind of deficiency that does not erode my faith in their essential pursuit of the good, the true, the beautiful, and the just.[21]

Unfortunately, so much of the influence of the philosophy that these entities promote has not proven out to be "good, true, beautiful and just." There are many people who have been destroyed, or have barely escaped destruction, by a power which at first seemed so benevolent. They found that the "mind power" they worked so hard to cultivate could not be relied upon when needed most, and that it eventually sought to destroy them. In one of hundreds of similar letters received by the authors as a result of their research, a young woman writes:

> I recall how exciting it seemed to be part of a global federation of youth, given a new vision of peace, love, and brotherhood, bonded by drugs and music.
>
> It all seemed so new and wonderful going in. Coming out was another story. I was fortunate to get out with my mind intact, though it took me years to recognize and be freed of the spiritual bondage I'd entered.
>
> Other friends were not so lucky. Deaths, broken minds and spirits were the order of the day. I was just a straight Baptist kid dabbling in fun like drugs and forms of Satanism I didn't recognize then but do now. . . .
>
> Today I see it for what it is and am amazed at how I was deceived earlier. I've talked with other friends and we have looked back on it in disbelief, as if we'd been hypnotized for a time.

Doug Glover is another of the thousands of people who have had similar experiences. At the height of his involvement in the New Age movement, Doug was one of America's leading rebirthers. His story is too long to relate, with its apparently unstoppable success that disintegrated into a nightmare world of fear and confusion. Looking back, Doug says:

> Rebirthing is a powerful occult technique that some have called "Yoga for the West." It is in fact closely related to Paramahansa Yogananda's Kriya Yoga, and one of the most popular books among rebirthers has been Yogananda's *Autobiography of a Yogi*.
>
> Somewhat like Jungian depth analysis, rebirthing makes it possible to seemingly peel off layers of consciousness much like peeling an onion, to eventually get to the core of one's being and reach the coveted state of Self-realization as a god.
>
> It has to be done again and again. I began to see that a deception was involved, that I was being drawn ever deeper into confusion and control by other beings.

In the five years since I left the movement I have struggled to regain the ability to think clearly and be unafraid. I know of others who, like myself, have been left drained and mentally fogged for years even after they stopped rebirthing.

After lengthy observation of the entire New Age scene, I am convinced that these techniques (rebirthing, Yoga, TM, visualization of inner guides, etc.) have an intrinsic power in themselves. They work because they are designed specifically to *blow open doors and knock down barriers that God has placed in the human spirit to prevent a takeover by demonic beings that I came to realize are real and very destructive.*[22]

Getting Everyone to Play the Mind Games

No one is better at knocking down these barriers and opening the doors of perception than Jean Houston. She and Robert Masters wrote the classic *Mind Games* in 1972. It is a book so dangerous that by merely following its directions one can induce an altered state of consciousness. Consequently it contains, throughout its pages, periodic eye-catching patterns with the large caption underneath: **WAKE UP!** That will, say the authors, ". . . take you back into your ordinary state, your cultural trance, or what is described sometimes as an 'alert, normal waking consciousness' . . . the state in which we all dream the same dream, more or less, and call it: reality." The ultimate goal is to deliver the entire world from this dream, "until we will one day look back astounded at the impoverished world of consciousness we once shared, and supposed to be the real world—our officially defined and defended 'reality.' "[23]

The chanting of the Hindu *OM* is a routine part of the preparation process for playing the mind games. The connection to ancient shamanism is both admitted and cultivated throughout the exercises. Players are even taken back in deep trance to experience real-as-life visitations to temples in India, Tibet, and Nepal, joining the monks in their chanting and rituals. In another trance the following experience is orchestrated:

> And you're going to come to a clearing, where a very powerful ritual involving chanting and drumming is

being performed by primitive people. This is an extremely wild and elemental rite.

You will perceive it first as a spectator, seeing the fire in the center of the clearing, the naked, glistening bodies dancing, hearing, resonating to the ever-more-compelling beating of the drums until your own body is throbbing with that beat, until you are caught up in the ritual, feeling in your body what those primitive people are doing, feeling just everything they are feeling, knowing everything they are knowing, as they dissolve the individual consciousness of the participants in the ritual, creating one collective consciousness.[24]

These are but samples of the "advanced state of consciousness" that Masters and Houston want us to adopt as a way of life to replace the ordinary consciousness which they consider inferior. And if those of us who are too old and conservative to go along with the new game of life can't be converted, they are confident that as psychologists they have access to children and youth through the public schools and can accomplish their goal by that means. "There should and must be mind games for persons of all ages," Masters and Houston declare with missionary zeal, "including small children, and in the future such mind games will be routine in education at all levels." The fulfillment of that ambition has all but become history.

Similar games are now, in fact, routine at all levels of public education. "Wizards" is a representative game in use in Southern California public schools. It is supposed to teach spelling. The vocabulary is unusual, to say the least. "Wizards" promotes demonology and sorcery and humorously portrays Satan as a great achiever and leader. Much of the credit for such infiltration of American schools with mysticism and occultism must go to dedicated educators such as Deborah Rozman, "a psychology instructor for the San Lorenzo Valley [California] adult school program [and] an education consultant to many school districts." Rozman's methods are presented in her book *Meditating With Children: A Workbook on New Age Educational Methods*, which has received wide praise. The *San Jose Mercury* newspaper declared enthusiastically, "Educators who once turned to Ritalin and other drugs for hyperactive children . . . are now turning to daily meditation exercises instead—with positive results."

Meditating With Children is dedicated to "the Universal Mother of Compassion found in all nature" and to "Paramahansa Yogananda for some of the exercises and much of the inspiration for writing this book [and] above all . . . to The One. . . ." Its basic premise is "the Divine Nature of Childhood," and its stated purpose is to help "Children everywhere . . . evolve towards their spiritual destiny." The book is a compendium of blatant Hindu religious symbols and practices, from chanting the OM and Yoga exercises to Self-realization. Yet *East-West Journal* not only praises Rozman's book as "among the most enlightening of the new teaching books . . . a well-illustrated tool of practical psychology," but astonishingly declares: ". . . the absence of a religious point of view in the book makes this volume an excellent learning vehicle."[25]

A comparable workbook dedicated to Jesus Christ and filled with Christian doctrine and prayers would be excluded (and rightly so) from public schools. Yet Rozman's Hindu handbook (and many like it) is accepted and praised as nonreligious. We are told that the separation of church and state forbids creationism to be taught even as an alternate theory to evolution, yet pantheism's All-is-One is welcomed because it supports evolution. It is a strange fact that, particularly in the Western world, orthodox Islam, Judaism, and Christianity are readily identifiable as *religion*, while Hinduism and Buddhism masquerade as *science*.

The American Civil Liberties Union would quickly file suit against any public school, government agency, or major corporation that pushed Southern Baptist or Catholic or Jewish beliefs and rituals on its students or employees. This watchdog organization remains strangely silent, however, when Hindu and Buddhist occultism and other forms of Eastern mysticism or American Indian shamanism are promoted in the name of science by public institutions. Nor does the public at large seem to recognize the heavy doses of mysticism it is receiving through the media. As a result, an Eastern worldview is now almost taken for granted in the Western world.

Children are being brainwashed into a shamanic worldview not only in our public schools but through television cartoons, movies, comic books, toys, and games. Science fiction exerts a powerful influence for Eastern mysticism. Once looked upon as pure fantasy, sci-fi now has a long track record of accurately foretelling what legitimate science would eventually accomplish. Thus its fantastic stories hold out the promise, particularly to youth, that similar exploits can be accomplished by all those who learn the secret of the "Force." This influence begins at a very early age. A recent issue of *Shaman's Drum* announced triumphantly:

> Every Saturday morning millions of kids of all ages are treated to lessons in shamanic practice on the "Ewoks" cartoon show, produced by George Lucas of *Star Wars* and *Raiders of the Lost Ark* fame.
>
> Nearly every show involves good Ewok shaman Logray doing battle with his arch enemy Morag, and the word *shaman* is used directly. Clairvoyant dreams, talking trees, magical spells, amulets, and wisdom teachings are gently woven into this entertaining and popular series.[26]

Don't Drop the Shield

There is a fascinating correlation between many of the television and comic book characters and the gods and demons in classic religious mythology of the past. Unlike Grimm's fairy tales, however, today's magical fantasy is placed in the context of *science*, which makes it very believable to children growing up in an era of space travel and computers, where the sky is no longer the limit and the dream that anything is possible seems to be in the process of literal fulfillment. The seduction is powerful and the vulnerable child has no suspicion of what is happening.

It should be understood that we are not referring merely to ideas or beliefs, but to the contact with independent and deceitful spiritual entities that comes as a result of particular practices being taught on all levels. The ultimate parlor game presented by Masters and Houston involves the materialization of an entity which they call the "Group Spirit." It is created, they inform us, by a "method known and practiced for thousands of years in Tibet, where such entities are known as *thought-forms*, or *tulpas.*" While it is described as "an expression of the collective consciousness of all of the players," the Group Spirit cannot be explained in that manner. It can be seen, heard, and touched by members of the group and in response to questions presents answers from a source of knowledge "inaccessible to [the players] by any other means."

While pushing the psychological "collective unconscious" explanation, Masters and Houston suggest the possibility of something more than that. They remind us that "many of the best scientific minds of our time . . . hold it to be completely reasonable to suppose that intelligent life exists in many places throughout the universe at this present time . . . [perhaps] in dimensions which overlap our own space-time, and . . . in some ways and places we have not even thought about. Moreover, it is also quite possible that some of these life forms . . . can communicate with us. . . ." In fact, they agree with Doug Glover's statement that shamanic techniques are specifically designed to knock down natural barriers to the invasion of human personality by these entities. They write:

> . . . the very best way and perhaps for the present the only way [of contact with these entities] is within the context of an altered state of consciousness.
>
> And this may be true for the reason that within that range of states we think of as normal, conscious contact with these other life forms has been made impossible by some kind of shielding against it. . . .
>
> By altering consciousness we sometimes drop the shield, and the contacts become possible.[27]

It is our contention that rather than being representations of the collective unconscious, the preponderance of evidence demands the recognition that the entities produced by shamanic techniques (from Ulene's "Corky" to Siegel's "George"), are forms taken by demonic spirits that exist in their own right and independently from human consciousness. We also believe that because of who these entities actually are, no one should ever "drop the shield." Yet Masters and

Houston (like so many others) promise that if you "trust the guide and have confidence in the ability of the guide to protect you, then you will be safe from harm." It sounds hauntingly like something the disguised wolf might reassuringly whisper to Little Red Riding-hood.

16

Important Distinctions

Karl Marx predicted that religion would soon die. Marx is dead, and religion is more alive than ever before even though Marx's followers have imprisoned and murdered millions of people in the process of liberating the masses from the harmful "opiate" of religion. In every corner of the world—in every culture and at every level of society—one comes face-to-face with the compelling power of belief in some higher power controlling human destiny and the compulsion to strike a self-serving bargain with that force. In spite of computers and space exploration and communication satellites, neither the gods nor the rituals have changed.

On the roof garden of a fashionable Istanbul hotel, wealthy businessmen (who also regularly pray in Islam's time-honored way) consult a spiritualist at their monthly meeting, while at home their wives "read" the coffee grounds left in their cups. Both are practices forbidden by Islam. In Romania, top Communist officials, in spite of the official stance against fortune-telling, secretly consult an Indian Yogi, whom they have brought into the country as part of a circus. In Beverly Hills, an attorney and his college professor guest and their wives rest fingers lightly on an empty, overturned wine glass after dinner and watch expectantly as it is impelled across the table by some unseen power, in response to their earnest questions. In New York, driven by the same compulsion, a successful Wall Street trader consults his astrologer to determine when to buy or sell.

After the ritual dancing and drumbeating have stopped, a Luo tribe witch doctor in Kenya, with the approval of the United Nations

World Health Organization, listens carefully as ancestral spirits speak through the mouths of patients in deep trance. At the same time, on Long Island an Episcopal priest and several of his parishioners hold a seance to communicate with dead relatives in order to seek advice from those who had little wisdom upon earth but have somehow become all-knowing since reaching the "other side." In the steamy town of Recife in northern Brazil, Orisha gods and goddesses, imported from Nigeria and Dahomey, and now called by the names of Catholic saints, take violent "possession" of participants in a Macumba ceremony. Far away, at Massachusetts Institute of Technology, a Ph.D. candidate in solid state electronics with an open *I Ching* book on his lap solemnly drops 12 yarrow sticks and studies the resultant pattern. He is seeking guidance for a major decision in his life. Nearby at Harvard, a chemistry professor meditates beneath a mail-order pyramid. And deep in the Amazon jungle, natives drinking *yage* prepared from the *banisteria caapi* vine slip into an altered state of consciousness and begin to describe events taking place at that very moment in a distant village.

In Tibet, lamas carry on, in secret, ancient practices now forbidden by the Chinese: Spirit mediums transmit the messages of gods, demons, and the dead, while the *naljorpa* feast on corpses of the enlightened in order to increase their own psychic powers, or engage dead bodies in a mystic dance climaxed by sexual intercourse with the spirit-animated corpses. On the Island of Hawaii, a *kahuna* engages in a secret *huna* ritual to gain control over "life energy" for a wealthy client who carefully keeps his connection with native religion hidden from his business associates. And in Hollywood, California, in an occult bookstore, a pair of teenage girls, whose parents take them each Sunday to fundamentalist Christian churches, browse through the parentally forbidden shelves on witchcraft, eager to discover for themselves the promised powers.

Two Sources of "Revelation"

Recognizable in all the examples cited above is a common philosophical foundation: the pantheistic/naturalistic worldview. The persistence of such beliefs in this modern age is remarkable enough. Even more significant, however, is the consistency of belief and practice that has prevailed for thousands of years in every corner of the earth without, in many instances, any contact between isolated or hostile peoples and within otherwise completely dissimilar cultures. That fact points inescapably to a common, intelligent source that transcends time and distance, and which has throughout history been universally ascribed to ancestral spirits or gods, but which the Bible identifies as Satan and his minions.

Considering all of the evidence that we have reviewed to this point, there are only two possible worldviews: chance or design, naturalism or supernaturalism, pantheism/polytheism or monotheism. Neither can be "proved by science" any more than can love or truth or consciousness. Both views come by revelation and must be accepted or rejected by faith. The differing manner, however, in which these two opposing revelations are received is significant.

The perennial philosophy is a revelation that consistently comes in altered states of consciousness, when one is cut off from any basis for making an objective evaluation. It often comes on drugs or in deep meditation or under hypnosis or as a sudden insight while reveling in nature. It also comes as direct teaching from the channeled entities, whether they call themselves spirit guides, spirits of the dead, ascended masters, space brothers in UFO's, or archetypal symbols from the collective unconscious. There is no way to check the identity and reliability of the source, and there is considerable evidence that at least on occasion it lies.

Supernaturalism/monotheism comes through a revelation which is contained in the Bible. It has existed as a written record for thousands of years and has been subject to careful scrutiny and criticism by both believers and critics. In contrast to the scriptures of other religions, the Bible speaks of verifiable historic events, places, peoples, and nations. It also contains prophecies involving real places and events, many of which have already been fulfilled and all of which can be checked. In contrast, other scriptures, such as the Hindu Vedas, the Baghavad-Gita, or Ramayana, are clearly mythological accounts, of which there are conflicting versions.

The promise of a coming Jewish Messiah is a prime example of a biblical prophecy. There are more than 300 references in the Old Testament giving the place and manner of his birth, life, and death. Even the day the Messiah would triumphantly enter Jerusalem, hailed by tumultuous crowds (now celebrated by Christians as Palm

Sunday), and his crucifixion a few days later, were prophesied hundreds of years in advance.[1] Millions of former skeptics have been convinced that these prophecies were literally fulfilled in Jesus of Nazareth.

The Jewish people themselves present an astonishing evidence of the validity of the Bible. When they first entered the land of Palestine, Moses made a remarkable and detailed prophecy: If the Israelites fell into the same occult practices as the nations they were displacing (sorcery, mediumship, hypnosis, and divination, which were an abomination to God), they would be scattered across the earth in judgment. Moses also foretold, as did numerous subsequent Hebrew prophets, that in the "last days" prior to the Messiah's second coming Israel would be gathered once again into her land.[2] These events are history and stand as powerful evidence to the validity of the Bible—evidence that anyone today may examine for oneself.

Never has any other nation remained identifiable after 2500 years of dispersion to the four corners of the world, much less returned to its former homeland to become a nation once again. Moreover, that this seemingly worthless piece of desert and swamp, abandoned for centuries, should not only be inhabited again by the descendants of the ancient Israelites and become fruitful and prosperous, but that this tiny nation should become the focus of the entire world's attention, is again incredible. Yet this is exactly what prophecy after prophecy in the Bible boldly declared, and in our day it has come to pass.

The staggering fulfillment of such prophecies authenticates the Bible as the writings of no other religion have ever been authenticated. One would expect that the human race would choose to believe the revelation that is supported by such evidence, rather than the grandiose promises of godhood coming from deceitful spirits. It seems clear, however, that revelation is accepted or rejected more on the basis of its appeal than by its factuality. The biblical gospel that calls mankind into account for its rebellion against God has never been popular. The opposing revelation of pantheism/naturalism, however, has always held a strong appeal. It panders to our natural desire to create our own reality and thereby control our own destiny and be accountable to no one but ourselves.

Israel was warned not to attempt to contact the "spirits" that spoke through mediums and manifested themselves in trance (no matter how induced). According to the Bible, these entities, which still seduce in our day, are evil spirits bent upon deception, whether they masquerade as spirits of dead relatives or ascended masters or whatever else. Whether one wishes to heed it or not, the counsel of the great Hebrew prophet Isaiah and the warning of coming judgment spoken to Israel 2700 years ago seem remarkably relevant today:

> So why are you trying to find out the future by consulting witches and mediums? Don't listen to their whisperings and mutterings. Can the living find out the future from the dead? Why not ask your God?
>
> "Check these witches' words against the Word of God!" he [God] says. "If their messages are different than mine, it is because I have not sent them; for they have no light or truth in them."
>
> O pleasure-mad kingdom, living at ease, bragging as the greatest in the world—listen to the sentence of my court upon your sins. You say, "I alone am God! . . . That is why disaster shall overtake you suddenly—so suddenly that you won't know where it comes from. And there will be no atonement then to cleanse away your sins.
>
> Call out the demon hordes you've worshiped all these years. . . . You have advisors by the ton—your astrologers and stargazers, who try to tell you what the future holds. But they are as useless as dried grass burning in the fire. They cannot even deliver themselves! You'll get no help from them at all.[3]

A Society of Sorcerers

For the past 200 years, scientific materialism has sought to discredit revelations from either God or spirit entities by denying the existence of a spirit world. Yet belief in spiritual power and the various sorceries fostered by that belief has persisted. And now there is an explosive revival of ancient occult beliefs and practices in the new wrappings of anthropological and psychological euphemisms, which have given sorcery the pseudoscientific respectability required for popular acceptance in our day.

The possibility of possessing the godlike mind powers promised by New Age human-potential gurus is a very seductive idea, but only so long as one imagines having this power exclusively for oneself. The realization, however, that the same mind power would be available to others as well turns this dream into a nightmare. Life would become a terrifying struggle of an entire society of sorcerers competing with each other to see whose power was the strongest. Instead of God being in charge of his universe, there would be billions of little gods shuffling around reality by the power of belief to suit individual tastes. Instead of the promised paradise—chaos.

Imagine the scenario: every mind open to be read or influenced by others, and a free flow of clairvoyant images with no barriers. No physical or mental privacy. Psychic might makes right, and mind power is the only law. No moral conscience, no right or wrong. And even if such concepts were acknowledged, there would be an utter impossibility to place responsibility. For example, an auto runs up on the sidewalk and kills several people. The driver's defense is that his car had come under the control of an enemy whose sorceries were more powerful than his own. An investment advisor or corporate president makes disastrous decisions, but he claims that a rival had put a hex on him. How could it be proved otherwise?

For a practical example of what such a society produces, one need only look at the terror which grips the members of thoroughly shamanized primitive cultures. These exist not only in the Amazon jungles today, but in "civilized" countries such as Haiti, where voodoo is an ever-present terror in spite of the claim that it is used only for good. The ability of naturalism/pantheism to dominate a presumably monotheistic society is seen in the common expression that "Haiti is 85 percent Catholic and 110 percent vodoun." The futility of opposition from the Catholic Church can be seen in the fact that every voodoo ceremony begins with a Catholic prayer—then proceeds in a manner that undermines Christianity.

If it seems farfetched that similar conditions could exist in America, remember that millions of eager New Agers are involved in the pursuit of the same shamanic powers through scores of self-improvement courses such as we have discussed, and through the popularization of witchcraft by various other means in modern as well as ancient form. Consider what is happening now in the sophisticated and very American Hawaiian Islands. The current revival of native religion, which is being hailed as the recovery of lost tradition, has brought into the open witchcraft practices that survived in secret under a thin veneer of professed Christianity and now threaten to explode. In a recent interview, a follower of native Hawaiian religion (who had been speaking freely up to that point) was asked to give an example of the revived use of "evil spells." There was a long, uncomfortable hesitation. At last the worshiper cried out:

> I cannot! I'm terrified of it. Nobody talks about the religion. Hawaiians are still being prayed to death by other Hawaiians.[4]

Deeper into the Maelstrom

Something similar, though under many different names, is happening across America, particularly in her major cities. There are an estimated 500,000 followers of voodoo in New York alone. The *Los Angeles Times Magazine* recently did a feature story on the rise of Santeria in Southern California, where a society of sorcerers is emerging and playing an increasingly visible role. The statement of Monife Balewa, a follower of Santeria, was typical and gave a frightening insight:

> I have been possessed by Oshun, and I've prayed that it not happen again. It's usually the drum that brings it on. The last time, I don't remember what happened, but I've been told I jumped out a second-story window. I lost a $250 watch, and made a statement that a person would die because of disrespect. Oshun can be very stern and correct. A week later, that person died.[5]

Another follower of Santeria declared with considerable fear, "I'm afraid of what would happen if I messed up. A mistake can kill you." Giving some indication of the growing influence of this religion around the world, the article reported that "the winner of the Nobel Prize for Literature in 1986, Wole Soyinka of Nigeria, is a believer in the Yoruba gods. Most of his works are about the *orishas* [Santeria spirits]. . . . It is the majority religion in Brazil, in Haiti, in Cuba."

A Santeria priest numbers among his clients in the Los Angeles South Bay area "doctors, lawyers, business executives as well as laborers." He says, "There are hundreds and hundreds of people who live around here that are into this. You would be surprised, typical, blond hair, blue-eyed Americans. . . . There are Santeros all over."[6] One police officer said that he personally knew of "police officers in Miami, Chicago, New York and Los Angeles who practice some form of Santeria."[7]

The criminals, too, are tapping the same source of power to their advantage. Drug dealers pay Santeria priests huge sums to obtain the protection of the gods. Sergeant Richard Valdemar of the Los Angeles Sheriff's Department, who works with gangs in East Los Angeles and calls Santeria "a satanic cult," declares:

> I believe occult religions like Santeria help certain gang members commit criminal acts. . . . They believe their demon god protects them from any harm that could possibly happen, even from bullets. With that kind of belief, they do things they wouldn't normally do.[8]

Even without the actual acquisition of the powers of sorcery, the problems can be extreme where it is only imagined that such powers are possessed. There is a growing number of victims of mind dynamics and other self-improvement courses who thought they were gaining "personal empowerment" but lost control. With the accelerating shamanization of America that number will continue to increase. Attorney Gerald Ragland, who recently won an 800,000-dollar judgment for client Deborah Bingham against Lifespring (a derivative of Werner Erhard's est), has a number of other cases pending. Among them are the following, which give some insight into the serious problems that arise under the delusion that a paranormal "power" is available for us to tap into and use to our own ends:

A woman who, driving home from the [Lifespring] training, believed she could control the traffic lights; a man who showed up for the last day of basic convinced that Lifespring wanted him to take over the training; and a man who, a few days after the training, thought God was telling him to sacrifice his baby son.[9]

It should be clear to even the most skeptical observer that a sweeping movement is taking American society into an ever-deeper involvement in shamanism and mysticism. What is not generally recognized, however, is that this transformation of Western beliefs and culture under the influence of Eastern religions (principally Hinduism and Buddhism) has not come about by chance, but by deliberate planning and diligent effort.

Evangelists from the East

There has been much criticism, some of it no doubt justified, of the Western missionaries who went to Africa, China, and India to spread the message of Christianity and in the process Westernized other cultures. In strange contrast, there has been little or no criticism of Buddhist and Hindu missionaries who have aggressively pushed their religion upon an unsuspecting Western world. In our naivete we imagine that the invading gurus, Yogis, swamis, and lamas are not missionaries at all and have no interest in converting others to their faith.

It comes as a great surprise to most Westerners to learn that the largest missionary organization in the world is India's Vishva Hindu Parishad (VHP). Its constitution states that its primary purpose is "to establish an order of missionaries, both lay and initiate, [for] the purpose of propagating dynamic Hinduism [represented] . . . by various faiths and denominations, including Buddhists, Jains, Sikhs, Lingayats etc. [and to spread] . . . spiritual principles and practices of Hinduism . . . in all parts of the world. . . ." None of the VHP publications, though produced in massive quantity, are available in bookstores or libraries even in India. The Vishva's operations are so secret that even most Indians are not aware of its existence.

The Vishva-sponsored 1979 World Hindu Conference in Allahabad, India, was chaired by the Dalai Lama of Tibetan Buddhism.

Again most Westerners would be surprised by this close connection between such seemingly rival religions as Hinduism and Buddhism. The conference's 60,000 participants were told that the VHP's goal of the destruction of Christianity and the establishment of Hinduism as the world religion was moving forward successfully.

Why is *Christianity* singled out as *the enemy*, when we have noted all along that the Bible of Jews, Moslems, and Christians opposes the pantheistic/naturalistic worldview? The answer no doubt lies in the fact that the Jewish and Islamic view of these scriptures puts the burden upon mankind to save itself—which in that respect is in agreement with the perennial philosophy. Christianity, on the other hand, is based upon the belief that Christ had to do something for us that we ourselves could not accomplish. As the only viable alternative to New Age shamanism/pantheism, Christianity merits a careful and unbiased evaluation.

As part of the most massive missionary effort in history—aimed directly against Christianity—every guru who has come to the West (from Maharishi Mahesh Yogi to Bhagwan Shri Rajneesh to Baba Muktananda) was sent here by his guru specifically to win converts to the Hindu/Buddhist pantheistic faith. Yogananda, for example, who was one of the forerunners of this mass evangelism campaign, personally initiated more than 100,000 disciples into Kriya Yoga. Maharishi Mahesh Yogi has initiated millions. Yet the Hindu/Buddhist missionaries all protest that they are not teaching religion but the *science* of Yoga, health, and higher states of consciousness. That this subterfuge is accepted and defended should stretch the thinking individual's credulity to its outer limits.

We can register no legitimate complaint against those who seek to share with others what they sincerely believe to be important truth. However, those claiming to represent truth should not misrepresent their purpose or their product. We have already mentioned the ploys of the Maharishi, including the solemn avowal that transcendental meditation has nothing to do with religion, when in fact it is unadulterated Hinduism from beginning to end. The other representatives of Eastern religions have been similarly guilty. A comparable deception would be for the Catholic Pope in his travels around the world to pretend that he represented an organization of great scientists instead of a church, and to deny specifically that his mission had anything whatever to do with religion. He would be soundly condemned—yet the Yogis and lamas are lauded in spite of such deceit.

The Hindu/Buddhist worldview is now taken for granted at almost every level of Western society. One can only imagine the hue and cry that would be raised if Christian missionaries attempted a similar feat in India. It simply would not be allowed. In fact, that country has excluded foreign missionaries from entering its borders since shortly after it gained independence. Yet India's missionaries are being sent out to the whole world, protesting their tolerance for all religions and deliberately denying their true mission. This absolute intolerance posing as the most generous tolerance is one of the most frustrating features of New Age shamanism.

The Embrace That Smothers

The "openness to everything" that results in an unacknowledged closed-mindedness (which, as Allan Bloom so ably points out, is the bane of today's relativistic society) has its roots in Hindu doctrine. If "All is One," and if even the All is an illusion of the mind, then nothing really matters. Opposites are identical and even contradictory beliefs have the same meaning. This attitude is endemic to Eastern philosophy and reveals itself in many ways. For example, William Divine, chairman of the California Acupuncture Association, recently declared:

> Oriental medicine is like that. You could bring one patient in, five different practitioners could look at him and come up with five different diagnoses, and nobody's wrong.[10]

In Eastern religions there can be no right or wrong, and as we have seen, this is the message of the spirit entities. On the basis of what "Ramtha" has said, J.Z. Knight declares that we can be delivered from the idea of a judgmental God by understanding that "there is no sin, therefore no reason for guilt."[11] Of course, if no one is wrong, then no one is right either. Indeed, the very thought that someone might claim to be *right* is anathema in today's "anything goes" society. As Wade Davis insisted during an interview on the nationally syndicated *Geraldo* talk show of March 22, 1988: ". . . there is no such thing as right or wrong in religion . . . that's where wars come from."

This denial of distinctions is the worst kind of narrow-mindedness because it masquerades as broad-mindedness. It is exemplified in the person who purports to agree with everyone and insists that even the widest differences are only a matter of "semantics." Ironically, such professed tolerance of other viewpoints destroys them, not by a frontal assault, but simply by refusing to acknowledge those viewpoints for what they are. An antagonist who disagrees and is willing to discuss the issues is worthy of more respect than the one who, in his broad-minded desire to embrace everything and reject nothing, denies that there are any issues.

Imagine the chaos if pharmacists or medical doctors took the attitude that "All is One," that there is no difference between cyanide and aspirin, that a person who needed his tonsils removed would be just as well served by having his heart or lungs removed. Yet this is the prevailing attitude today when it comes to ethics or morals or religion, as though in the fleshly matters of life we must insist upon truth, but when it comes to the soul and our relationship to God, anything goes.

To many people such an "everybody-wins" attitude is the only decent way to go. But if "loser" is to be dropped from our vocabulary, then "winner" must go as well. Frustrated with programs put forth by the psychology profession to solve social problems, but which at the same time hold no one accountable for being *wrong*, T. H. Fitzgerald wrote in an *AHP Perspective* article: ". . . if people are not responsible for their acts, what implications does that have for all our other values?" Of course there can be no values. Fitzgerald stated the problem clearly:

> The sense I still get around AHP is . . . that everybody is somehow right "from their perspective" because there can be no ultimate arbiter. Dennis Jaffe writes . . . about the Search for Excellence, but if there is to be Excellence, must there not also be Non-Excellence, and what do we say when we meet it on the road? . . . Even the language for the discussion of moral issues has been

corrupted by psychological cant and the vocabulary of positivist scientism.[12]

One of the most common examples of this absolute intolerance that poses as total tolerance is found in the well-known aphorism, most often used in reference to religion: "We're all taking different roads to get to the same place." While that declaration sounds broad-minded to a fault, it clearly represents the ultimate in narrow-mindedness. Although "different roads" are seemingly tolerated, they are not allowed to lead to different places—everyone must go to the "same place." So much for the tolerance embodied in this allegedly broad-minded principle.

It is by such sophistry that Hinduism has gained its reputation for tolerance toward all religions. Hinduism does indeed embrace all faiths, but in the process they are absorbed into Hinduism through the "embrace that smothers." Whatever the Hindu in his proverbial broad-mindedness seems to accept loses its former identity and is recast in a Hindu mold. This new concept is then passed off as an improvement. Thus an acceptance becomes, in effect, a destructive metamorphosis.

Hinduism is quite willing, for example, to embrace Christ. After all, with 330 million gods, adding one more changes nothing. Of course, Jesus is not accepted for who he claimed to be—the one and only "way, truth, and life." He becomes merely another Hindu avatar, another incarnation of Vishnu. Thus in embracing him Hinduism destroys the Jesus of the Bible and creates its own "Christ." Certainly everyone is free to reject him, but Hinduism perverts Christ's claims under the pretense of embracing him. This false embrace is no more honest than the recent cynical statement attributed to Cuban dictator Fidel Castro: "I never saw a contradiction between the ideas that sustain me and the ideas of Jesus."

Confusion and Perversion

New Age leader Barbara Marx Hubbard provides a further example of the "embrace that smothers." Hubbard claims to have had a powerful "born-again" experience, even including an overwhelming sense of the presence of the resurrected "Jesus." The words he spoke to her, however, like those of the "Jesus" who dictated the

Course In Miracles to Helen Shucman, are a very clever perversion of what the biblical Jesus had to say. There is a reinterpretation of meanings which effectively destroys historic Christianity and replaces it with a Hindu/Buddhist pseudo-Christianity. [13]

This is cynicism of the worst sort.

According to Hubbard, the "Christ" who speaks to her is: "an evolutionary mutation . . . sprung out of the genetic pattern of Homo sapiens with an enhanced capability to attune to the God-force." This "Jesus" communicated to Hubbard a pseudoscientific rehashing in modern evolutionary terms of the same pantheism/polytheism that the spirit guides consistently preach: "God" is a universal, evolutionary "Force" that is "not kind [and] does not care for the feelings of individuals." [14]

Are we not justified in concluding that the "Jesus" which Hubbard and Shucman encountered is not the Jesus Christ of the Bible at all, but a seducing spirit only too eager to pose as "Jesus" while preaching the Hindu/pantheistic gospel?

In *Mind Games*, Masters and Houston equate the Christian experience of being "born again" with "satori," "samadhi," "nirvana," and "cosmic consciousness." They certainly are entitled to believe in and offer such experiences to others, but to associate them with Christianity is to be guilty of the most flagrant perversion. Jesus Christ declared that those who received him as their Savior and Lord, believing that he had died for their sins, would be "born of the Spirit" into the family of God, becoming the children of God and receiving eternal life as a free gift of God's grace. It is on this basis alone that one can be "born again" in the Christian meaning of that term. Certainly "satori," "samadhi," etc. have nothing whatever to do with believing in Jesus Christ, but are mystical experiences achieved in altered states of consciousness.

Here once again Christian terminology is adopted, but its meaning is immediately destroyed by equating it with Hindu/Buddhist experiences that are in the clearest opposition to Christian concepts. This broad-mindedness amounts to a declaration that the peculiarly Christian significance of these terms is insignificant, that they can be taken to mean anything and that any other substitute will do just as well. To think otherwise, it is implied, would be narrow-minded and unacceptable dogmatism.

Somehow the freedom to choose one's own religious or spiritual remedy (which certainly ought to be granted) has become confused with the insistence that all remedies must be equal. But if all the options offered are the same, then the "freedom to choose" between them is meaningless. Clearly the choice of remedy should depend upon the diagnosis of the problem; and in both of these naturalism and supernaturalism differ radically—so radically, in fact, that a reconciliation between them is impossible. For anyone to attempt to gloss over these deep differences as though they are of no consequence is fundamentally dishonest. Yet this is the attitude of most New Agers, and it results in confusion and perversion.

The Broad-Minded Opposition to Christianity

The major complaint leveled against Christianity by New Agers is that it claims to be *right*, which by implication means that other religions which disagree are *wrong*. Christianity's validity ought to be determined on the basis of its truth or falsehood. Instead, however, it is rejected for being "narrow-minded." That is an odd accusation. Certainly those who claim that no one is either right or wrong cannot legitimately accuse Christianity of "narrow-mindedness," since they themselves, by insisting that all roads lead to the same place, are the most dogmatic of all. Jesus was not so narrow-minded as to insist that everyone, though taking different roads, must inevitably arrive at the same destination. He declared that there were two destinations—heaven or hell—and that no one was forced to go to either. Each one's ultimate destination is a matter of free choice. For a decision of such magnitude, one ought to be as certain as possible of the facts.

Christianity is based upon the claims Christ made about himself and the eyewitness accounts of his life, death, and resurrection as recorded in the New Testament and verified by Old Testament prophecies—claims which Jews and Moslems reject, thereby further identifying their particular opposition to Christianity. Certainly the claims of Christ are *unique*: that he was God come as a man (the only sinless, perfect man) in order to die for the sins of the world, and thus that he was the only Savior of mankind. Neither Buddha, Mohammed, Confucius, nor any other religious leader made such claims. His resurrection (not reincarnation) also marks Christ as unique and is foundational to Christianity.

One may journey to Mecca to visit the grave of Mohammed, or elsewhere to visit the tombs of other great saints and founders of religions. The grave of Jesus Christ, however, unlike any other, stands empty. Jesus claimed to be more than a teacher who came to show the way by example and instruction; he claimed to *be* "the way, the truth, and the life." Thus it is essential not just that his teachings live on but that he himself be alive and able to impart eternal life to those who receive him.

Certainly Christ's claims that he *is the truth* and *the only way to God* not only stand alone, but indict all other ways as false. Everyone is entitled to reject such claims, but it is a cynical perversion to suggest that Jesus was just another guru teaching basically the same thing as all the rest. Certainly anyone familiar with the New Testament would immediately recognize such a suggestion as preposterous. It has, however, gained some credibility through reports that Christ studied in India under the gurus in order to prepare for his mission. This theory, which represents the strongest attack against Christ's unique claims, is consistently taught by the channeled entities and has been popularized in various speculative books such as *The Aquarian Gospel*.

Jesus and the Gurus

How did such an idea surface? A certain Nicholas Notovitch, while traveling in Tibet in the late 1800's, was allegedly told by Tibetan lamas that a record existed in a Himalayan monastery reporting the visit of Jesus. In the early 1900's another visitor to Tibet was allegedly told the same thing. However, no one capable of reading and translating such "records" ever saw them, no copy was brought to the West for examination, and now the story is that the "records" have been destroyed.[15]

If the Bible were based upon no better evidence than that, the critics would justifiably have ripped it to shreds long ago.

Not only is there not a particle of historical evidence that Jesus ever visited India, much less *studied* there, but this theory is refuted by everything that Jesus said and did during his ministry. The New Testament account, which holds together consistently, is not compatible with Jesus ever being absent from Israel for any extended period of time. The people in his hometown of Nazareth knew him only as "the carpenter," not as a Jewish Marco Polo, and they were astonished when he suddenly began to preach and travel about Galilee, accompanied by great crowds. To family and neighbors it was a scandal for Jesus to take the guise of a religious teacher. They treated him with a contempt born of familiarity, not with the awe they surely would have given one who had traveled widely and studied in such exotic lands as India and Tibet.

As we have already noted, every guru who comes to the West lauds and honors his Master, for every Hindu must have a guru, including the gurus themselves. Yet Jesus never referred to his guru or to any religious writings except the Jewish Scriptures, which he quoted repeatedly. He claimed to have been sent from his "Father in heaven," a term unknown to the gurus and hated by the rabbis. The gurus claim to be men who, through Yoga and ascetic practices, have become "Self-realized" gods. Jesus, in contrast, did not claim to be a man struggling upward to godhood, but God who had stooped down to become a man. The gurus deny the existence of sin, whereas Jesus said he had come to call sinners to repent and to save them from eternal judgment by himself dying for the sins of the whole world.

The gurus are all vegetarians, whereas Jesus was not. He ate the Passover lamb, fed the multitudes with fish, and even after his resurrection ate fish as a demonstration to his doubting disciples that he was bodily resurrected and not a "ghost" as they supposed. There have been thousands of gurus, but Jesus claimed to be the one and only Son of God. The gurus teach that there are many ways to God, but Jesus declared: "I am the way and the truth and the life; no one comes to the Father except through me."[16]

The Requirements of Moral Law

To reject Christ is every person's right, but it is intellectual dishonesty of the worst sort to insist that his teachings are perfectly compatible with Hindu-Buddhist pantheistic philosophies. This must be so, concludes one writer, because "all the New Agers I've met love Jesus and Buddha and Krishna and anyone, regardless of race or language or religious preference. . . ."[17]

The idea that love somehow renders the question of truth and right and wrong irrelevant is a basic fallacy underlying much of the

New Age. On the contrary, genuine love motivates one to correct a fellow human being whom one perceives to be in serious and life-threatening error.

One of the major fallacies in pantheism is that its "All is One" philosophy does not allow for any difference between a physical law and a moral law. Yet that distinction is extremely important. A moral law, for example, cannot be used for one's own ends, though a physical law could be used in that way. Moral laws cannot become the source of personal empowerment, which is the big goal in the New Age movement. Universal moral laws which are binding upon all can only be prescribed by the Supreme God of supernatural monotheism, who himself in his own character sets the standard of righteousness, love, purity, and goodness.

In spite of the attempt to educate modern man to believe that there are no moral absolutes, every member of the race has a conscience and knows that he or she has violated moral laws. Moreover, we recognize that a penalty is required and that the solutions offered by Eastern mysticism simply do not satisfy the claims of justice. Everyone knows that even the simplest violation of law, such as a parking ticket, cannot be made right by practicing Yoga or meditation or chanting OM in an altered state of consciousness. Nor would it seem reasonable to satisfy Infinite Justice by such techniques—which is why Eastern mysticism by very definition denies moral justice.

Nor can the violation of moral law be rectified by keeping the law. It would be absurd to expect a judge to waive a speeding fine because the offender had obeyed the speed limit more often than he had exceeded it. Yet the popular idea persists that all will be well if one's "good deeds outweigh the bad." And to those who would plead, "Please let me off this time and I promise never to break the law again," the judge would simply reply: "If you never break the law again, you will only be doing what the law requires, and you get no extra credit for that, from which to pay for having broken the law in the past."

In contrast to Eastern mysticism, Christianity teaches that the moral laws of God's infinite justice have been violated. There is no way that finite man can pay the infinite penalty. By his own choice man has consigned himself to eternal separation from the God who created him. God, being infinite, could pay the penalty, but it would not be just, because he was not one of us. In the supreme act of love, God became a man in order to satisfy the claims of his own law and died the death which his justice demanded for our sin.

The triumphant cry of Jesus just before he expired upon the cross—"It is finished"—is an accounting term in the original New Testament Greek (*teleo*, to discharge a debt). The infinite penalty for sin had been paid. According to the Bible, all man needs to do is humble himself to admit that he as a sinner deserved what Christ suffered in his place, and to receive the pardon that is offered as a free gift of God's grace and love—a pardon he could never merit or earn. Certainly the staggering nature of such claims (there could be no better news if these claims are true) would demand a careful investigation. Famed Harvard University law professor Simon Greenleaf (in his day the highest authority on legal evidence and a confirmed skeptic who accepted the claims of Christ only after careful research) declared in an appeal to his colleagues to make a similar investigation:

> These are no ordinary claims; and it seems hardly possible for a rational being to . . . treat them with mere indifference or contempt.[18]

In contrast, there is a palpable emptiness to the New Age gospel. Not only doesn't it ring true either to logic or ordinary experience, but it lacks those qualities which the human heart aspires after. Righteousness and truth are missing altogether—yet surely the question of *truth* ought to far outweigh feelings, personal preference, or mystical experience. Of what value is the most ecstatic experience, if it is mere fantasy, or worse yet, a fraud? To barter away the eternal benefits of truth for the feelings of the moment is a bad bargain indeed.

Moreover, in the Hindu/Buddhist New Age philosophy the forgiveness is absent for which every honest heart yearns. No wrong is admitted, even though our consciences tell us otherwise and long for release. Thus there is no thankfulness or gratitude to God for forgiving and saving us, for we are our own gods and saviors—yet forgiveness and gratitude are universally recognized to be among the noblest human qualities and greatest blessings. Nor is there a taste of mercy or grace, for the same reason.

As an answer to man's deepest longings and need, naturalism/pantheism offers an impersonal cosmic Force with dark and light sides. Instead of love, the greatest virtue and highest experience, we are left with a void.

America: The Sorcerer's New Apprentice

The effectiveness of the Eastern gurus (aided by innumerable "spirit guides" and fellow travelers) to convert the Western world to the Hindu/Buddhist/shamanic faith has been unprecedented in all of history. America is in the process of a radical transformation. The success of this effort owes much to America's homegrown evangelists who have surfaced from such a broad spectrum of professional credibility: the Siegels, Simontons, Bensons, Rays, Houstons, Jampolskys, Denvers, Lennons, and Learys. Most of these New Age zealots seem to be motivated by a sincere desire to help a suffering world. Whatever the motivation, however, the determined undermining of Christianity is well on its way, and the establishment of an ecumenical New Age shamanism as the world religion has made astonishing progress everywhere except in Islamic countries. The full impact upon every area of society promises to be beyond present comprehension.

Many of America's largest and most powerful corporations, with branches in numerous countries, have now joined this unprecedented worldwide missionary effort. Management-experts-turned-missionaries are taking to the whole world the same Eastern mysticism which the gurus brought to the West, but now incorporated into and redefined as the latest techniques for successful personal and business performance. The sophistication, advanced degrees, and affluence of these new jet-set missionaries lend a credibility that makes their seductive gospel almost irresistible.

These are a new breed of business leaders who talk about the interconnectedness of all things, getting back in touch with nature, and the divine spark within us all as the basis for a new planetary unity. They especially want to share the psychospiritual technologies of the mind, which they hope will help mankind to realize its full potential and thereby turn this suffering world into paradise at last. It sounds so good.

As we have seen, the ancient shamanic techniques for contacting spirit guides have been introduced to the masses under the umbrellas of science, medicine, psychology, education, and business, but with the entities explained away psychologically. Yet no amount of scholarly rationalization can change the fact that these consciousness-altering techniques consistently bring contact with, and in many cases possession by, seducing spirits.

Seemingly unaware of the grave danger, America, once the world's leader in finance, business, science, and technology, is reasserting its leadership position, but now in a new enterprise— the rise of New Age shamanism. The implications are staggering. An inescapable choice which will determine our destiny confronts us. Shouldn't that choice be made on the basis of the evidence and in firm commitment to ultimate truth?

Notes

CHAPTER 1 — A TURNING POINT?
1. Robert Lindsey, *New York Times*, cited in *Los Angeles Herald Examiner*, September 29, 1986, p. B-8.
2. Max Planck, *Where Is Science Going?* (Norton, 1932), p. 160.
3. *Noetic Sciences*, Autumn 1987, Willis Harman, p. 23.
4. *Science Digest*, John Gliedman, "Scientists in Search of the Soul," p. 78.
5. *Seattle Times*, January 18, 1987, Bill Dietrich, "A New Age: The 1980's Low-Dogma Approach to Religion."
6. *American Health*, April 1985, Lise Spiegel, "New-Age Shrinks," p. 18.
7. *San Jose Mercury News*, June 14, 1986, Joan Connell, "The Spiritual Frontier," p. 1C.
8. *U.S. News & World Report*, February 9, 1987, "Mystics on Main Street," p. 67.
9. *American Health*, January/February 1987, Andrew Greeley, "Mysticism Goes Mainstream," p. 47.
10. Ibid., pp. 47-48.
11. *Australia's New Age News*, September 1987, Douglas James Mahr and Francis Racey, Ph.D, "Tired Of The Program? Change Your Channel," p. 9.
12. Aldous Huxley, *The Perennial Philosophy* (Harper, 1944).
13. *Los Angeles Times*, December 5, 1986, Lynn Smith, "The New, Chic Metaphysical Fad of Channeling," Part V, p. 1ff.
14. *The Los Angeles Times*, Smith, Ibid., p. 30.
15. Ruth Montgomery with Joanne Garland, *Ruth Montgomery: Herald of the New Age* (Fawcett Crest, 1986), pp. 71-111.
16. *SCP Journal*, Vol. 7, No. 1, 1987, "A Matter of Course: Conversation with Kenneth Wapnick," pp. 9-17.
17. Whitley Strieber, *Communion* (William Morrow, 1987), p. 13.
18. See also *Omni*, December 1987, pp. 53ff.
19. *Geo*, February 1982, "GeoConversation," an interview with Dr. Robert Jastrow, p. 14.
20. *The Gandhi Reader: A Source-Book of his Life and Writings*, ed. Homer A. Jack (London, 1958), pp. 229-30.
21. Sir John Eccles, with Daniel N. Robinson, *The Wonder of Being Human—Our Brain & Our Mind* (New Science Library, 1985), p. 54.
22. *Life Times: Forum For A New Age*, Number 3, p. 48, originally published in South Africa's New Age magazine, *Odyssey*.
23. Arthur C. Clarke, *Childhood's End* (Ballantine Books, 1953), p. 181.
24. Planck, *Where?*, p. 168.
25. Sir Arthur Stanley Eddington, *The Nature of the Physical World* (Macmillan, 1929), cited in *Quantum Questions: Mythical Writings of the World's Great Physicists*, ed. Ken Wilber (New Science Library, 1984), p. 5.
26. Erwin Schroedinger, cited in *Quantum Questions*, pp. 81-83.
27. Wilber, *Quantum*, pp. 5,6,x.
28. Sir James Jeans, *The Mysterious Universe* (The MacMillan Company, 1930), p. 140.
29. Wilber, *Quantum*, p. 170.
30. *Omni*, December 1986, Patrick Tierney, "The Soviets' Peace Program," p. 89.
31. *Critique: A Journal of Conspiracies & Metaphysics*, Issue 25, Dennis Stillings, "Ramtha, Channeling & Deception," pp. 106, 110-11.
32. John A. Keel, *The Eighth Tower* (Signet, 1975), pp. 197-99.
33. Daniel Lawrence O'Keefe, *Stolen Lightning: The Social Theory of Magic* (Continuum Publishing Company, 1982), pp. 569-70.

CHAPTER 2 — SORCERY: THE NEW PARADIGM
1. *The Occult In America: New Historical Perspectives*, ed. Howard Kerr and Charles L. Crow (University of Illinois Press, 1986).
2. Sir Arthur Eddington, *The Nature of the Physical World*, (Macmillan, 1953), p. 344.
3. *Research in Parapsychology 1972* (special dinner address by Arthur Koestler), p. 203.
4. *The Nature of the Physical World*, op. cit., p. 317.
5. *Los Angeles Times Magazine*, December 6, 1987, Alice Kahn, "Esalen at 25: How California's Legendary Human-Potential Mecca Has Changed and Why the Magic Remains," p. 41.
6. Jay Stevens, *Storming Heaven: LSD and the American Dream* (The Atlantic Monthly Press, 1987), p. 345.
7. Quoted from *Life* in David Henderson, *'Scuse Me While I Kiss The Sky: The Life of Jimi Hendrix* (Bantam Books, 1981), pp. 206, 233.
8. *The Christian Science Monitor*, November 24-30, 1986, "Agenda for the 21st century," p. 18.
9. *Rolling Stone*, Vol. 1, p. 410.
10. Carlos Castaneda, *The Power of Silence* (Simon and Schuster, 1987), Front fly of jacket, Foreword, etc.
11. Baba Ram Dass, "The Transformation: Dr. Richard Alpert, Ph.D., into Baba Ram Dass," *The Inward Journey*, edited by Joseph F. Doherty and William C. Stephenson (New York, 1973), pp. 287-320.
12. Herbert Benson, *The Relaxation Response* (William Morrow, 1975), pp. 59-65.
13. Marilyn Ferguson, *The Aquarian Conspiracy: Personal and Social Transformation in the 1980s* (Los Angeles, 1980).
14. *New York Times*, op. cit.
15. Walter Bromberg, *From Shaman to Psychotherapist* (Henry Regnery Co., 1975), p. 336.
16. *The Futurist*, March-April 1987, Marsha Sinetar, "The Actualized Worker," pp. 21-25.
17. Robert Lindsey, *New York Times*, cited in *St. Petersburg Times*, December 6, 1986, p. 7E.
18. *Los Angeles Times*, February 17, 1987, Part I, pp. 4, 16.
19. *Los Angeles Times*, January 25, 1987, Part I, pp. 1, 31.
20. Marilyn Ferguson, *The Aquarian Conspiracy* (J.P. Tarcher, 1980), inside jacket.
21. *Life Times: Forum For A New Age*, Number 3, p. 48, originally published in South Africa's New Age magazine, *Odyssey*.

22. *Master of Life*, Issue 35, July 1987, p. 3.
23. Available from Box 5491, Fullerton, CA 92635. February, 1988 edition sold for $14.95.
24. *U.S. News & World Report*, op. cit.
25. *Newsweek*, May 4, 1987, "Corporate Mind Control: New Age gurus want to change employee thinking," p. 38.
26. *Los Angeles Times*, November 17, 1987, p. 6, Part IV.
27. Cited from an undated Esalen newsletter signed by Michael Murphy.
28. *The Wall Street Journal*, December 3, 1986, Robert S. Greenberger, "East Meets Est: The Soviets Discover Werner Erhard," pp. 1, 23.
29. Ibid.
30. *Training*, September 1987, Ron Zemke, "What's New In The New Age?" p. 26.
31. Ibid.
32. *New York Times*, April 17, 1987, Robert Lindsey, "Gurus Hired to Motivate Workers Are Raising Fears of 'Mind Control.' "
33. *Newsweek*, op. cit., p. 39.
34. *New York Times*, April 17, 1987, op. cit.

CHAPTER 3 — *CAVEAT EMPTOR:* LET THE BUYER BEWARE

1. *New York Times*, April 17, 1987, op. cit.
2. *Training*, op. cit., p. 29.
3. *New York Times*, April 17, 1987, op. cit.
4. Ibid.
5. Ibid.
6. *Training*, December 1985, "Issues," p. 96.
7. Richard L. Watring, "New Age Management," unpublished paper in conjunction with a master's thesis.
8. Barbara Clark, *Growing Up Gifted* (Merrill Publishing, 1979), pp. 367-68; Nel and Norma Gabler with James C. Hefley, *What Are They Teaching Our Children?* (Victor, 1985), p. 28; *Educational Leadership*, December 1964, Harold D. Drummond, "Leadership For Human Change," p. 147, etc.
9. *Training*, September 1987, op. cit., p. 33.
10. *What Is*, Summer 1986, Dick Sutphen, "Infiltrating The New Age Into Society," p. 14.
11. *USA Today*, May 26, 1987, Deidre Donahue, "A cosmic trend in hardcover," p. 2D.
12. Timothy Leary, "Daring to be Different," from audiotape of the speech at the AHP 22nd Annual Meeting at Curry College, Boston, August 21-26, 1984.
13. *Yoga Journal*, September/October 1987, Georg Feuerstein, "A Brief History of Hatha Yoga, Part Two," p. 67.
14. *Whole Life Monthly*, September 1987, Art Kunkin, "Transcendental Meditation on Trial, Part Two," pp. 14, 17.
15. Ibid., p. 17.
16. Ibid., pp. 15-17.
17. Ibid., p. 17.
18. Ken Wilber, Jack Engler & Daniel P. Brown, *Transformations of Consciousness* (New Science Library, Shambhala Publications, 1986), see especially Chapter 2 by Mark D. Epstein and Jonathan D. Lieff, "Psychiatric Complications of Meditation Practice," pp. 53-63.
19. *Yoga Journal*, September/October 1987, Catherine Ingram, "Ken Wilber: The Pundit of Transpersonal Psychology," p. 43.
20. R. D. Scott, *Transcendental Misconceptions* (San Diego, 1978), pp. 37-38, 115-29.
21. Ibid., p. 119.
22. *Brain/Mind Bulletin*, March 1987, p. 1.
23. *AHP Perspective*, February 1986, Naomi Steinfeld, "Passages In: For People in Spiritual Crisis," p. 9.
24. Ibid.
25. *Science Digest*, January 1982, Flo Conway and Jim Siegelman, "Information Disease: Have Cults Created a New Mental Illness?" pp. 86-88.
26. *Brain/Mind Bulletin*, July 12, 1982, p. 3.
27. Walter Truett Anderson, *The Upstart Spring* (Addison-Wesley, 1983), pp. 199-202, 234-37.
28. *Los Angeles Weekly*, December 6, 1987, Alice Kahn, "Esalen at 25: The Legendary Human-Potential Mecca Has Changed—but the Magic Remains," p. 22.
29. *The Esalen Catalog*, September 1985-February 1986, p. 8.
30. *New Realities*, March/April 1987, Stanislav and Christina Grof, "Holotropic Therapy: A Strategy for Achieving Inner Transformation," p. 11.
31. W. Brugh Joy, M.D., *Joy's Way* (Tarcher, 1979), pp. 8-9.
32. Ibid.
33. *The Skeptical Inquirer*, Winter 1986-87, quoted by Kendrick Frazier in "The 'Whole Earth' Review of the Fringe," p. 197.
34. *Training*, September 1987, op. cit., pp. 25-26.
35. *U.S. News & World Report*, op. cit., p. 69.

CHAPTER 4 — POPULARIZING SPIRITUALITY

1. Herbert Benson with William Proctor (Random House, 1987), pp. 16-22.
2. Jon Klimo, *Channeling* (Jeremy P. Tarcher, Inc., 1987), p. 20.
3. Undated brochure advertising *Common Boundary*, "Helps you discover a whole new world of possibilities," distributed in late 1986.
4. *New Age Journal*, May/June 1987, M. Scott Peck, "A New American Revolution," pp. 32-55; see also the editorial by Florence Graves, p. 4.
5. Association for Humanistic Psychology *Newsletter*, February 1984, Jon Spiegel, "AHP Leadership in the Profession," p. 22.

6. *Los Angeles Times*, August 20, 1986, Part V, p. 1.
7. *Shaman's Drum*, Summer 1986, p. 9.
8. *Yoga Journal*, September/October 1985, Shepherd Bliss, "Humanistic Psychology Reaches Toward the Transcendent," p. 8.
9. Herbert Benson, M.D., *The Mind/Body Effect* (Simon and Schuster, 1979), p. 61.
10. *The Harmonist*, Vol. 1, No. 2, 1986, "Interview: Fritjof Capra," p. 22.
11. David Bohm and F. David Peat, *Science, Order and Creativity* (Bantam Books, 1987).
12. *Omni*, October 1987, Marion Long, "In Search of a Definition," p. 160.
13. Napoleon Hill, *Grow Rich With Peace of Mind* (Fawcett Crest, 1967), pp. 218-19 etc.
14. Ibid., p. 159.
15. *Prabuddha Bharata*, 1979 (Calcutta), 84, Rakhahari Chatterji, "Vivekananda and Contemporary India," p. 192.
16. Vivekananda, *The Complete Works of Vivekananda*, 8 volumes (Calcutta, 1970-71), Vol. 2, pp. 12-13.
17. Swami Abhedananda, *Christian Science and Vedanta* (Vedanta Society, 1902), p. 1. See also Wendell Thomas, *Hinduism Invades America* (Beacon Press, 1930) and Raymond J. Cunningham, "The Impact of Christian Science on the American Churches, 1880-1910," in *American Historical Review*, 72 (1967):885-905, cited in *The Occult In America: New Historical Perspectives*, ed. Howard Kerr and Charles L. Crow, "The Occult Connection? Mormonism, Christian Science, and Spiritualism," R. Laurence Moore, p. 143.
18. Mary Baker Eddy, *Science and Health* (1878), Volume 2, pp. 143-44.
19. Michael Ray and Rochelle Myers, *Creativity In Business* (Doubleday, 1986), pp. 36-38.
20. *Shaman's Drum*, Spring 1987, "Menninger Foundation Finds Interest in Shamanism," p. 6.
21. C. G. Jung, *Memories, Dreams, Reflections* (Pantheon Books, 1963), p. 50.
22. According to an article by Swiss Parliamentarian Albert Oeri, student friend of Jung's, in the daily newspaper *Basler Nachrichten*, written in honor of Jung on his 61st birthday.
23. *Tomorrow*, Spring 1961, in which the English translation was published of an earlier article by Jung's personal secretary, Aniela Jaffe, in the German parapsychological journal *Zeitschrift für Parapsychologie und Grenzgebiete der Psychologie*, Vol. IV, No. 1, 1960. See also Aniela Jaffe, *From the Life and Work of C. G. Jung* (Harper & Row, 1971), p. 2.
24. Nandor Fodor, *Freud, Jung and Occultism* (University Books, 1971), p. 86.
25. Brad Steiger, *Gods of Aquarius* (New York, 1976), p. 222.
26. *Journal of Defense and Diplomacy*, September 1985, Charles Wallach, "The Science of Psychic Warfare."
27. Eddy, *Science and Health* (1881, 3rd ed.), Vol. 2, p. 42.
28. *Omni*, October 1987, Marion Long, "In Search of a Definition," p. 80.

CHAPTER 5 — NATURALISM, SCIENTISM, AND SUPERNATURALISM

1. *Los Angeles Times Magazine*, December 6, 1987, op. cit., pp. 20, 22.
2. Ibid., p. 22.
3. Jean Shinoda Bolen, M.D., *The Tao of Psychology: Synchronicity and the Self* (Harper & Row, 1979), pp. 95-97.
4. *Los Angeles Times Magazine* (op. cit.).
5. Howard Kerr and Charles L. Crow, eds., *The Occult In America: New Historical Perspectives* (University of Illinois Press, 1986), pp. 58-78.
6. *Penthouse*, Timothy White, "Daryl Hall's Magic," p. 60.
7. *The Occult In America* (op. cit.), p. 162.
8. Vivekananda, *Complete Works*, op. cit., Vol. 2, pp. 12-13.
9. *Wholemind Newsletter: A User's Manual to the Brain, Mind, and Spirit*, Vol. 1, No. 1, p. 5.
10. William Irwin Thompson, *Passages About Earth* (Harper & Row, 1973), pp. 160-83.
11. Deuteronomy 4:19; 17:2-5; Jeremiah 8:1-6; Romans 1:18-32; etc.
12. *Science Digest*, November 1981, Mary Long, "Visions of a New Faith," p. 39.
13. Carl Sagan, *Cosmos* (Random House, 1980), p. 243.
14. *Essays Catholic and Critical*, ed. Edward Gordon Selwyn (Macmillan, 1926), pp. 74-77.
15. Ernest Jones, *The Life and Work of Sigmund Freud* (Basic Books, 1953), Vol. III, p. 381.
16. *The Harmonist*, Vol. 1, No. 2, 1986, "INTERVIEW: Fritjof Capra," pp. 23, 25.
17. The Ojai Foundation (P.O. Box 1620, Ojai, CA 93023) for 1985, p. 5.
18. *Los Angeles Times Book Review*, December 27, 1987, James S. Gordon, review of *Jung, A Biography*, by Gerhard Wehr, p. 13.
19. The Ojai Foundation (op. cit.).
20. Michael Harner, *The Way of the Shaman: A Guide to Power and Healing* (Harper & Row, 1980), p. xi.
21. *Science Digest*, November 1981, op. cit., p. 39.
22. Carlos Castaneda, *The Power of Silence: Further Lessons of don Juan* (Simon and Schuster, 1987), Foreword.
23. Arthur Koestler, *The Roots of Coincidence* (New York, 1972), p. 50.
24. Eddington, *Nature*, pp. 344-45.
25. Thompson, *Passages*, p. 129.
26. *The Harmonist*, op. cit., p. 22.
27. *Life Times: Forum For A New Age*, Number 3, p. 48, originally published in South Africa's New Age magazine, *Odyssey*.
28. *New Realities*, Vol. III, No. 6, December 1980, Roland Gammon, "Scientific Mysticism: New Faith for the '80s?" p. 10.
29. *Los Angeles Times*, December 11, 1987, Gregg Wager, "Musicians Spread the Maharishi's Message of Peace," p. 12, Part VI.
30. *U.S. News & World Report*, February 9, 1987, "Mystics on Main Street," p. 69.
31. *The 1988 Guide to New Age Living*, Jonathan Adolph, "What is New Age?" p. 11.
32. *Los Angeles Times*, December 21, 1986, p. 1.
33. *Los Angeles Times Magazine*, December 6, 1987, op. cit., p. 16.

34. Ibid., pp. 40-41.
35. Esalen *Catalog*, January-June 1980, and subsequently.
36. Walter Truett Anderson, *The Upstart Spring* (Addison-Wesley, 1983), pp. 302-05.
37. Franz Cumont, *Astrology and Religion Among the Greeks and Romans* (Dover Publications, 1960), p. 56.

CHAPTER 6 — THE RESURGENCE OF NATURE RELIGION

1. *Insight*, January 11, 1988, Derk Kinnane Roelofsma, "Battling Satanism a Haunting Task," p. 49.
2. *The Daily Breeze*, January 27, 1985, p. A3.
3. *Los Angeles Times*, July 9, 1986, View, pp. 1, 4.
4. Herbert Schlossberg, *Idols For Destruction* (Thomas Nelson, 1983), p. 171.
5. Sir John Eccles & Daniel N. Robinson, *The Wonder of Being Human: Our Brain and Our Mind* (New Science Library, 1985), p. 61.
6. Eccles & Robinson, *Wonder*, p. 71.
7. Howard Kerr and Charles L. Crow, eds., *The Occult In America* (University of Illinois Press, 1986), p. 2.
8. *Pasadena Weekly*, February 5-11, 1987, D. G. Fulford, "Wicca Ways," pp. 1, 8.
9. Kerr and Crow, *The Occult*, p. 3.
10. *Los Angeles Times*, March 16, 1982, Elizabeth Mehren, "Goddesses of Coming New Age Probe the Meaning of It All," p. 1, View Section.
11. Ibid.
12. *Daily News* (Indio, CA), November 30, 1987.
13. *Army Times*, "Witches, Pagans in Military Demand Rights" by Grant Willis, October 26, 1987, pp. 1, 26.
14. Leonard Orr and Sondra Ray, *Rebirthing In The New Age* (Berkeley, Celestial Arts, 1983), p. 144.
15. *Life Times: Forum For A New Age*, Number 3, p. 48, originally published in South Africa's New Age magazine, *Odyssey*.
16. Michael Denton, *Evolution: A Theory in Crisis* (Adler & Adler, 1986) p. 77.
17. Cited in Eccles & Robinson, *Wonder*, p. 38.
18. C. G. Jung, *Psychology and the Occult* (Princeton University Press), 1977, p. 130.
19. *Update*, September 1982, Johannes Aagaard, "Hindu Scholars, Germany and the Third Reich."
20. Maharishi Mahesh Yogi, *Inauguration of the Dawn of the Age of Enlightenment* (Fairfield, Iowa: MIU Press, 1975), p. 47.
21. *Psychology Today*, March 1983, "A Conversation With Jonas Salk," p. 53.
22. Ibid., p. 52.
23. B. F. Skinner, *Science and Human Behavior* (Macmillan, 1953), p. 447.
24. Allan Bloom, *The Closing of the American Mind* (Simon and Schuster, 1987), pp. 199-204.
25. *The 1988 Guide to New Age Living*, op. cit., p. 12.
26. Eccles & Robinson, *Wonder*, p. 71.
27. Cited by historian Eric Voegelin in his *Order and History, Vol. 2, The World of the Polis* (Louisiana State University Press, 1957), p. 179.
28. *Psychology Today*, March 1983, "A Conversation With Jonas Salk," p. 56.
29. Ibid.
30. Eccles & Robinson, *Wonder*, p. 43.

CHAPTER 7 — FREUD, JUNG, AND THE OCCULT

1. Carl R. Rogers, *A Way of Being* (Houghton Mifflin Company, 1980), pp. 90-91; William Kirk Kilpatrick, *The Emperor's New Clothes* (Crossway Books, 1985), p. 176.
2. Rogers, *Being*, pp. 90-91.
3. Ibid., pp. 99-102.
4. Kilpatrick, *Emperor's*, pp. 176-77.
5. *American Health*, January/February 1987, Andrew Greeley, "Mysticism Goes Mainstream," pp. 47-48.
6. Ibid.
7. Ibid.
8. *Time*, December 4, 1972, p. 12.
9. Immanuel Kant, *Dreams of a Spirit-Seer*, translated by Goerwitz, pp. 88, 92.
10. Fanny Moser, *Spuk: Irglaube Oder Wahrglaube? [Ghost: False Belief or True?]* (Baden, 1950), from the foreword by Carl Jung; Aniela Jaffe, *Apparitions and Precognition* (New York, 1963), from Jung's foreword; cited in Jung, *Occult* (op. cit.) pp. 144, 154.
11. C. G. Jung, *Psychology and the Occult* (Princeton University Press, 1977), p. vii. This is a collection of Jung's writings on this subject, translated by R. F. C. Hull.
12. Nandor Fodor, *Freud, Jung, and Occultism* (University Books, 1971), pp. 219-20.
13. Originally published as "Seele und Tod" in Berlin, 1934; cited in C. G. Jung, *Psychology and the Occult* (Princeton University Press, 1977), p. 131.
14. Moser, *Spuk*, from the foreword by Carl Jung.
15. Moser, *Spuk*, cited in C. G. Jung, *Psychology* (op. cit.), pp. 146-52.
16. Aniela Jaffe, *From the Life and Work of C. G. Jung* (Harper & Row, 1971), pp. 6, 9.
17. Originally translated by H. G. Barnes from a German manuscript and published in *Proceedings of the Society for Psychical Research* (London, 1920), p. 109.
18. Jaffe, *Life and Work*, pp. 7-8.
19. C. G. Jung, *Memories, Dreams, Reflections* (Pantheon Books, 1963), p. 183.
20. Ibid., p. 155.
21. Bernard Gittelson, *Intangible Evidence* (Simon & Schuster, 1987), p. 213.
22. Fodor, *Freud, Jung*, pp. 129-30.
23. Cited in Gittelson, *Intangible*, p. 136.

24. Stoker Hunt, *Ouija: The Most Dangerous Game* (Harper & Row, 1985), p. 110.
25. See *New Directions in Parapsychology*, ed. John Beloff (London, Paul Elek Ltd., 1974); Guy Lyon Playfair, *This House Is Haunted: An Investigation of the Enfield Poltergeist* (Souvenir, 1980); Alan Gauld and A.D. Cornell, *Poltergeist* (Routledge & Kegan, 1979).
26. Lawrence LeShan, *The Science Of The Paranormal: The Last Frontier* (The Aquarian Press, 1987), p. 31.
27. Loyd Auerbach, *ESP, Hauntings and Poltergeists* (Warner Books, 1986), pp. 50-51.
28. Allan Bloom, *The Closing of the American Mind* (Simon and Schuster, 1987), pp. 199-204.
29. Martin L. Gross, *The Psychological Society* (Random House, 1978), pp. 43-44.
30. Sir Arthur Eddington, *Science and the Unseen World* (Macmillan, 1937), pp. 53-54.
31. Michael Polanyi, *The Tacit Dimension* (Anchor, 1967), p. 37; cited by LeShan, *Paranormal* (op. cit.).
32. Eccles & Robinson, *Wonder*, p. 37.
33. Watring, "New Age" op. cit.
34. Carl Jung, *Collected Letters, Vol. 1, 1906-1950* (Princeton University Press, 1973), p. 43.
35. C. S. Lewis, *The Screwtape Letters* (Spire, 1976), p. 45.
36. Harold Sherman, *Your Mysterious Powers of ESP* (New York, 1969), p. 120.

CHAPTER 8 — PSYCHOTHERAPY: THE RELIGIOUS "SCIENCE"

1. Gross, *Society*, pp. 3-4.
2. Garth Wood, *The Myth of Neurosis: Overcoming the Illness Excuse* (Harper & Row, 1987), p. 265.
3. *The American Scholar*, Autumn 1973, Sigmund Koch, "The Image of Man in Encounter Groups," p. 636; *Psychology Today*, September 1969, Sigmund Koch, "Psychology Cannot Be a Coherent Science," p. 66.
4. Robert N. Beck, ed., *Perspectives in Philosophy* (Holt, Rinehart, Winston, 1975), Karl Popper, "Scientific Theory and Falsifiability," p. 343.
5. Lee Coleman, *The Reign of Error* (Beacon Press, 1984), p. xii-xv.
6. *The National Educator*, July 1980, Roger Mills, "Psychology Goes Insane, Botches Role as Science," p. 14.
7. Mary Stewart van Leeuwen, *The Sorcerer's Apprentice* (InterVarsity Press, 1982), p. 49.
8. Thomas Szasz, *The Myth of Psychotherapy* (Doubleday, 1978), pp. 139, 146.
9. Ibid., pp. 104-05.
10. Bernie Zilbergeld, *The Shrinking of America: Myths of Psychological Change* (Little, Brown and Company, 1983), p. 3.
11. *Journal of Consulting and Clinical Psychology*, Vol. 48, Allen Bergin, "Psychotherapy and Religious Values," quoting Carl Rogers, p. 101.
12. *Chronicles*, March 1986, "Psychology Today, Psychology Tomorrow, Psychology Forever," p. 48.
13. Martin and Deidre Bobgan, *Psychoheresy*, (EastGate Publishers, 1987), p. 23.
14. Thomas Szasz, *The Myth of Psychotherapy* (Anchor/Doubleday, 1978), p. 28.
15. *Chronicles*, op. cit., p. 51.
16. Peter Breggin, telephone commentary cited in *The Esalen Catalog* (Volume XXIV, Number 3, 1985), "Misuse of Psychiatric Drugs—East and West," p. 6.
17. Peter Stansky, ed., *ON 1984* (Stanford Alumni Association, 1984), pp. 209-10.
18. Arthur Jensen, Oscar Krisen Buros, eds., *The Sixth Mental Measurements Yearbook* (The Gryphon Press, 1965), p. 501.
19. *The Planetary Vision Quest*, a brochure promoting a series of three workshops conducted by Marilyn Ferguson, Fritjof Capra, and Jean Houston on successive weekends in Chicago during June 27-July 13, 1986, and sponsored by The Institute of Cultural Affairs.
20. Wood, *Neurosis*, pp. 273-74.
21. Ibid., pp. 268-69.
22. *Los Angeles Times*, March 23, 1980, Lance Lee, "American Psychoanalysis: Looking Beyond the 'Ethical Disease,' " Part VI, p. 3.
23. Bernie Zilbergeld, "The Myths of Psychiatry," in *Discover*, May 1983, pp. 66, 71, 74.
24. *American Psychologist*, 33 (1978), J. McCord, "A Thirty-Year Follow-Up of Treatment Effects," pp. 284-89; cited in Wood, *Neurosis* (op. cit.), pp. 280-81.
25. Swami Rama, Rudolph Ballentine, M.D., Swami Ajaya, Ph.D., *Yoga and Psychotherapy: The Evolution of consciousness* (Honesdale, PA: Himalayan International Institute, 1976), back cover.
26. Daniel Goleman and Richard Davidson, eds., *Consciousness: Brain, States of Awareness, and Mysticism* (Harper & Row, 1979), Jacob Needleman, "Psychiatry and the Sacred," p. 209.
27. *Psychology Today*, January 1981, Daniel Goleman, "An Eastern Toe in the Stream of Consciousness," p. 84.
28. Lawrence LeShan, *How To Meditate* (Boston, 1974), pp. 150-51.
29. *Los Angeles Times*, November 23, 1987, Beth Ann Krier, "The Medicine Woman of Beverly Hills," Part V, pp. 1, 4.
30. E. Fuller Torrey, *The Mind Game* (Emerson Hall Publishers, Inc., 1972), p. 8.
31. Richard Feynman et al, *The Feynman Lectures on Physics, Vol. 1* (Addison-Wesley, 1963), pp. 3-8.
32. Klimo, *Channeling*, pp. 150-51.
33. *New Age Journal*, November/December 1987, David Ruben, "A Deadly Case of Mental Teasing?" p. 9.
34. Benson, *Maximum*, p. 38.
35. *Training*, September 1987, op. cit., p. 30.
36. Benson, *Maximum*, pp. 207-08.
37. Aldous Huxley, *The Doors of Perception* (Harper & Row, 1954), p. 78.
38. Peter R. Breggin, *Psychiatric Drugs: Hazards to the Brain* (Springer Publishing, 1983), p. 4.
39. *Wholemind*, op. cit., p. 5.
40. William Wolff, *Healers, Gurus, and Spiritual Guides* (Los Angeles, 1969), pp. 79, 185.
41. Jung, *Memories*, pp. 188-89.
42. Wade Davis, *The Serpent and the Rainbow* (Warner Books, 1985), pp. 214-16.
43. Loyd Auerbach, *ESP, Hauntings and Poltergeists; A Parapsychologist's Handbook* (Warner Books, 1986), p. 218.

CHAPTER 9 — GHOSTS IN THE MACHINE

1. *Proceedings of the English Society for Psychical Research*, 23:1-121, William James, "Report on Mrs. Piper's Hodgson Control."
2. *ReVISION*, Spring 1984, Ken Wilber, "Of Shadows and Symbols: Physics and Mysticism," pp. 6-7.
3. Arthur Koestler, *Roots of Coincidence* (New York, 1972), p. 62.
4. *Parapsychology Review*, May-June 1983, p. 8.
5. Arthur Koestler, *The Roots of Coincidence* (London, 1972), p. 11.
6. Sir James Jeans, *The Mysterious Universe* (The Macmillan Company, 1939), p. 147-58.
7. *Chronicles*, April 1987, Herbert Schlossberg, "Reenchanting the World," p. 26.
8. Jeans, *Mysterious* (op. cit.), pp. 150-51.
9. Zechariah 10:2; Habakkuk 2:18; 1 Corinthians 10:18-20; etc.
10. Herbert Benson, M.D., with William Proctor, *Your Maximum Mind* (Random House, 1987), pp. 24-25.
11. Ibid., p. 46.
12. Ibid., pp. 8-9, 28-37, 63, 177-78, 196-97, etc.
13. Michael Ray and Rochelle Myers, *Creativity In Business* (Doubleday, 1986), pp. 106-07.
14. C. S. Lewis, *They Asked for a Paper* (London, 1962), pp. 164-65.
15. Ray and Myers, *Creativity*, pp. 197-98.
16. Klimo, *Channeling*, interview with author, p. 253.
17. Ibid., p. 313.
18. Paul Hawk in, *The Magic of Findhorn* (Bantam Books, 1976), pp. 103-04.
19. Hunt, *Ouija*, p. 90.
20. Edmond C. Gruss (with John G. Hotchkiss), *The Ouija Board: Doorway to the Occult* (Moody Press, 1979), pp. 17-52.
21. William F. Barrett, "On Some Experiments with the Ouija Board and Blindfolded Sitters," in *Proceedings of the American Society for Psychical Research*, September 1914, pp. 381-94; cited in Gruss, *Ouija* (op. cit.), pp. 53-57.
22. Thelma Moss, *The Probability of the Impossible* (J. P. Tarcher, 1974), p. 240.
23. Irving Litvag, *Singer in the Shadows* (Popular Library, 1972), cited in *Gnosis Magazine*, No. 5, Fall 1987, p. 11.
24. From Anita M. Muhl, *Automatic Writing: An Approach to the Unconscious*, cited in Hunt, *Ouija* (op. cit.), pp. 128-31.
25. Klimo, *Channeling*, p. 182.
26. Maya Deren, *Divine Horsemen: Voodoo Gods of Haiti* (Chelsea House, 1970), pp. 247-49.
27. M. Scott Peck, *People Of The Lie* (Simon & Schuster, 1983), pp. 184, 188.
28. Ibid., p. 196.
29. Eddington, *Nature*, pp. 258-59.
30. Peck, *People*, p. 215.
31. *Life Times*, Issue Number 3, Carl Rogers, Ph.D., "The New World Person," p. 47.
32. Jung, *Occult*, p. 112.
33. Klimo, *Channeling*, p. 249.

CHAPTER 10 — IN SEARCH OF SPIRIT ENTITIES

1. Leviticus 19:31; 20:6; Deuteronomy 18:9-14; Isaiah 8:19,20; etc.
2. Robert R. Leichtman, *From Heaven to Earth: Edgar Cayce Returns* (Ariel Press, 1978), p. 13.
3. *The Wall Street Journal*, April 1, 1987, Kathleen A. Hughes, "For Personal Insights, Some Try Channels Out of This World," p. 1.
4. Allen Spraggett, *The Unexplained* (New York, 1967), p. 95.
5. F. LaGard Smith, *Out On A Broken Limb* (Harvest House, 1986), pp. 101-02.
6. Allan Angoff, *Eileen Garrett and the World Beyond the Senses* (New York, 1974), p. 77.
7. Ibid.
8. Eileen J. Garrett, *Many Voices: The Autobiography of a Medium* (Dell Publishing, 1968), p. 43; Angoff, *Garrett*, p. 78.
9. Spraggett, *Unexplained*, pp. 68-71.
10. Ibid.
11. *Noetic Sciences*, op. cit., p. 24.
12. C. D. Broad, *Religion, Philosophy and Psychical Research* (New York, 1953).
13. Klimo, *Channeling*, from author's interview with DiMele.
14. *Reader's Digest*, June 1979, condensation of a book by John G. Fuller, *The Airmen Who Would Not Die*, pp. 196-246.
15. *Reader's Digest*, op. cit., p. 196.
16. Smith, *Limb*, pp. 42-46; see also Ira Progoff, *The Image of an Oracle*.
17. Ken Carey/Raphael, *The Starseed Transmissions* (UNI-SUN, 1982).
18. Ken Carey, *Vision* (UNI-SUN, 1985), p. vii.
19. Carey/Raphael, *Starseed*, pp. 68-70.
20. 1 Timothy 4:1, *New Testament in Modern English*, translated by J. B. Phillips, Christianity Today Edition, 1965.
21. Klimo, *Channeling*, p. 245.
22. Klimo, *Channeling.*, in an interview by the author with Truzzi, pp. 11, 248.
23. *Noetic Sciences*, op. cit., p. 25.

CHAPTER 11 — MINDS FROM BEYOND

1. *New Age*, October 1985, p. 11.
2. *Omni*, February 1987, Jerome Clark, "Censoring The Paranormal," p. 33.
3. *U.S. News & World Report*, February 9, 1987, "Mystics on Main Street," p. 67.
4. Bernard Gittelson, *Intangible Evidence: Explore the world of psychic phenomena—and learn to develop your psychic skills* (Simon & Schuster, 1987), p. 88.

5. *Los Angeles Times*, April 23, 1987, review by Jonathan Kirsch, "Worshiping at a Shrine of Agnosticism," p. V-18.
6. For an excellent introduction to this field see Hans J. Eysenck and Carl Sargent, *Explaining the Unexplained: Mysteries of the Paranormal* (London: Weidenfeld & Nicolson, 1982).
7. John J. Heaney, *The Sacred & The Psychic* (Paulist Press, 1984), p. 5.
8. See Alan Gauld, *The Founders of Psychical Research* (Schocken Books, 1968) for an excellent account of the pioneers in this field.
9. Ibid., p. 142.
10. Norman & Jeanne MacKenzie, *The Fabians* (Simon and Schuster, 1977), Acknowledgements, p. 18.
11. *The Tarrytown Letter*, June/July 1983, Jean Houston, "The New World Religion," p. 5.
12. Louisa E. Rhine, *Mind Over Matter, Psychokinesis: The astonishing story of the scientific experiments that demonstrate the power of the will over matter* (Macmillan, 1970), pp. 389-90.
13. *Science Digest Special*—September/October 1980, Laurence Cherry, "Physicists Explain ESP," p. 85.
14. *Research In Parapsychology*, Annual Report of the Parapsychological Association (New Jersey, 1975), p. 234.
15. *Journal of Humanistic Psychology*, Winter 1981, Willis W. Harman, "Rationale for Good Choosing."
16. *Los Angeles Times*, January 11, 1988, Part II, p. 5.
17. *Los Angeles Times*, February 11, 1979, Part I, pp. 3, 22-23.
18. *Los Angeles Times*, March 31, 1987, Part II, page 8.
19. *Omni*, September 1984, Daniel Kagan, "Psi For Hire," p. 20.
20. Ibid.
21. *Los Angeles Times*, December 4, 1987, pp. 1, 32.
22. *Critique: A Journal of Conspiracies and Metaphysics*, Spring/Summer 1986, "Psi-War," p. 9.
23. *The Atlantic*, October 1978, Michael Brown, "Getting Serious About the Occult," p. 102.
24. *The New American*, December 9, 1985, Edith Kermit Roosevelt, "Will ESP Be a Weapon of the Future? U.S. and USSR research in this unique field continues," p. 6.
25. *U.S. News & World Report*, May 7, 1984, p. 73.
26. *Bottom Line*, July 30, 1984, Keith Harary, "Your Innate Psychic Abilities . . . And How to Use Them," p. 9.
27. *The Atlantic*, October 1978, op. cit., pp. 100, 102.
28. *U.S. News & World Report*, May 7, 1984, op. cit.
29. *U.S. News & World Report*, May 4, 1987, p. 19.
30. *Psychology Today*, July 1974, Andrew Weil, "Parapsychology, Andrew Weil's Search for the True Geller, Part II: The Letdown," pp. 74-82.
31. John H. Heaney, *The Sacred & The Psychic* (Paulist Press, 1984).
32. Stanley Krippner, *Song of the Siren* (New York, 1975), pp. 260-61.
33. Andrija Puharich, *Uri: A Journal of the Mystery of Uri Geller* (New York, 1975), pp. 166-70.
34. Michael Harner, *The Way of the Shaman: The Guide to Power and Healing* (Harper & Row, 1980), pp. 42-43.

CHAPTER 12 — CREATING YOUR OWN REALITY

1. Jane Roberts, *The Nature of Personal Reality* (Prentice Hall, 1974), p. 509.
2. Klimo, *Channeling*, p. 34.
3. Ibid., p. 43.
4. Wilber, *Quantum*, p. 8.
5. *The Harmonist*, Vol. 1, No. 2, 1986, "Interview: Fritjof Capra," p. 22.
6. Fritjof Capra, *The Tao of Physics* (Shambala, 1975), p. 11.
7. Edgar D. Mitchell, "Implications of Mind Research," an address to members of Congress and Congressional staff on behalf of the Congressional Clearinghouse on the Future, printed in *Institute of Noetic Sciences Newsletter*, Spring & Summer 1980, Volume 8, Number 5, p. 5.
8. *Master of Life: Tools & Teachings To Create Your Own Reality*, Valley of the Sun Publishing Co., Box 38, Malibu, CA 90205.
9. Mitchell, "Implications," op. cit.
10. "The Viewpoint in the Science of Mind Concerning Certain Traditional Beliefs" (Science of Mind Publications); Ernest Holmes, *The Science of Mind* (textbook), p. 30, cited in *Science of Mind*, September 1983, p. 47.
11. Klimo, *Channeling*, p. 311.
12. *New Age*, November/December 1987, Dennis Livingston, "Taking on Shirley MacLaine," p. 79.
13. *Science of Mind*, March 1978, pp. 19, 107-08.
14. *Science of Mind*, March 1978, "Victim or Master," pp. 3-4.
15. *Spokesman-Review*, Spokane, WA, June 17, 1987.

CHAPTER 13 — FROM SLIME TO DIVINE

1. *Whole Life Times*, October/mid-November 1984, No. 38, Shepherd Bliss, "Jean Houston: Prophet of the Possible," pp. 24-25.
2. Roszak, *Unfinished*, pp. 110-14.
3. Harner, *Shaman*, p. 57.
4. From an interview by AP correspondent George W. Cornall, quoted from *Times-Advocate*, Escondido, California, December 10, 1982, pp. A 10-11.
5. *Los Angeles Times*, June 25, 1978, Part VI, pp. 1, 6.
6. *Harpers*, February 1985, pp. 49-50.
7. Douglas Dewar and L.M. Davies, "Science and the BBC," *The Nineteenth Century and After*, April 1943, p. 167.
8. Roszak, *Unfinished*, pp. 101-02.
9. Michael Denton, *Evolution: A Theory in Crisis* (Adler & Adler, 1986), p. 342.
10. *Los Angeles Times*, December 10, 1980, Hugh A. Mulligan, *AP Special Correspondent*, " 'Big Bang': Evolutionists on the Defensive," Part V, pp. 8-9.
11. Colin Patterson, personal communication to Luther D. Sunderland on April 10, 1979.

12. *The Guardian Weekly*, November 26, 1978, p. 1.
13. Michael Denton, *Evolution: A Theory in Crisis* (Adler & Adler, 1986), p. 117.
14. Eccles and Robinson, *Wonder*, pp. 18-19.
15. Alfred Russel Wallace, *The World of Life* (London: Chapman & Hall, Ltd., 1910), p. 184.
16. Barbara Brown, *Supermind* (Harper & Row, 1980), pp. 6-7, 19.
17. Ferguson, *Aquarian*, p. 67.
18. Theodore Roszak, *Unfinished Animal* (Harper & Row, 1975), pp. 74-75.
19. Alan Watts, *This Is It* (Random House, 1972), p. 90.
20. Herbert Schlossberg, *Idols for Destruction* (Thomas Nelson, 1983), p. 40.
21. Peck, *Road*, pp. 266-83.
22. David Spangler, *Reflections on The Christ* (Findhorn, 1978), pp. 36-37.
23. Wilber, *Eden*, p. 6.
24. Timothy Leary, "Daring to be Different," op. cit.
25. Bernie S. Siegel, M.D., *Love, Medicine & Miracles* (Harper & Row, 1986), p. 99.

CHAPTER 14 — SATANISM, ROCK, AND REBELLION
1. From a written transcript of the show, available from Oprah Transcripts, Journal Graphics Inc., 267 Broadway, New York, NY 10007.
2. Robert Masters and Jean Houston, *Mind Games* (Dell Publishing, 1972), p. 214.
3. Bloom, *Closing*, p. 27.
4. *The Common Boundary*, September/October 1986, "Debating the Identities of Entities," p. 13.
5. *The Oprah Winfrey Show*, November 20, 1986, Transcript #8644, p. 6.
6. *ABC NEWS, 20/20*, "The Devil Worshippers," May 16, 1985, transcripts available from Box 2020, Ansonia Station, New York, NY 10023.
7. Jerry Hopkins and Daniel Sugerman, *No One Here Gets Out Alive* (Warner Books, 1980), back cover.
8. *The Playboy Interviews with John Lennon and Yoko Ono* (Berkeley, 1982), p. 169.
9. Ibid., p. 114.
10. Ibid., p. 203.
11. *Rolling Stone*, May 5, 1977, p. 55.
12. *Playboy Interviews*, op. cit., p. 106.
13. *Circus*, January 31, 1984, p. 70.
14. Charles White, *The Life and Times of Little Richard* (Harmony Books, 1984), p. 206.
15. James Douglas Morrison, *The Lords and New Creatures* (Simon & Schuster, 1970).
16. *Time*, December 16, 1974, p. 39.
17. Sound track from the film *Jimi Hendrix*, Interview with Fayne Pridgon (Side 4).
18. Curtis Knight, *Jimi* (Praeger Publishers, 1979), p. 127.
19. Willis Harman, "Hope for the Earth, Connecting our Social, Spiritual and Ecological Visions," *Institute of Noetic Sciences Newsletter*, Fall 1982, Volume 10, Number 2, p. 24.
20. 2 Thessalonians 2:1-12; Revelation 13; etc.
21. *Saturday Evening Post*, August 8, 1964.
22. Ray and Myers, *Creativity*, pp. 40-48.
23. William C. Miller, *The Creative Edge: Fostering Innovation Where You Work* (Addison-Wesley Publishing, 1987), pp. 84-97.
24. Ray and Myers, *Creativity*, pp. 43, 105.
25. *Time*, June 22, 1987, p. 69.
26. *New Republic*, January 18, 1988, Andrew Sullivan, "Flogging Underwear," p. 22.
27. *Creem*, March 1985, p. 64.
28. *Rock*, April 1984, p. 30.
29. Maya Deren, *Divine Horsemen*, p. 250.
30. Jerry Hopkins and Daniel Sugerman, *No One Here Gets Out Alive* (Warner Books, 1980), pp. 158-60.
31. Wade Davis, *Serpent*, pp. 43-45.
32. Ray and Myers, *Creativity*, p. 37.
33. Wade Davis, *Serpent*, pp. 76-77, 104, 114.
34. See Dave Hunt, *Peace, Prosperity and the Coming Holocaust* (Harvest House Publishers, 1983), pp. 129-54.

CHAPTER 15 — SHAMANISM ON THE RISE
1. From the brochure advertising the conference.
2. Michael Harner, *The Way of the Shaman* (Harper & Row, 1980), p. 136.
3. Ibid., pp. 20, 43-44.
4. Art Ulene, *Feeling Fine* (J. P. Tarcher, Inc., 1977), p. 259.
5. Siegel, *Love*, pp. 147-49.
6. Ibid., p. 156.
7. Errol R. Korn and Karen Johnson, *Visualization: The Uses of Imagery in the Health Professions* (Dow Jones-Irwin, 1983), pp. 94-95, 130.
8. Ulene, *Feeling*, pp. 97-99.
9. Stephanie Matthews-Simonton, O. Carl Simonton, M.D., James L. Creighton, *Getting Well Again* (Bantam Books, 1980), p. 198.
10. Watring, "New Age," op. cit.
11. Klimo, *Channeling*, p. 138.
12. Harner, *Way*, p. 50.
13. Puharich, *Uri* (op. cit.), p. 213.
14. Davis, *Serpent*, pp. 109-10.

15. Siegel, *Love*, pp. 19-20.
16. *Yoga Journal*, January/February 1988, Bill Thomson, "Spiritual Values in the Business World," p. 52.
17. Benson, *Maximum*, p. 7.
18. *Orange County Resources*, Phil Friedman, Ph.D., "Interview with Gerald Jampolsky, M.D.," p. 3, from Jampolsky's book *Teach Only Love*.
19. Siegel, *Love*, pp. 19-20.
20. *Critique: A Journal of Conspiracies and Metaphysics*, #27, Bob Banner, "A Summary Report on the Angels, Aliens and Archetypes Conference," p. 64.
21. Puharich, *Uri* (op. cit.), p. 213.
22. From a personal interview.
23. Robert Masters and Jean Houston, *Mind Games* (Dell Publishing, 1972), pp. 13, 229-30.
24. Masters and Houston, *Games*, p. 134.
25. Deborah Rozman, *Meditating with Children: A Workbook on New Age Educational Methods* (University of Trees, 1975), from endorsements in the front of book.
26. *Shaman's Drum: A Journal of Experiential Shamanism*, Summer 1986, "Shamanism on Television," p. 19.
27. Houston and Masters, *Games*, pp. 70-71.

CHAPTER 16 — IMPORTANT DISTINCTIONS

1. Sir Robert Anderson, *The Coming Prince* (Kregel, 1975), p. 127.
2. Deuteronomy 28:15,37,64; 30:1-4; Isaiah 11:11; 66:20; Jeremiah 23:3-8; 32:37-40; 33:14-26; Ezekiel 36:24-38.
3. Isaiah 8:19,20; 47:8,11-14, *The Living Bible*.
4. *Los Angeles Times*, February 9, 1988, Tamara Jones, "Fire Goddess Defended: Harnessing of Volcano Is Hot Hawaii Issue," Part I, pp. 1, 18.
5. *Los Angeles Times Magazine*, February 7, 1988, Rick Mitchell, "Power of the Orishas: Santeria, an Ancient Religion From Nigeria, Is Making Its Presence Felt in Los Angeles," p. 32.
6. *The Daily Breeze*, January 27, 1985, Janet Barker, "Secrets of Santeria," p. A3.
7. *Los Angeles Times Magazine*, op. cit., pp. 18, 32.
8. *Daily Breeze*, op. cit.
9. *The Washington Post Magazine*, October 25, 1987, Marc Fisher, "I Cried Enough To Fill A Glass," p. 26.
10. *Los Angeles Times*, February 13, 1988, Part II, p. 1
11. *Minneapolis Star and Tribune*, November 27, 1986, p. 6, quoting Robert Lindsay from the *New York Times*.
12. *AHP Perspective*, December 1984, T. H. Fitzgerald, "Practical Problems," p. 13.
13. Barbara Marx Hubbard, *The Book of Co-Creation: An Evolutionary Interpretation of the New Testament*, a three-part unpublished manuscript dated 1980, pp. x-xiv.
14. Barbara Marx Hubbard, *The Evolutionary Journey; A Personal Guide to a Positive Future* (Evolutionary Press, 1982), pp. 75, 114-16.
15. *Washington Times*, November 27, 1987, Larry Whitham, "Book backs theory Jesus visited India before public life," p. E6.
16. John 14:6, New International Version.
17. *The Source* (Koloa, HI 96756), January/February 1988, Jack Underhill, "Some New Age Myths And Truths," p. 19.
18. Simon Greenleaf, *Testimony of the Evangelists* (Baker Book House), Introduction.

Dear Reader:

We would appreciate hearing from you regarding this Harvest House nonfiction book. It will enable us to continue to give you the best in quality literature.

1. What most influenced you to purchase *America: The Sorcerer's New Apprentice*?
   - ☐ Author
   - ☐ Subject matter
   - ☐ Backcover copy
   - ☐ Recommendations
   - ☐ Cover/Title
   - ☐ _____

2. Where did you purchase this book?
   - ☐ Department store
   - ☐ General bookstore
   - ☐ Christian bookstore
   - ☐ Grocery store
   - ☐ Other

3. Your overall rating of this book:
   - ☐ Excellent ☐ Very good ☐ Good ☐ Fair ☐ Poor

4. How likely would you be to purchase other books by this author?
   - ☐ Very likely
   - ☐ Somewhat likely
   - ☐ Not very likely
   - ☐ Not at all

5. What types of books most interest you?
   (check all that apply)
   - ☐ Current Issues
   - ☐ Self Help/Psychology
   - ☐ Bible Studies
   - ☐ Women's Books
   - ☐ Marriage Books
   - ☐ Fiction
   - ☐ Biographies
   - ☐ Children's Books
   - ☐ Youth Books
   - ☐ Other _____

6. Please check the box next to your age group.
   - ☐ Under 18
   - ☐ 18-24
   - ☐ 25-34
   - ☐ 35-44
   - ☐ 45-54
   - ☐ 55 and over

Mail to: Editorial Director
Harvest House Publishers
1075 Arrowsmith
Eugene, OR 97402

Name _____

Address _____

City _____ State _____ Zip _____

Thank you for helping us to help you in future publications!

OTHER BOOKS BY DAVE HUNT

BEYOND SEDUCTION
A Return to Biblical Christianity

THE SEDUCTION OF CHRISTIANITY
Spiritual Discernment in the Last Days
with *T.A. McMahon*

THE GOD MAKERS
by *Ed Decker* and *Dave Hunt*

PEACE, PROSPERITY AND THE COMING HOLOCAUST

THE CULT EXPLOSION

DEATH OF A GURU
by *Rabi Maharaj* with *Dave Hunt*

FEAR NO MAN
by *George Reed* with *Dave Hunt*

SECRET INVASION
by *Hans Kristian* and *Dave Hunt*